Wildlife Law, Regulation, and Falconry

An Analysis of Legal Principles

Wildlife Law, Regulation, and Falconry
An Analysis of Legal Principles

William J. Murrin
&
Harold M. Webster, Jr., J.D.

WESTERN SPORTING
SHERIDAN, WY
USA

Text by
William J. Murrin & Harold M. Webster, Jr., J.D.

Edited by
Robert A. Murrin

Cover Design by
David Gatti

© 2013 William J. Murrin

Published by
Western Sporting
730 Crook Street
Sheridan, WY 82801
www.westernsporting.com
sales@westernsporting.com

Library of Congress Cataloging-in-Publication Data

Murrin, William J.
 Wildlife law, regulation, and falconry : an analysis of legal
principles / written by William J. Murrin & Harold M. Webster,
Jr., J.D. ; edited by Robert A. Murrin.
    pages cm
 ISBN 978-1-888357-26-4 (alk. paper)
1. Wildlife conservation–Law and legislation–United States.
2. Endangered species–Law and legislation–United States. 3.
Falconry–United States. I. Webster, Harold Melvin, 1920- II.
Murrin, Robert A. III. Title.
 KF5640.M85 2012
 346.7304'69516–dc23

                                        2012023042

Printed in the United States of America

ISBN 978-1-888357-26-4

Wildlife Law, Regulation, and Falconry
An Analysis of Legal Principles

Patrons

James M. Ingram III, M.D. .... *Nebraska, USA*

Brian McDonald .... *Texas, USA*

William G. Meeker .... *Texas, USA*

Harold M. Webster, Jr. J.D...................... *Montana, USA*

Sponsors

George Bristol .... *California, USA*

Jason Jones.................................. *Wyoming, USA*

Troy Morris................................ *California, USA*

Kirk Williams................................ *Illinois, USA*

Contributors

Richard Hoyer .... *Oregon, USA*

Jeffrey Clay Odell............................. *Wyoming, USA*

Lars Sego................................. *New Mexico, USA*

This book is dedicated to Frank L. Beebe for the invaluable lessons he provided in wildlife politics, for his unsurpassed contributions to falconry, and for his discovery of breeding techniques for peregrine falcons in captivity that were used by release projects across North America. Too few are aware of his pioneering work in this regard.

We would also like to make the reader aware that the raptor illustrations used throughout this book were drawn by Frank L. Beebe. It is a tribute to the greatest raptor enthusiast of the 20th century.

Table of Contents

Artwork by Frank L. Beebe

Tables

Praise for Wildlife Law, Regulation, and Falconry

Few people know or understand the vital role that the law of animals has played over the ages in organizing our understanding of individual liberty, private property rights, and government regulation. With a special nod to the sport of falconry, Murrin and Webster thoroughly canvass this complex topic from its Roman law origins to its modern regulatory state, and show how from a strong classical liberal perspective, much modern regulation has deviated from sound principles of state regulation. What looks to be a narrow field of human endeavor casts light on some of the most difficult questions of political theory.

Richard Epstein
- •Laurence A. Tisch Professor of Law, New York University School of Law,
- •Peter and Kirsten Bedford Senior Fellow, Hoover Institution,
- •James Parker Distinguished Service Professor Emeritus of Law and Senior Lecturer, University of Chicago Law School.

Bill Murrin and Hal Webster, Jr. take us on a fascinating journey through the history, philosophy, and principles underlying American wildlife law and regulation. Along the way they provide a new perspective of natural resource management, which will contribute to the ongoing debate of how best to preserve the environment while protecting individual rights.

Robert F. Kennedy, Jr.
- •President, Waterkeeper Alliance.

The authors have produced a fascinating and controversial look at wildlife law and policy. The book includes impressive research and learned presentations on key issues, their historical roots— philosophical and legal—and the implications for modern wildlife policy. They challenge established thinking on a host of matters including important topics such as the public trust doctrine and the Fourth Amendment to the U.S. Constitution. Their conclusions and prescriptions are controversial, thought provoking, but grounded in history. I found particularly interesting the exploration of the roots of modern environmentalism—Rousseau, the Transcendentalists, John Muir—and the contrast with the traditional Western view of nature. If you want to delve into history and challenge contemporary thought about wildlife law and policy, you ought to read this book.

William Horn
- •Former Member of the National Academy of Sciences Environmental Sciences Board.,
- •Former Assistant Secretary of the Interior for Fish, Wildlife and Parks.

Acknowledgments

A great deal is owed to Brian McDonald for his guidance in sorting out fact from fiction in falconry and peregrine falcon politics. He contributed much to making this a far more accurate work and improved its reliability as a resource for law and policy. In addition to this, Brian funded the design of the cover in order to provide dignity to an honest effort to set the record straight on the abuse of law as it relates to falconry in particular and wildlife management in general. We also wish to thank Lee Grater for his insights into the role agricultural chemicals have played in raptor population dynamics. Lee's education and experience in chemistry and raptor biology provided a more transparent view through which we may better approach the truth. We also wish to thank Rob Sulski for the time he took to explain peregrine falcon migration dynamics. His insights are used extensively in the chapter on peregrines. His explanations demonstrate the complexity of counting peregrines and the inaccuracy of using migration counts to determine wildlife management policy.

We are indebted to Robert Murrin for his invaluable time to edit this work with patience and accuracy. His mastery of the English language will surely make this a more agreeable treatise to read than it otherwise would have been. We also wish to beg his forgiveness for not necessarily accepting every change he recommended. While we recognize the need for some consistency in structural issues of our language, writing is as much a mechanical matter as it is a creative one. Therefore in some cases we chose to pursue our own style of expression over accepted contemporaneous rules. Consequently, any deviation from these rules is of our own choice and personal preference, holding the Editor blameless for any shortcomings the reader may encounter. Finally, we would like to thank Bill Meeker for his contributions on the peregrine falcon chapter regarding eggshell thinning. We have come a long way in understanding raptor embryos in relation to the dynamics of incubation, moisture content, and shell thickness, compared to the period when we were blaming DDT for "eggshell thinning" and the reduction of peregrine populations.

Preface

This work offers lawyers and jurists insight into an area of law they typically are not exposed to. It is a collaboration between Webster, a J.D., and myself, one who studied constitutional law and Natural Law outside of the academy, providing a unique perspective rarely seen these days. Since I am not a lawyer and have not been trained to bow to precedent, I have based my contribution to this work more on fundamental legal principles and have used precedent to support such principles, where applicable, rather than using it as an omnipotent legal authority.

Colleges that offer wildlife management degrees can utilize this work as a teaching tool. Environmental law colleges may benefit from it as well by viewing a rare glimpse at an understanding contrary to the established doctrines in which "political indoctrination has replaced open intellectual discourse, and ideas are evaluated not on their merits, but on their agreement with 'progressive' ideology," (Arnn, 2010). Lastly, those who wish to see the political philosophy our Founders embraced be applied to specific public interests will appreciate the analysis in this work.

The views presented here will prove useful to those with open minds in the academic community since these views come from a traditional American perspective on the subject of liberty—a rarity in this community—versus the statist view so dominant in contemporary academia. The academic bias has become narrowly focused with its own prejudices, nuances, and limits – i.e. it has become stagnant. Reading only academic essays on the subject of law and policy tends to create a culture of intellectual poverty due to the narrow-mindedness of many in the academic community.

I personally approach these topics without any preconceived factional ideas (since I belong to no faction), and am not contaminated by academic biases[1] or by any concern for a career in law, government employment, or politics. In addition, Webster has no career aspirations since he is now 92 years old and is more concerned about truth and the rule of law than about any personal gain.

---

1   In a letter to Peter Carr on Aug. 10, 1787, Thomas Jefferson wrote, "State a moral case to a ploughman & a professor. The former will decide it as well, & often better than the latter, because he has not been led astray by artificial rules."

My contribution comes from a common sense approach by one who has studied outside academia, based on what the Founders read (i.e., Enlightenment treatises which they referenced in forming our government) and what they themselves wrote. While the Constitution is not perfect, as was so well articulated by the anti-federalists during the ratification period, it is nonetheless the best system yet devised by man. Perhaps the way to improve it is to revisit the arguments made by the anti-federalists and to amend it based on that which they predicted would take place: that is, a government in which so much power could so easily be centralized because of insufficient checks and balances.

The arguments made in this work point to issues that must be addressed and rectified. It is extremely important to the survival of the art and sport of falconry, as well as to all other wildlife related endeavors, since the arguments are based on the very premise of liberty. Whether it is an issue of natural resource harvest, free speech, the right to bear arms, etc., an overreaching government is the antithesis of liberty. It is the intention of Webster and myself to demonstrate how the Federal government, and in some cases State governments, have exceeded their delegated authority and to show how to realign many of the issues with our Federal and State constitutions. It will therefore be necessary to periodically broaden the discussion to general principles of politics and government, since there is no real separation between general and specific public interests.

Bill Murrin
July 4, 2012

Introduction

Falconry is a benign endeavor that is regulated as though it could threaten the health, safety, or security of the country, thereby "justifying" infringements of several of the enumerated constitutional rights possessed by citizens. While regulation is important to a harmonious society, if taken too far, regulation can be used to deny legitimate rights and liberties based on prejudices emanating from particular sectors of society, such as factions. This is destructive to the social harmony that regulation is intended to maintain, thereby defeating the very purpose of regulations.

When prejudices are asserted against a sector of society—through regulations, for example—retaliation is typically forthcoming, and this creates a hostile social environment. It then becomes apparent that a balancing act is required in the establishment and application of regulations if we hope to maintain peace and harmony. Regulation must be implemented and enforced only to the degree that it truly serves the public good. Sound constitutional law and science, grounded in ethics, must be the guiding light. Any faction that embraces a prejudice against a benign activity is free to assert restrictions upon its own members, but not upon the rest of society. This is an important principle that helps define a free society, and without it, freedom does not exist, or exists only to the degree factions remain dormant on a given issue. This, of course, is not a very secure freedom, and contradicts the very purpose of a constitutional republic. Quigley (1961) points out that when a social system meets the society's needs, it prospers; however, when factions (which he refers to as institutions) develop and use government to serve their own needs at the expense of the rest, this is when civilizations decline and eventually fall. James Madison points out that factions were the common cause of the failure of every republic, and therefore must be resisted at every turn. Identifying factional influence, then, is the first step toward this resistance.

Having laid down the principles this work encompasses, we will seek insight into the structure of wildlife law as it relates to our culture and the American system of government. We first need to analyze this body of law in broad terms before we can understand how it applies to falconry regulation. Therefore, the first section of this work, *Evolution of Wildlife Law and Management,* will analyze how we inherited the present regulatory system. An examination of general historic political forces of the nineteenth and early twentieth centuries is crucial to our analysis of this evolution because these forces determined the course of regulations. We beg your indulgence while this subject is covered in some depth in this chapter.

Before we delve into law, let's first consider where falconry fits into the scheme of things within our Western heritage. Falconry is an art, and has components of sport in it. It is an ancient cultural heritage that deserves international respect and recognition. As a matter of fact, the United Nations Educational Scientific and Cultural Organization (UNESCO) Intergovernmental Committee for the Safeguarding of the Intangible Cultural Heritage added falconry to its List of the Intangible Cultural Heritage of Humanity in 2010.[2]

Much of European history is tied to falconry: falconry was inextricably linked with European politics from the time of the Crusades to the French Revolution; many great works of art incorporate falconry; literature references it (including Shakespeare); words in our language are derived from it; laws for the taking and possession of raptors were established for the benefit of particular classes; many contemporary hunting dogs were originally bred for falconry; and even the payment of ransoms were made with falcons, all of which demonstrates the pervasiveness of falconry in our Western heritage. This was no idle activity. Falconry has a rich cultural tradition spanning many centuries and has played an important role in the development of Western culture. Even some of the British King's Charters for the colonies in the new lands of America had provisions for falconry, demonstrating the importance of it in the lives of so many British subjects.

Brian McDonald, a pioneer of early falconry in our country, informs us that falconry is more of an art than a sport.[3]

The historical literature of falconry clearly states that falconry is in fact an art, which can be found throughout the writings of many centuries, untold civilizations, and

---

2   See http://www.unesco.org/culture/ich/en/RL/00442

3   McDonald was born in 1927 and observed much of the history of American falconry and played a key role in the founding of a national organization that promoted falconry and the protection of raptors, i.e. birds of prey.

untold languages. Falconry today is the culmination of all of its artistic endeavors, passed down through generations and disseminated across the planet. It has, for the most part, been an individual art. (Brian McDonald, personal communication, 2010).

Dr. George Allen, Branch Chief, Division of Migratory Bird Management, U.S. Fish and Wildlife Service (FWS), states, "Falconry is as much an art as anything else," (Payne). Schluter (Frederick II, 1250/1943, p. 451) states that falconry "was the favorite sport of all classes and was regarded as a high art."

Falconry encompasses the care of raptors, the taking of wild raptors, the conservation of wild populations, breeding, selling, training, and finally hunting with them, which is the point at which art and sport meet. There is no one way to care for, train, and hunt with raptors. Falconers develop relationships with their birds that are as unique as the personalities of the individual falconer. A falconer expresses himself by practicing this art in a manner that suits his esthetic sensibilities.

When it comes to the hunting aspect, it is the experience of the chase that defines the falconer's art. Take of quarry is secondary to the artist but primary to many sportsmen. The artist is more concerned about the style of the chase as expressed through the coordination of the players (i.e., falconer, dog, raptor, and quarry). The artist would rather see his bird miss the quarry than take it out of style. Contrast this with the sportsman, who is typically more concerned about bag count than style. There is room for both personalities in this endeavor, but it is the artist that has raised falconry to the cultural heritage level, and it is based on this understanding that McDonald informs us that falconry, as an art form, is deserving of greater legal protection. Both art and sport are certainly inalienable rights, but McDonald points out that *art* has historically garnered greater legal recognition than *sport,* since art falls under the First Amendment right of free speech, which includes freedom of expression. Some in our society would deny us this First Amendment right. In particular, FWS Law Enforcement Division asserts that falconry is a "privilege" and not a right.

Falconry is indeed an endeavor of expression, albeit a dynamic form of art. It evokes powerful emotions that transcend description, and therefore needs to be understood as a way of life that must be defended from all attacks—emanating from both public and private sectors—that seek to marginalize or potentially eliminate it.[4]

Nagle (2005) raises the point that wilderness experiences have spiritual aspects to them. Access to nature has spiritual values to many, and many falconers would agree that this art draws spiritual awareness out of the most devout practitioners (if not categorized as spiritual, then at least it could be described as highly emotional). For some, it draws out an awareness of creation, a sense of purpose, and a deeper understanding of the orderliness of existence. It could certainly be categorized as a religion, though not of the organized variety (it could be considered akin to American Indian religions), which arguably places it under another clause of First Amendment protections.

Later, we will consider the positive and negative aspects of nature worship in a system of government that prides itself on the separation of church and State. For present purposes, it is important to understand that falconry is much broader and deeper than a simple sport that is exposed to the caprice of fickle constituencies. The anti-majoritarian principles instituted in our republican form of government (i.e., where there is no public welfare issue at stake, citizens are at liberty to seek their own happiness, free of majority, as well as minority, tyrannies) demand that endeavors such as falconry incorporate the full force of legal protections, just as any other pursuit of self-determination. It is no different than pursuing a religion, a livelihood, education, self-expression, establishing a family, etc. Benign activities citizens pursue are understood as liberties, which require no permission from anyone. It is a self-evident truth that those activities that do not infringe upon others are rights inalienable to law-abiding citizens, requiring no explicit protection in the Constitution. That which is not prohibited by sound constitutional law is, by implication, a liberty, as the Ninth Amendment[5] instructs.[6]

Contrary to this, government has no power to act on matters not

---

4   McDonald points out how art has been controlled in the past. "Typical examples of government tyranny as applied to art and artists can be found during the first half of the 20th century. Throughout the Axis powers, Hitler, Mussolini, and Tojo dictated the arts in their spheres of influence. This was done, allegedly, 'for the welfare of the state.' Stalin's Soviet Union held a tight rein on art – particularly in literature."

5   "The enumeration in the Constitution of certain rights shall not be construed to deny or disparage others retained by the people." Ninth Amendment, U.S. Constitution.

6   The Greek word *adiaphora* means *things which are neither commanded nor prohibited* which designates things outside of moral law. This symbolizes the principle the Ninth Amendment encompasses.

expressed in ratified constitutions or in constitutionally sound statutes (in spite of rogue judicial decisions, which the twentieth century is teeming with), since the purpose of a constitution is to surround government with barriers it is not allowed to surmount unless amended. Government requires permission from citizens, expressed collectively through their constitutions, to act on any subject. The Necessary and Proper and the General Welfare Clauses[7] provide government authority to manage the country without explicitly defined authority for each action that needs to be taken (obviously, this would be impossible to do); however, these clauses provide the power and authority that must be understood as remaining strictly within the confines of the four corners of the document. In other words, if there is no provision within the Constitution that provides for the authority to act on a given subject, no matter how small, then the power remains with the States or with citizens, as the Tenth Amendment[8] instructs. The Ninth and Tenth Amendments were incorporated into the Constitution because the Founders understood that if these were omitted, future generations would interpret the Constitution and its amendments as defining the limits of the people and not the limits of government. This would cause the Constitution to be a worthless scrap of paper.

In providing instruction in the meaning of the Tenth Amendment, Tucker (1803, p. 246)[9] offers:

> All the powers of the federal government being either expressly enumerated, or necessary and proper to the execution of some enumerated power; and it being one of the rules of construction which sound reason has

---

7   "The Congress shall have power to ... provide for the ... general welfare of the United States.... To make all laws which shall be necessary and proper for carrying into execution **the foregoing powers**, and all other **powers vested by this Constitution...**" (Article One, Section Eight, U.S. Constitution; emphasis added). These Clauses demonstrate that the intent of the Framers was to limit the power of the Federal government and for it to remain within the confines of the Constitution.

8   "The powers not delegated to the United States by the Constitution, nor prohibited by it to the States, are reserved to the States respectively, or to the people," (Tenth Amendment, U.S. Constitution).

9   "St. George Tucker's *View of the Constitution of the United States* was the first extended, systematic commentary on the Constitution after it had been ratified by the people ... and amended by the Bill of Rights. Published in 1803 by a distinguished patriot and jurist, it was for much of the first half of the nineteenth century an important handbook for American law students, lawyers, judges, and statesmen. Though nearly forgotten since, Tucker's work remains an important piece of constitutional history and a key document of Jeffersonian republicanism," (Wilson, page vii).

adopted; that, as exception strengthens the force of a law in cases not excepted, so enumeration weakens it, in cases not enumerated; it follows, as a regular consequence, that every power which concerns the right of the citizen, must be construed strictly, where it may operate to infringe or impair his liberty; and liberally, and for his benefit, where it may operate to his security and happiness, the avowed object of the constitution: and, in like manner, every power which has been carved out of the states, who, at the time of entering into the confederacy, were in full possession of all the rights of sovereignty, is in like manner to be construed strictly, wherever a different construction might derogate from the rights and powers, which by the latter of these articles, are expressly acknowledged to be reserved to them respectively.

In referencing Article VI, the Supremacy Clause, Tucker (1803, p. 304) states that

a law limited to such objects as may be authorized by the constitution, would, under the true construction of this clause, be the supreme law of the land; but a law not limited to those objects, or not made pursuant to the constitution, would not be the supreme law of the land, but an act of usurpation, and consequently void.

Let us now consider how wildlife law evolved.

Note to the reader: Italicized comments are inserted in brackets within quotes throughout the text for continuity's sake. Also, the contemporary view that using the general masculine pronoun is somehow sexist is a politically correct effort to redefine our language and culture that the authors will take no part in, especially since we are in complete disagreement with the collectivist agenda it represents. The use of "he" is genderless when used in the general sense. We refer to ships and the Earth in the feminine, which reflects affection. This is not sexist or offensive to men, it is simply the way our language developed and it has become proper to do so. "He/she" and all other attempts to be gender sensitive are improper English and should be avoided since they only add to the burden of communication. In addition, political correctness such as this promotes hypersensitivity and the sense of being victimized, both of which contribute to divisiveness and the loss of social harmony.

Wildlife Law, Regulation, and Falconry
An Analysis of Legal Principles

Mature male peregrine and immature female peregrine falcon.

Evolution of Wildlife Law
and Management

Reflection on the history of our wildlife management culture is critical to a thorough understanding of where we now stand in regards to law, policy, and regulations. Our perspective has been molded by our American experiences and our European roots, which come primarily from Roman and British law. These need to be analyzed before we can understand why we manage wildlife the way we do.

Roman Law

If we look at Roman property law, we naturally find a close resemblance to our own.

Roman law determined that no one owned wildlife—including the State—until possession took place. Let's consider Rome's classification of property, which had two broad categories:
1. Things owned by someone
2. Things owned by no particular person
   a. State owned (an example might be public buildings)
   b. Commonly owned (such as public trust property, e.g., waterways)
   c. Corporate owned (such as property owned by a municipality)
   d. Not owned until possession takes place (such as air, water, and wildlife – true of Roman and U.S. law, but not British). In the legal lexicon, this is known as *res nullius*, or unowned property. There has been a concerted effort for over a century to eliminate *res*

nullius from our understanding of unowned property since it is a barrier to factional interests.

The Institutes of Justinian, a "systematic and elementary treatise on the law"[10] that was codified in AD 535, provides in Book II, Division of Things:

1. By the law of nature these things are common to mankind—the air, running water, the sea, and consequently the shores of the sea. [*Notice no reference is made to ownership.*]

2. All rivers and ports are public; hence the right of fishing in a port, or in rivers, is common to all men. [*The port and rivers are part of the Public Trust Doctrine (trust) under U.S. law, whereas the fish belong to no one. The trust is common property that provides access to natural resources in general for individual use, as well as for transportation.*]

5. The public use of the seashore, too, is part of the law of nations[11], as is that of the sea itself; ... the shores may be said to be the property of no man, but are subject to the same law as the sea itself, and the sand or ground beneath it. [*Nineteenth century U.S. Supreme Courts used this reasoning when they established the Public Trust Doctrine.*]

11. Things become the property of individuals in various ways; of some we acquire the ownership by natural law ... of others by the civil law. It will be most convenient to begin with the more ancient law; and it is very evident that the law of nature,

---

10   www.historyguide.org/ancient/justinian.html

11   Reference to the "law of nations" is part of Natural Law and is grounded in ancient Greek and Roman understanding of the natural rules that govern man's interaction with his environment and with one another. It is the ancient philosophy—reawakened, expanded upon, and embraced by Enlightenment political philosophers—that shaped American law and government. It was departed from due to philosophers like Kant and Hume and to the Romantic rebellion in the early nineteenth century. Also, "Many Protestants saw the Enlightenment as synonymous with religious unbelief.... The Romantic rebellion was originally a European movement and featured the following characterizations: A sense of admiration for, and harmony with, nature (Rousseau); a revolt against reason as senseless formality and cold logic; the glorification of emotion, or 'the sublime'; a new understanding of language; and the cult of the artist," (Professor Guelzo, et al., 2003). Natural Law is more like science, and one could accuse science of having the same attributes of Natural Law that the Romantics rebelled against. It appears that the Romantics simply wished to discard mature and responsible behavior for the more attractive temptation of the passions and emotions. It's possible the Romantics were reacting to dogmatism that was too harsh and strict at the time, which occurs periodically. The reactionary pendulum swung too far and the Romantics threw the baby out with the bath water and caused great harm to our legal and political system. Hopefully the damage they caused will eventually be rectified.

established by nature at the first origin of mankind, is the more ancient, for civil laws could then only begin to exist when states began to be founded, magistrates to be created, and laws to be written. [*Access to natural resources must be understood as part of Natural Law, for how could individuals, both prehistoric and contemporary, have survived without them? Natural Law was present long before the establishment of civilization, and will remain long after its demise. Physical laws are a subcategory of Natural Law; physicists seek to discover physical laws and how to use them, and are therefore on the path to understanding Natural Law. Besides the physical sciences—which were previously called natural philosophy—Natural Law philosophers seek to understand laws that govern man's behavior and harmonize the interaction between men so that all may benefit—not just a few and not just most, but all men. Hence the Natural Law assertion that all men are created equal. The English and American legal practitioners of the seventeenth and eighteenth centuries sought to discover these human laws through court decisions as they apply to a civil society. Court precedent has social consequences, and these consequences reveal whether a court's decision has good or bad qualities for society, i.e. does precedent provide a positive atmosphere that promotes healthy social intercourse or inhibit it. Precedent exposes a deeper understanding over time, until it is refined to the point where it becomes settled law, i.e., law that is no longer questioned but is understood as an objective social good that benefits all. For example, we know that murder, rape, and theft are social evils—this is now settled, but at one time it was not. Under a state of nature, such behavior would have been acceptable to the offender, but unacceptable to the victim or his close relations. Reprisals would have, in all likelihood, been forthcoming, creating a state of war we refer to as feuds. Such discord is antagonistic to the peace of a region, and extensive suffering is the result. The discovery of law based on the principle of providing peace, harmony, safety, and security for ALL is an evolutionary process that will require a great deal of time to complete.*]

12. Wild beasts, birds, fish and all animals, which live either in the sea, the air, or the earth, so soon as they are taken by anyone, immediately become by [Natural Law] the property of the captor; for natural reason gives to the first occupant that which had no previous owner. And it is immaterial whether

a man takes wild beasts or birds upon his own ground, or on that of another [*This establishes our understanding that resident wildlife is not the property of land owners, which distinguishes Rome and the United States from British feudalism*]. Of course any one who enters the ground of another for the sake of hunting or fowling, may be prohibited by the proprietor.... [*This demonstrates the same respect for private property that we hold dear.*] Whatever of this kind you take is regarded as your property, so long as it remains in your power....

14. Bees also are wild by nature. Therefore, bees that swarm upon your tree, until you have hived them, are no more considered to be your property than the birds which build their nests on your tree; so, if any one hive[s] them, he becomes their owner.

15. Peacocks, too, and pigeons, are naturally wild, nor does it make any difference that they are in the habit of flying out and then returning again, for bees, which without doubt are naturally wild, do so too. Some persons have deer so tame, that they will go into the woods, and regularly again return; yet no one denies that deer are naturally wild. But, with respect to animals which are in the habit of going and returning, the rule has been adopted, that they are considered yours as long as they have the intention of returning, but if they cease to have this intention, they cease to be yours, and become the property of the first person that takes them. These animals are supposed to have lost the intention, when they have lost the habit, of returning.

19. All that is born of animals of which you are the owner, becomes by the same law your property.[12]

The inclusion of the various wildlife mentioned above is to provide a framework of understanding, a foundation of reasoning, and a cohesive structure of natural resource law. Rome had centuries of trial and error to work through these issues to form a well reasoned understanding; therefore, we may benefit from Rome's experiences. Certainly, the Founders looked to Rome for guidance, as has our Supreme Court on numerous occasions; for the older a principle is, the more it has been tested. Hence the reason "settled law" is known by that term.

---

12   www.fordham.edu/halsall/basis/535institutes.html#II. Natural, Common, and Civil Law.

An important distinction between Roman emperors and feudal European monarchies is Roman emperors were not the proprietors of the Roman Empire. Rather, they were its rulers in a sovereign—versus proprietary—capacity, whereas medieval European kings actually possessed both the sovereign and proprietary power of their respective kingdoms. All land and natural resources were the property of the king, to be assigned to his nobles so long as they remained loyal to him. Wildlife was his to do with what he willed. He could provide privileges to his favorites and arbitrarily prohibit all others from access and use of any and all wildlife. His decisions were law, and subjects had a limited right to object since any rights they may have had were, in fact, not actually rights, but privileges that could easily have been taken away at the king's discretion. (The debate over the divine right of kings was controversial not because it questioned the power of the king, but because it questioned the source of his power—was it derived from divine or human authority? Natural Law philosophers said it was derived from human – i.e. the people – authority.) The simultaneous possession of sovereign and proprietary power provided feudal British monarchs (i.e., prior to the Glorious Revolution of 1688) control over everything and everyone in Britain (though the nobility did have certain rights kings did not dare violate), whereas in Rome, the Emperor possessed the political or sovereign power, but not the proprietary power of the empire. This is a very important distinction as it relates to ownership of wildlife, and has consequences for American wildlife law. That is, in making and interpreting law, are contemporary legislatures and courts influenced by a feudal or a republican past? Let us view the history of British wildlife law to consider this question.

British Law

Norman England began as a feudalistic monarchy established by William the Conqueror (Hume, 1778, p. 455), but over the centuries it adopted republican principles. Liberty and the franchise, as we know them, were predominantly the possessions of the nobility. Adam Smith (1776, p. 386-87) informs us that serfs were slaves tied to the land, and were only allowed enough nourishment to survive. It wasn't until the late nineteenth and early twentieth centuries that commoners acquired the right to vote (Hall, Albion, & Albion, 1946, pp. 796-97).

Blumm (2005, p. 107) informs us:

> Under the laws of England, limitations on wildlife appropriation by private individuals were pervasive.... Property owners generally possessed only those rights granted to them by their superiors in the feudal hierarchy [*"rights" is a misnomer; "privileges" would be more accurate*], and those superiors, most notably the king, could withdraw and reassign rights under many circumstances [*hence the reason they are not rights*]. Concerning animals *ferae naturae* [*of a wild nature*], the king employed his sovereign and proprietary powers to diminish his subjects' right to take wildlife by creating an elaborate land-classification system, including royal forests, and by limiting hunting to royal grantees.

This is a privilege-based system where rights were, for all intents and purposes, non-existent; though nobles had enough power to challenge the king if they collaborated, as they did when faced with a tyrant like King John, from whom they exacted Magna Carta. Privileges can be dispensed or extracted at the arbitrary will of those in power, whereas rights are far more enduring and can be modified only through sound legal justification and procedure. Consider the hurdles our Founders erected in order to amend our Constitution (though courts, legislatures and certain presidents have managed to amend and usurp it without sanction of law, with exceptional circumstances used as excuses). This was established in order to minimize factional and arbitrary power.

Regarding the King's proprietary and sovereign power over wildlife, Blackstone (1766, vol. 2, pp. 410-16) provides some insight into the evolution of this situation from Roman free-principles to a British feudal monarchy:

> [A]nother species of prerogative property ... the property of such animals *ferae naturae*, as are known by the denomination of *game*, with the right of pursuing, taking, and destroying them: which is vested in the king alone, and from him derived to such of his subjects as have received the grants of a chase.... This may lead us into an enquiry concerning the original of these franchises....

[I]t cannot be denied, that by the law of nature every man, from the prince to the peasant, has an equal **right** of pursuing, and taking to his own use, all such creatures as are *ferae naturae*, and therefore the property of nobody, but liable to be seized by the first occupant ... [as] it was held by the imperial law [of Rome], even so late as Justinian's time.... But it follows from the very end and constitution of society, that this **natural right**, as well as many others belonging to man as an individual, may be restrained by positive laws [*which in contemporary times defines the right to drive an automobile as well as hunt, though this is denied by most States*] enacted for reasons of state [*which defines the need for regulation*], or for the supposed benefit of the community.... Many reasons have concurred for making these constitutions: as, 1. For the encouragement of agriculture and improvement of lands.... 2. For preservation of the several species of these animals, which would soon be extirpated by a general liberty. 3. For prevention of idleness and dissipation ... which would be the unavoidable consequence of universal license. 4. For preventing of popular insurrections and resistance to the government, by disarming the bulk of the people: which last is a reason oftener meant, than avowed, by the makers of forest or game laws. [*We observe this in the United States, where anti-gun factions are attempting to repeal the Second Amendment incrementally.*] (Emphasis added)

Yet, however defensible these provisions in general may be, on the footing of reason, or justice, or civil policy, we must notwithstanding acknowledge that, in their present shape, they owe their immediate original to slavery. [*The conquered became serfs—i.e., slaves—of the conquerors.*]

[I]t will be found that all forest and game laws were introduced into Europe at the same time, and by the same policy, as gave birth to the feudal system; when those swarms of barbarians issued from their northern hive, and laid the foundation of most of the present kingdoms of Europe, on the ruins of the western [Roman] empire. For when a conquering general came to settle the economy of a vanquished country, and to part it out among his soldiers ... it behooved him, in order to secure his new acquisitions, to keep the … natives of the country … in as low a condition as possible, especially to prohibit them the use of arms. Nothing could do this more effectually than a prohibition of hunting and sporting: and therefore it was the policy of the conqueror to reserve this right to himself, and such on whom he should bestow it; which were only his … great barons. And accordingly we find, in the feudal constitutions, one and the same law prohibiting the natives in general from carrying arms, and also proscribing the use of nets, snares, or other engines for destroying the game. This exclusive privilege well suited the martial genius of the conquering troops, who delighted in a sport which in its pursuit … bore some resemblance to war.

[In England] the whole island [had] all sorts of game in the times of the Britons [*pre-fifth century AD*]; who lived in a wild and pastoral manner, without inclosing or improving their grounds, and derived much of their subsistence from the chase, which they all enjoyed in common [*not unlike natives of America*]. But when husbandry took place under the Saxon government [*post-fifth century*], and lands began to be cultivated, improved, and enclosed, the beasts naturally fled into the woody … tracts; which were called the forests, and, having never been disposed of in the first distribution of lands [*i.e., when lands were divided into private property based on agrarianism*], were therefore held to belong to the crown.… But every freeholder had the full liberty of sporting upon his own territories, provided he abstained from the king's forests … which indeed was the ancient law of the Scandinavian continent.…

However, upon the Norman conquest, a new doctrine took place; and the right of pursuing and taking all beasts of chase … was then held to belong to the king, or to such only as were authorized under him.[13]

This right, thus newly vested in the crown, was exerted with the utmost rigor, at and after the time of the Norman establishment; not only in the ancient forests, but in the new ones which the conqueror made, by laying together

---

13   McDonald makes a contemporary comparison here: "This paragraph quite easily describes falconry's current situation pertaining to the imposed laws and regulations which stifle the free exercise of its **free** practice by citizens. All that is required is to substitute the word 'government' (in the broad sense) for the word 'King.'"

vast tracts of country, depopulated for that purpose, and reserved solely for the king's royal diversion; in which were exercised the most horrid tyrannies and oppressions, under colour of forest law, for the sake of preserving the beasts of chase; to kill any of which, within the limits of the forest, was as penal as the death of a man.... The cruel and insupportable hardships, which these forest laws created to the subject, occasioned our ancestors to be as zealous for their reformation, as for the relaxation of the feudal rigors and the other exactions introduced by the Norman family....[14]

Goble and Freyfogle (2002, p.104) provide:

> In England the 'qualified and possessory property right in wild animals may arise in two ways:
> (i) *per industriam*, that is, 'by industry as by taking them, or by making them *mansueta* [tame].' The court emphasizes taming as a method of acquiring property *per industriam* and the durational limits imposed on such rights: 'in those [animals] which are *ferae naturae*, and by industry are made tame, a man hath but a qualified property in them ... so long as they remain tame, for if they do attain to their natural liberty, and have not *animum revertendi* [i.e., the spirit of returning], the property is lost.' See ... *Fines v. Spencer*, 3 Dyer 306b, 73 Eng. Rep. 692 (K.B. 1572) (tamed hawk).
> (ii) *Ratione impotentiae et loci*, that is, when the animal is powerless to leave 'by reason of inability and place,' i.e., 'as if a man has young shovelers or goshawks, or the like, which are *ferae naturae*, and they build in my land, I have possessory property in them, for if one takes them when they cannot fly, the owner of the soil shall have an action

---

14   This was the text used to study law by many in the Framer's generation until 1803, when St. George Tucker used Blackstone's *Commentaries* as a template to write *View of the Constitution of the United States*, the first treatise on the Constitution, which is now available once again through Liberty Fund and is highly recommended for those who wish to understand the true and original intent of the Founders. This is perhaps the only complete treatise that does so. Tucker had succeeded George Wythe (signer of the Declaration of Independence and legal mentor of Thomas Jefferson, John Marshall, James Monroe, and St. George Tucker himself) as professor of law at William and Mary College. The outcome of the Civil War changed our system of government regarding States' rights, without sanction of law, which caused Tucker's work to fall out of favor.

Immature northern goshawk.

of trespass.' See also *Keble v. Hickringill*, 11 Mod. 73, 88 Eng. Rep. 898 (K.B. 1706) (pleading ownership proper for young hawks).... This category thus was a recognition that the owner of land had a right to exclude others that implied a possessory interest resulting simply from the animal's presence on [his] land.' (Emphasis added)

Goble and Freyfogle (2002, p. 108) continue:

The court in *The Case of Swans* quoted Bracton [Bracton, ca. 1256, bk.2, ch. 1, ff. 8b-9] for the proposition that animals that had been 'tamed' belonged to the person who had tamed them as long as the animal returned. The quote comes from a discussion of the various classes of ownership that individuals might have in animals:

"Things are said to be *res nullius* [property of no one] in several different ways: by nature or the *jus naturale* [natural law],[15] as wildbeasts, birds and fish ... which formerly belonged to the finder by natural law but are now made the property of the prince [i.e. the State] by the *jus gentium* [human law]....[16]

By the *jus gentium* or natural law the dominion of things is acquired in many ways. First by taking possession of things that are owned by no one, and do now belong to the king by the civil law,[17] no longer being common as before, as wild beasts, birds and fish, that is, all the creatures born on the earth ... no matter where they be taken. When they are captured they begin to be mine...."

15   "Bracton offered the following definition of 'natural law': 'Natural law is defined in many ways. It may first be said to denote a certain instinctive impulse arising out of animate nature by which individual living things are led to act in certain ways. Hence is it thus defined: Natural law is that which nature ... taught all living things....'" Natural Law also encompasses the physical world; therefore, physicists attempt to discover natural law, as do chemists.

16   "Bracton defined *jus gentium* or 'human law' as 'the law which men of all nations use, which falls short of natural law since that is common to all animate things born on the earth.... The *jus gentium* is common to men alone.'" The law of nations falls under this category.

17   "Bracton provided the following definition of 'civil law': Civil law, which may be called customary law, has several meanings. It may be taken to mean the statute law of a particular city.... Civil law may also be called all the law used in a state or the like, whether it is natural law, civil law, or the *jus gentium*."

The Latin classifications of animals' legal status demonstrate the long history of their use. There are two general classes in which animals have been categorized: *domitae naturae* (of a domestic nature) and *ferae naturae* (of a wild nature). Animals of a wild nature had two subcategories once taken by man: *mansueta naturae* (tamed) and *animus revertendi* (returns to humans of its own accord—a tamed raptor returning to a falconer is an example). It has always been recognized that citizens have absolute title to animals *domitae naturae*, but have qualified title to animals *ferae naturae*. The qualification of ownership for animals taken from the wild has been limited by two conditions, as previously mentioned: either the citizen maintains possession of the animal and does not lose it, or if the animal is allowed to roam freely, it returns of its own accord. If the animal reverts back to the wild and is lost or loses its propensity of returning to the owner, it then becomes *ferae naturae* once again and may be taken by another. But until the animal reverts back, it remains the sole property of the one who took it—it remains classified as *mansueta naturae*.[18] Goble and Freyfogle (2002, pp. 10-14) offer an in depth analysis of common law classifications of the legal status of animals.

Goble and Freyfogle reference the ranking of nobles represented by the privileges and protections provided to them:

> Animals have often served as status symbols. This role was particularly well-developed in the hierarchical feudal societies of Christendom and Islam from 500 to 1600. Even more important than swans as status symbols were falcons where, at least for some commentators, each social rank had its particular falcon or hawk. *The Boke of Saint Albans* (1486) provided such a detailed listing....

---

18   Let us look to the meaning of the word domestication and how it is tied to the word "tamed": Oxford English Dictionary provides the following for domesticating animals:
Domestic – Of animals: Living under the care of man, in or near his habitations; tame, not wild.
Domesticable – Capable of being domesticated or tamed.
Domesticate – To accustom (an animal) to live under the care and near the habitations of man; to tame or bring under control.
Domestication – The action of domesticating, or the condition of being domesticated.
    The falconry term for taming is *manning* or to *man*, which probably has its origins in the Latin word *mansueta*. A raptor that has been tamed has been *manned*. Though this term may be lost in our contemporary English language, it is still an integral part of the falconry lexicon.

[M]uch of the English law on wildlife reflects and reinforces the hierarchical structure of English society—and a good deal of American law is based on a rejection of that social system.

"[In England] there were three types of ... game laws: (1) statutes directly regulating the taking of wildlife, (2) qualification statutes specifying who might hunt, and (3) statutes imposing penalties on those who 'stole' deer and other game from the landed gentry's parks and warrens. (2002, p. 113)

Regarding the qualification statutes that specified who might take wildlife, after the Glorious Revolution of 1688, Parliament passed these laws requiring English subjects to possess a predetermined amount of land and money in order to be given the privilege to hunt, even on their own land. This reflected feudal ideology in order to maintain class distinctions rather than promote conservation interests. Horn[19] and Lampp point to the evolution of English law where

the landed gentry succeeded in shifting the right to take wildlife from the [Crown] to the landowners. This included ... the doctrine of *'ratione soli'* whereby a landowner was considered to have constructive possession of all animals on his property, (2008).

In addition to these restrictions, Englishmen also had gear restrictions enacted in 1423, bag limits placed on fish in 1558, plus the prohibition of the taking of eggs from nests of wild birds and the taking of molting birds enacted in 1553, prohibition of commerce in wildlife in 1755, "qualification statutes" addressing the "privilege of hunting" being reserved for those who met the wealth requirements in 1671, and the most notorious of all was the Black Act, which provided for capital punishment for illegally taking certain wildlife.

The Black Act was the favorite example when American judges wished to remind their readers of the tyranny that game laws could produce.... The Georgia

---

19   William Horn is Counsel for American Falconry Conservancy and U.S. Sportsmen's Alliance, amongst others, and is one of the foremost wildlife attorneys in the U.S.

Supreme Court … opined that English game laws were "productive of tyranny." The game laws were "founded upon a tender solicitude for the amusement … of the aristocracy of England. It was made to protect from the violation or profanation of the people, the forest of his majesty or the park of a peer." (Goble & Freyfogle, 2002, pp. 765 & 767)

Compare these last two sentences to the efforts of contemporary environmental protectionists—perceiving themselves as an aristocracy or as superior to all others—who view average citizens touching wildlife as profaning it.

The concept of aristocratic privileges of England for the few was rejected by Americans, and was instead applied as rights to all American citizens. The impetus of this transition was based on Natural Law principles where all men are understood to be equally endowed with liberty (hence the disgust the Founders had with the ancient and global institution of slavery right from the start – but how to overcome the entrenched institution was the question). This included discarding English traditions as they related to access, use, and ownership of wildlife because of their offensiveness to natural rights, which demand that all have access to our natural resources. The British system was an arbitrary one based on the subjective interests of the monarch and the aristocracy. The Founders understood that such power lodged in the hands of a group of men could be nothing but arbitrary because of biases and self-interests. There are no angels here who will see to it that power will not be abused.

American Law

Originally, in colonial America, wildlife dominated the environment. In such a setting, regulation of harvest had no place. Access and use of wildlife was a necessity for existence, and it created no conflict since human numbers were too small to have any effect on wildlife populations.

To demonstrate the conditions of early America, Tober (1981) quotes an 1868 Massachusetts report in which commissioners reflect on their forefathers' experiences in a new land:

[M]en were scarce and wild animals were plenty. In a new country, the first settlers may properly have, not only liberty, but in some things license; license to till land anywhere, to cut wood anywhere, to shoot and trap game anywhere, to catch fish anywhere and in any way. All such things are then too plenty. As population increases, land and wood become PROPERTY.... This is the march of civilization.

When European settlers came to the New World, they brought with them the cultural perspective of their homeland. It was understood that land was to be adapted to the uses of mankind, based upon a fundamental belief that this earth and everything on it was for man's use (not unlike how all other animals see this world as exclusive for themselves, albeit in far simpler terms). Undeveloped lands were considered a waste. It was a place where wild and dangerous beasts awaited unsuspecting travelers. It was a "Godless no-man's-land" where some ventured into unknown places, never to be seen again. But the rewards that awaited risk-takers were well worth the gamble compared to the desperate environment experienced by many commoners of Europe, where there was little to no hope of advancing one's condition because of the multitude of laws and regulations erected as barriers against one sector of society for the protection of another—a direction the United States has been following over the course of many years.[20]

From our comfortable twenty-first century vantage point, we tend to judge early Americans without fully understanding their world. Culturally, they came from European nations where liberty had once been known under the Roman Republic, but had long since been lost and was in the process of rediscovery through the Enlightenment era under Natural Law philosophy. Those in the upper European classes felt the blessings of liberty, but the lower, i.e., the majority, were denied them. Physically, the lower classes had hard lives with little hope of social or economic advancement. In the new lands of America, all of this changed, and with hard

---

20   Compare our present state of affairs to what Alexis de Tocqueville so eloquently expressed in his 1835 classic *Democracy in America*, where he warned us about the regulatory pitfalls France had succumbed to and that America was likely to follow if not vigilant. Such barriers trap many commoners in a perpetual state of poverty, and when an opportunity arises to escape, they will immigrate to lands that offer greater freedom and opportunity. Based on the present trajectory we are on, as of 2011, it may not be long before we will be a nation of emigrants rather than immigrants. The question will then be, what nation offers greater liberties and opportunities than the U.S.?

work and no interference from a rigidly regulated system that used government to restrain opportunity, upward mobility was likely; though in England, upward mobility was far easier than in most of Europe because of the respect for capitalism, private property, and the rule of law.

Besides the promise of free land, in order to motivate subjects to colonize America, the English government promised the freedom to hunt and to possess arms in the new lands, heretofore unknown to the lower classes. Of course, these freedoms were necessary for survival purposes and were sure to have been well-received by English subjects. Free land, liberty, and the right to bear arms would have been intoxicating for brave, risk-taking individuals, and was something worth fighting and possibly dying for.

The renowned Boone family is a good example. Squire Boone Sr., born in 1696 in Devonshire England, immigrated to Philadelphia, Pennsylvania at seventeen years of age, seeking opportunity in America. He raised eleven children, two of whom became famous in their day. One of them, Daniel, we still remember in our history books (though this has probably changed in recent years because of statist/collectivist/multiculturalist efforts to marginalize and degrade America's heroes). Daniel and his younger brother, Squire Jr., journeyed into the uncharted region of Virginia known as Kentucky, where "game was abundant beyond belief," (Conway, 1994). They faced tremendous hardships, fought the natives and the elements to carve out their place in the world, and were confronted by death on numerous occasions. They hunted and trapped in this unexplored region, and sold furs in their home colony of North Carolina to accumulate enough money to establish a settlement in 1775, known as Boonesborough. Their abilities to survive off the land, fight for their place in the sun, and utilize the natural resources for economic advancement is what allowed these men to succeed and be remembered as trailblazers in American history. In addition, both Daniel and Squire served as delegates in the Virginia legislature. Conway informs us that Squire was one of the signers of Virginia's ratification of the U.S. Constitution. Only in America could men of such humble origins and with this sort of fortitude reach such heights. Such men are to be admired for their abilities and ingenuity.

In these early days of incredible risk, the only limits on hunting were on enclosed fenced land, land that had been cultivated, and posted (no trespassing) land. Other than these limitations, property owners had no power to exclude others from hunting on their lands. This came to be known as the *free-take* policy.

The taking of wildlife was seen as beneficial, given the fact that settlers perceived wildlife as competition in one fashion or another. Wild ungulates competed in the foraging of pastureland and ate settlers' crops; lynx, bobcat, fox, and weasel took the fowl from farmyards; rabbits ate vegetables in gardens; rodents ate stored grains; wolves, bears, and cougars took livestock and occasionally humans; insects, such as locusts,[21] devastated crops; and so forth. Such competition would have been unnerving when one's life depended on the fruits of his labor. Wildlife was not perceived as something to romanticize or be sentimental over, as individuals like John Muir later advocated; it was seen as a threat that needed to be killed for food and clothing or exterminated as a menace. Only after the continent has been largely tamed— i.e., shaped to the uses of man—are we at luxury, as a society, to embrace the romanticism of John Muir.

This perspective needs to be appreciated in order to see the evolution of our culture and its relation to wildlife. It wasn't until settlements had grown sufficiently and trade between the mother country and the new lands had developed to a healthy level that some security was felt. The production of food had to reach a point where people could not only provide for their families, but also build surpluses to sell to other regions of the world. At this point, the need to hunt diminished somewhat, and an influx of immigrants, who were more risk-averse than their predecessors,

---

21   The Rocky Mountain Locust was a plague to Midwest farmers in the late nineteenth century. Huge swarms estimated at 12.5 trillion locusts and covering 198,000 square miles were recorded, causing incredible agricultural damage. By 1902, this locust became extinct (around the same time and for the same reasons as the passenger pigeon - i.e. due to the loss of habitat) because of farming practices (one can only imagine how many bird species, such as prairie grouse, were affected by the loss of this prey base), yet we heard no cry for the locust like we did for the passenger pigeon, nor for the elimination of farming like we did for market hunting. It becomes obvious that factions pick and choose what serves their agendas, and disregard facts that are inconvenient. The Migratory Bird Treaty Act (MBTA) was based on the demonization of market hunting, yet we have no similar, far-reaching statute protecting insects and demonizing farming practices—the true cause of the loss of so many species—in the name of saving insects, as well as saving birds. To the farmer, insects are a menace, but to the entomologist, insects are as precious as song birds are to ornithologists or game birds are to sport hunters. This demonstrates that the MBTA was based on arbitrary assertions and therefore needs serious amendment to bring it into compliance with constitutional principles.

began to flood the colonies.[22]

Even though the need to hunt may not have been as important, it was still an integral part of the American culture and was understood as a fundamental right of the first order. Goble and Freyfogle (2002, p. 138) point out, "The importance of hunting—whether as **a symbol of freedom** or as a source of food—can be seen in its protection in colonial ordinances and early state constitutions." (Emphasis added)

However, over time, the unrestricted right to hunt conflicted with other rights, thereafter requiring some limitations to balance the competing rights. For example, the *free-take* policy, useful in a sparsely populated region, created problems in an ever-increasing human population.

> Inevitably the common right, of free hunting and fishing came into conflict with another much-cherished institution, the private ownership of land. As Americans understood private property in land, it included the right to exclude others, whether or not they interfered with an owner's use of the land. Landowners possessed the inherent power to close their lands to hunting.... The public ... might still [have a right to access and use of wildlife], but for the landless, opportunities to capture dwindled. (Goble & Freyfogle, 2002, p. 139)

> One sign of the law's [adaptation to conflicting rights and community interests as it relates to harvest of wildlife] was its adoption of the legal rule that a hunter acting wrongfully had to relinquish captured wildlife. A hunter who trespassed or who violated game laws did not lawfully acquire title, and therefore could claim no ownership [since his pursuit was done under unlawful circumstances]. No longer could the hunter merely pay nominal damages for the trespass or pay a nominal fine for violating game laws,

---

22   Most of these immigrants attained a respectable position in the community as businessmen or landowners, and were referred to as the "Better Sort" and "Middling Sort" in that period. However, there were those who were not motivated to establish themselves in the community, but rather wished only to depend on other people and remain laborers. These were known as the "Meaner Sort" of that period. "They were not 'mean' necessarily in a moral sense but rather 'demeaned' by their dependence upon and servitude to others," (Carson, 1983, pp. 94-95). The former dominated the colonial and founding periods; the latter dominated subsequent periods. In the latter part of the nineteenth century, the former were identified disparagingly as defenders of *laissez faire*; the latter tended to gravitate toward Statism or collectivism in one fashion or another.

while keeping the game.... [T]respassers and [convicted] game-law violators are denied rights in their game as a means of deterring future wrongful acts. Unlawfully captured game goes to the landowner or to the state, not in recognition of [any] ownership rights, but simply as a means of implementing a policy of deterrence. (Goble & Freyfogle, 2002, p. 148-49)

As the population grew, frequent conflicts naturally occurred between individuals, which required legal intervention and subsequent legislation to address social discord. This takes us to the famous New York Supreme Court case *Pierson v. Post*, an 1805 case involving one man hunting a fox and another taking it before the first could actually take possession. This is a famous case regarding property rights, and is still referenced in law schools because it established the *rule of capture* in this country, which is relevant to natural resource acquisition. This case affirmed the American principle—adopted from Roman jurisprudence—that property that belongs to no one becomes the property of the first occupant or possessor.

As wealth was accumulated by a growing number of Americans (the majority of whom were previously from humble origins), the tendency of all men to identify themselves in an elite class spilled over into the harvest of wildlife. A trend developed whereby the wealthy class established game preserves for their own exclusive use. As the size of these preserves grew, with the best hunting lands being purchased for this purpose, the opportunities for the common man shrank. The exclusion of the many in pursuing and possessing wildlife was a primary element in what distinguished England from our Union regarding wildlife harvest. Here, all were to have an equal **right**, as opposed to a **privilege**, as it was for the elite class in England, to take game. Americans viewed all the English restrictions with contempt, and our courts reflected this in the language of their decisions. Goble and Freyfogle (2002, p. 137-38) quote a case, *Sterling v. Jackson*, 37 N.W. 845, 851 (Mich. 1888):

[In a] case pitting a hunting club against a duck hunter, both the majority and the dissent affirmed their allegiance to the principles that, "by the law of nature every man, of whatever rank or station has an equal right of taking, for his own use, all creatures fit for food that are wild by nature, so long as they do no injury to another's rights." The dissent was even more [animated]:

Game and forestry laws are not in harmony with the American idea, and are of late origin in the history of our country. Such laws can only be supported and justified on the ground that the game is fast disappearing, and ought to and must be protected and preserved for the use and benefit of the people—for the general public, and not for a specified few. Our fish and game laws have not been passed for the express benefit of clubs of wealthy sportsmen [*or for a wildlife management bureaucracy or wildlife watchers*], who can afford to buy up or lease all the land along the navigable streams and lakes of this state, and thus shut out the poor man who loves the rod or gun as well as they do, and who, in the spirit of our institutions, has a common **right** with them in the "fowl of the air and the fish of the sea."

The Pilgrim fathers, fleeing to the new world from the tyrannies of a despotic era in the history of the mother country, brought with them, not only religious ideas, but many other notions as to the rights of the common people not then prevalent or countenanced in England; and the old colony of Massachusetts Bay early adopted laws looking towards the establishment of a common **right** in the people to the fish and wild game then abounding in the waters and woods of the new world. (Emphasis added)

Id. at 855-56 (Morse, J., dissenting). See also *New England Trout & Salmon Club v. Mather*, 35 A. 323, 328 (Vt. 1896) (Thompson, J., dissenting) (condemning 'the iniquitous fish and game laws of England, enacted by the ruling class for their own enjoyment, and **which led to a system under which the catching of a fish or the killing of a rabbit was deemed of more consequence than the happiness, liberty, or life of a human being**'; see also *Hallock v Dominy*, 7 Hun. 52, 55 (N.Y. App. Div. 1876) (striking down county ordinance as analogous to English game laws, which 'are contrary to the spirit of our institutions'). (Emphasis added)

The heated rhetoric suggests that more was at stake than is immediately apparent. Limitations on taking game conflicted with American ideology. Repudiation of the English restrictions on hunting was a symbol of America's [belief in individual liberty] and its rejection of old world class structures.

As technological methods of wildlife harvest, transportation, and refrigeration advanced and the human population grew significantly—due predominately to immigration—harvest of shrinking wildlife populations increased, while habitat decreased at an alarming rate. This was a recipe for disaster. The term *the perfect storm* takes on new meaning.

The use of common pastures by agrarian communities exemplifies what can go wrong when property has no owner protecting the health of the property. Sax (1970, p. 534), responding to Hardin (1968), explains:

> [O]ne may observe behavior which is rational from the atomistic perspective of the actor, but which, from the perspective of the larger community, is highly disadvantageous. A typical example is that of citizens using a common pasture for grazing their animals. Although overgrazing is recognized as a problem, it is profitable for each individual to put one more animal out to graze; each such individual decision, however, brings closer the day when the common pasture will be useless to all.

Though wildlife is not the property of any, while in a free-roaming state it has a problem similar to that of the common pasture: a user population increasing to a level that is capable of decimating the resource.

In the latter part of the nineteenth century, the

> unrestricted rule of capture [was supportive of excessive] resource [utilization].... [S]peed and efficiency of capture became paramount.... By [not prohibiting unchecked wildlife harvest], America's [lack of a] harvest [management system] promoted investment in capture technology, encouraging hunters to purchase bigger nets, better guns [*such as cannon-like punt and swivel guns*], and more ammunition.... Nineteenth-century state legislatures, viewing nature

as inexhaustibly bountiful, allowed this unrestricted harvest by failing to regulate the taking of wildlife.... A radical change in American laws concerning animals *ferae naturae* was on the horizon. This change would see the free-take principle soon dislodged by **states' claims to superior rights** to wildlife in trust for their citizens....[23] [S]portsmen ... [asserted] that without regulation, market hunters would severely infringe on sport hunting [*and launched a propaganda campaign to utterly demonize the market hunter*].... By the late 1800s, many states had employed [jurisdictional authority] to regulate the use of fishing grounds, restrict hunting by seasons ... and terminate certain commerce in wildlife altogether.... The earliest regulations imposed bag limits and shortened or closed hunting seasons in an attempt to prevent excessive slaughter of fowl and other game. (Blumm & Ritchie, 2005, pp. 118-24) [Emphasis added]

It appears that legislators of this period were either ignorant of the real cause in the demise of so many species—that being the loss of habitat—or were unable to address the problems because of political forces. No doubt, unrestricted market and sport hunting contributed to the problem, but market hunters' harvest numbers of wildlife could not compare to the devastation that habitat loss created, but to have attempted to curtail westward expansion in the name of preservation would have been unthinkable as a policy in the nineteenth century. The establishment of Yellowstone as the fist National Park in 1872, the National Wildlife Refuge in 1903, and the National Park Service in 1916 exemplifies the recognition of the need for the preservation of nature, but these efforts pale in comparison to the efforts required to preserve habitat for healthy wildlife populations.

---

23   States, i.e. governments, do not possess rights, not to mention "superior rights" relative to citizens. However, states do have rights relative to the Federal government. States are to protect the rights of citizens. In the present context this means to manage wildlife harvest in a way that protects the right of access to wildlife in perpetuity. The term "superior rights" should be replaced with the term "management authority," for how can the State have superior rights over citizens when the claim is on behalf of citizens where the right and interest actually reside? This is a contradiction! The right would have to be extracted from citizens first, which can only be done by constitutional amendment.

The Beginning of a Culture of Regulation

Expansive regulation over all aspects of society, including wildlife harvest, became a legal movement in its own right across the American landscape because of a change in social forces in the latter part of the nineteenth century. Quigley (1961, p. 389) refers to this as the beginning of the era of "Irrational Activism," a term describing the irrational response a civilization has because of conflicts within the culture. We need to understand how volatile the forces and how irrational the responses were before we can understand how it affected the enactment of wildlife laws and the subsequent drafting of regulations.

> [B]y the end of the nineteenth century courts had developed new terminology to describe the sovereign power of states [*To clarify, citizens possess the sovereign power, not our governments (James Monroe, 1867).*] to act in the public interest. The chosen term was the "police power," [*an unfortunate choice of words; "regulatory authority" is more appropriate*] a term that originally signified the state's inherent power to enact laws in furtherance of the public good [*which in a free society, all laws are supposed to achieve, as Natural Law philosophers have historically advocated*]. Such laws, of course, restricted private activities, including private efforts to acquire, use, and dispose of private property [*but only to the degree it serves an objective social good and no more, which means protecting the rights of individuals as long as no mischief to the community is caused by individual actions*].
>
> The transition to the "police power" as the dominant metaphor for discussions of the power of the state occurred during the middle of the nineteenth century. (Goble and Freyfogle, 2002, p. 396-97)

Novak (1996) points out that regulation was nothing new to America, which, of course, is true. Local units of government had always embraced regulations that fit their local needs, and all civil governments throughout history have used regulation to maintain health, safety, security, peace, and harmony (governments have also used regulations to control economic activity to protect certain sectors of society that were able to institutionalize their interests, as will be explained shortly).

What changed in late nineteenth century America was the effort to disconnect regulatory authority from constitutional restraints in the name of some pending problem—that age old manipulative tactic of deceiving citizens in order to centralize power and control.

What would allow for severing constitutional constraints in such a young nation, when the memory of the drafting of the Constitution was so fresh in their minds? It was an evolutionary process with various interests influencing the change in the direction of big government, just as the anti-federalists predicted. Some interests were homegrown, some came from Europe.

Quigley (1961, p. 384) points out that in Europe during the Napoleonic Wars, there was

> a struggle between the new and the old. On the Napoleonic side we find ranged all the forces of mercantilism, meaning the theories and the vested-interest forces that believed that economic life had to be regulated by the government and regulated for largely political ends. This system played a very significant role in Western civilization in the period 1200-1800, but by the latter date it was clearly obsolete, and had to be replaced by a more advanced system. This newer system of economic management is known as *laissez faire* and, as is well known, it was associated with the period of expansion of the nineteenth century.

Interesting how Western civilization went from a highly regulated system under State mercantilism, from 1690 to 1810 (Quigley, 1961, p. 368), to a more free system of *laissez faire*, which provided for a dramatic improvement in the standard of living, but eventually went back to a highly regulated system by the late nineteenth century, which retards progress. This raises an extremely important question that demands an answer if we are to understand the nature of man within civilized society: Why do civilizations swing from an arrangement of relative liberty, with minimal government involvement, and where prosperity dominates, to an arrangement of intense regulatory controls in which prosperity incrementally diminishes as the march of regulation advances? One would think prosperity and freedom should prevail over poverty and authoritarianism every time, but they don't. It becomes apparent that in some cases, ignorance and envy drive certain sectors of society to demand that all must share misery equally. In other cases, it has to do with the desire of some to control others who are seen as inferior. And then another reason has to do with the behavior of the population of a society. Herrnstein & Murray (1994, p. 253-54) inform us:

> A free society demands a citizenry that willingly participates in the civic enterprise, in matters as grand as national elections and as commonplace as neighborliness. Lacking this quality—civility, in its core meaning—a society must replace freedom with coercion if it is to maintain order.
>
> … America's political system relies on the civility of its citizens—"civility" not in the contemporary sense of mere politeness but according to an older meaning which a dictionary close at hand defines as "deference or allegiance to the social order befitting a citizen." The wording of the definition is particularly apt in the American case. Civility is not obedience but rather "allegiance" and "deference"—words with old and honorable meanings that are now largely lost. The object of these sentiments is not the government but a social order. And these things are required not of a subject but of a citizen. Taken together, the elements of civility imply behavior that is both considered and considerate—precisely the kind of behavior that the Founders relied upon to sustain their creation, though they would have been more likely to use the word *virtue* than *civility*.
>
> The point is that, given such civility, a free society as envisioned by the Founders is possible. "Civil-ized" people do not need to be tightly constrained by laws or closely monitored by the organs of state. Lacking such civility, they do, and society must over time become much less free. That is why civility was relevant to the Founders' vision of a free society and also why it remains relevant today.

It may be the case that as a free society's wealth advances, the struggle for success diminishes, and with it the need for citizens to work together for mutual survival. Without the social bond that survival demands, people grow apart and indifferent to one another, and as generations pass, the lack of manners evolves into disrespect and incivility amongst citizens. Unless a large portion of the population embraces virtue and civility, freedom is not possible. Authoritarianism is then required to maintain order since contending factions are vying for dominance through any means at their disposal. But it must be remembered that socially responsible liberty provides for growth; authoritarianism establishes an environment for decay. Therefore, selfishness of factions leads to the loss of their own advantages over time—a form of self-inflicted wound or suicide is the only fitting analogy.

Quigley attributes the transition of civilizations from growth to decay to the transformation of *instruments of expansion*—which serve to improve society—into *institutions*, which serve only those the institution is made up of. Quigley states that institutions (which Madison referred to as factions) eventually destroy civilizations if they are not reformed or eliminated. Currently, our country accepts factional forces and the erection of institutions as part of the way our system is governed. If this is not seen as a social evil, we are doomed to the same fate as every other republic in history. Quigley explains the process by which this occurs:

> Since the levels of culture arise from men's efforts to satisfy their human needs, we can say that every level has a purpose. ... To satisfy these needs, there come into existence on each level social organizations seeking to achieve these. These organizations, consisting largely of personal relationships, we shall call "instruments" as long as they achieve the purpose of the level with relative effectiveness. But every such social instrument tends to become an "institution." This means that it takes on a life and purposes of its own distinct from the purpose of the level; in consequence, the purpose of that level is achieved with decreasing effectiveness. In fact, it can be stated as a rule of history that "all social instruments tend to become institutions." ...
>
> An instrument is a social organization that is fulfilling effectively the purpose for which it arose. An institution is an instrument that has taken on activities and purposes of its own, separate from and different from the purposes for which it was intended.... Every instrument consists of people organized in relationships to one another. As the instrument becomes an institution, these relationships

become ends in themselves to the detriment of the ends of the whole organization.... Moreover, as a second reason why every instrument becomes an institution, everyone in such an organization is only human and has human weakness and ambitions, or at least has the human proclivity to see things from an egocentric point of view. Thus, in every organization, persons begin to seek their own advancements or to act for their own advantages.... All of this reduces the time and energy devoted to the real goal of the organization and injures the general effectiveness with which an organization achieves its purposes.... [M]embers of any organization generally resist ... change; they have become "vested interests." Having spent long periods learning to do things in a certain way or with certain equipment, they find it difficult to persuade themselves that different ways of doing things ... have become necessary; and, even if they do succeed in persuading themselves, they have considerable difficulty in training themselves to do things in a different way. (Quigley, 1961, pp. 101-03)

Quigley points out that institutions erect defensive barriers around themselves—through government—in the form of regulations. As more and more institutions are formed across the political landscape, government regulations multiply in defense of these competing interests. Consider the American Medical Association, American Bar Association, construction trade associations, etc., with their barriers to entry in their respective fields. The manufacturing sector is not immune. Pharmaceutical companies use the Food and Drug Administration (FDA) for this purpose; oil companies who make automobile lubricants have erected performance parameters that are extremely expensive to test but have little to do with real world performance. The defense for barriers related to professions is to maintain high standards, which, of course, is important; however, in the name of high standards, limits on the number of new competitors are put in place in order to control supply so that demand remains high, which maintains high prices. The defense for the manufacturing sector's market-entry barriers—which is typically true of all such defensive claims—is that they maintain high standards, but what they actually do is restrain new and innovative competitors from entering the marketplace, while simultaneously maintaining elevated prices that are due to the cost of doing business in such highly regulated industries (as always, the poor get hit the hardest). Market forces are not allowed to play a part in these fields, which is the reason fewer and fewer people are able to afford such products or services. Medicine, in particular, is becoming less and less affordable and hence unavailable to a growing portion of our population because of the insidious expansion of regulations, which is the reason there has been a constant cry to socialize it. If we were to break down the regulatory barriers and remove the monopoly the AMA has over medical education, reduce the FDA's excessive regulatory control over pharmaceuticals,[24] break the stranglehold attorneys have on the Democratic Party so that tort reform can be accomplished—along with other changes—we would see prices plummet, which would allow the average citizen to afford to pay health care providers directly for average care and to afford insurance for catastrophic care. At that point, the demand for socialized medicine would dissipate and the quality of healthcare would be saved, which is the very reason why collectivist types would be against such deregulation – i.e., they want medicine socialized even if it means it is seriously degraded due to their ideology.

Because of the multiplication of institutions and their subsequent protective regulations, a society is incrementally and insidiously weakened and its prosperity diminished until institutions are reformed, eliminated, or invaders are able to easily conquer the civilization. The invaders experience little resistance because the majority of the members of the invaded society are so demoralized that they have no interest in defending a society that

24   For example: The Food and Drug Administration (FDA) places cost prohibitive market entry barriers on pharmaceuticals. "It takes on average 12 years and over $350,000,000.00 to get a new drug from the laboratory onto the pharmacy shelf," (www.drugs.com/fda-approval-process.html). We can assume that the pharmaceutical companies support this high cost of doing business since it places severe limits on competition, which allows for extreme price gouging. Of course, it is defended as a means to maintain high quality, but we need to compare how effective our system is in minimizing adverse reactions to drugs to other nations' costs and effectiveness. We must keep in mind that we can never provide a risk-free environment where drugs cause no adverse reactions. There will always be individuals who will react negatively to particular drugs no matter how extensive a testing regimen we put in place. There is a point of diminishing returns that is reached in testing and we must accept a certain percentage of problems. However, FDA and pharmaceutical companies would rather not inform the public of this since it allows for permanent jobs in the FDA and high prices for the drug companies. This is an example of how institutions work.

has erected regulatory barriers to defend factions at the expense of the whole; there is nothing in it for them to risk dying for. They may even see the invaders as liberators.

Quigley provides insight into our nature (to establish institutions) so that we may better understand how to avoid the pitfalls all races of men (not just whites, as multiculturalists seditiously assert in order to incite revolution) have a tendency to fall into. Of course, the Founders understood these pitfalls, albeit from another approach, and erected defenses in our Constitution to protect us from such forces. But these defenses are only as effective as the citizens' willingness to enforce them extends.

Taylor (1822) approaches the subject from a different perspective than Quigley. He states, "Ethics informs us that human nature is guided by self-interest. History proclaims in every page that governments exhibit conclusive proofs of this truth," (p. 9). He then analyzes abuses of power in European governments, pointing out how exclusive privileges, extravagance, and oppressive taxation lead to class warfare. He continues:

> Such is the policy which has arrayed class against class in Europe, and marshaled all its nations into domestic combinations, envenomed against each other by an ardour to get or to keep the patronage of their governments. These patrons make their clients pay the enormous fees they covet. As no government can patronize one class but at the expense of others, partialities to its clients beget mutual fears, hopes, and hatreds, and bring grist to those who grind them for toll. Even brothers, whom nature makes friends, are converted into enemies by parental partialities. Will the partialities of a government between different classes promote the harmony and happiness of society? Is not their discord the universal consequence of the fraudulent power assumed by governments, of allotting to classes and individuals indigence or wealth, according to their own pleasure? … What has produced our existing enmities?… Do they not all proceed from an imitation of the European policy deduced from the claim of a sovereign or despotic power in governments to distribute exclusive privileges, local partialities and private property, by their own absolute will and supremacy? (pp. 13-14)

Let us consider an abridged summary of the evolution of the later part of Western civilization—as it relates to excessive factional regulations versus *laissez faire*—for a panoramic view of what is involved.

A shift took place at the end of the feudal period and at the beginning of the commercial-capitalist system around 1440, which Quigley (1961, pp. 368-69) states was the beginning of the Renaissance in Europe proper (i.e., after its spread from the Italian States). It provided great wealth creation for a very large population, which in turn allowed for population growth. Prior to this point, European populations had been in serious decline for over a century and a half (Quigley, 1961, pp. 365-67), because of the institutionalized feudal system no longer being sustainable with its strict regulatory controls. Highly regulatory systems diminish economic opportunities, causing prosperity to decline, which is reflected in population dynamics. When there is sensible and objective government involvement in social intercourse, free societies flourish—which was observed during the Renaissance—and populations tend to grow.

By 1690, an amalgamation of State mercantilism and a form of institutionalized capitalism came to dominance until 1810, at which point it became obsolete, with the highly effective *laissez faire* system replacing it. As pointed out above, this didn't last very long. The draconian regulatory addiction came back in full force at the end of the nineteenth century. Here, the "police power" was expanded dramatically and combined with German statism to radically change the structure of our government. Three changes occurred here that brought about such a destructive transformation.

The first change was based on a great deal of propaganda being circulated throughout the Western hemisphere about the evils of capitalism and the wonders of the new religion—socialism. This argument took place because of the Industrial Revolution in America and England, creating a paradigm shift in economic and social forces, which broke down class barriers, allowing for the underclass to be recognized as a social institution with its own voice that could no longer be held down. Those on the side of free market capitalism wanted the poor to discover their talents and develop wealth under free conditions based on Natural Law (though as Taylor (1822) points out, the protective tariffs, bounties, exclusive privileges, and unequal taxation benefiting the manufacturing class at the expense of all others could hardly be considered a purely free market economy). Those on the side of socialism had no patience for such evolution and wanted to take all wealth and redistribute it based on their social regulatory engineering model, which was grounded in abstractions, fantasies, and dictates, rather than through natural systems.

To better understand what happened in America, we must reflect on England, since the effects of the Industrial Revolution are well documented here and the battle between collectivists and capitalists was most intense there (perhaps because of their closer proximity to the German States, where radical collectivist thought was developed to a high level and was deeply rooted). However, we need to keep in mind what Taylor (1822, pp.148-49) suggests regarding the difference between England and the United States: England had erected all kinds of regulatory barriers to protect the manufacturing interests at the expense of the working class. In the United States, there were no such regulatory barriers during Taylor's time, only burdensome protective tariffs that the working class and all others unjustly had to contend with.

Many of the economic and social forces brought about by the Industrial Revolution were outstanding changes; however, some were stressful to the lower classes (as Charles Dickens and others attempted to reveal in their fiction). Their agricultural labor was no longer in high demand due to the Agricultural Revolution, which became an "expansive force in England about 1730," (Quigley, 1961, p. 391). They immigrated to urban centers where opportunities were to be found (with a whole new set of social pressures needing to be resolved) rather than being spread across the countryside as peasants. But overall, the standard of living dramatically improved for absolutely everyone, yes even the lower classes in spite of what radical social engineers tell us. Consider England's population explosion, from 11 million in 1801 to 21 million in 1851, demonstrating significant improvements in living standards: better housing; increased food supplies at lower prices due to the earlier British Agricultural Revolution; lower transportation costs due to railroads, as well as improvements in canals and hard surfaced all-weather roads; improvements in communications due to the telegraph; increased life expectancy; fall in infant mortality rates; improvement in public health due to sanitation systems; discovery of ether (for surgery), vaccinations, and antiseptics;

the means to eliminate child labor for the first time in history (even slavery could finally be perceived as an evil rather than a social good); extensive private education for the masses; all of which was not possible under previous conditions. So what have the collectivists been complaining about all of these years? It is not Utopia, it is not perfect—here lies the problem for them.

Also consider mass production itself, which was not for the benefit of the wealthy, since they are such a small percentage of the population (besides, the wealthy prefer unique, one-of-a-kind products that, in their minds, separate them from the masses). Mass production was for the masses, achieved through economies of scale being reached, due to high demand, based on affordable prices—heretofore unattainable—and the available capital to a large population that could afford such consumer goods (Rogge et al., 2000). Given this truth, how could the standard of living for ALL not be raised? Under these conditions, cases of death by starvation declined dramatically, perhaps much to the chagrin of the collectivist types, who wish to use the misfortune of others to manipulate the interpretation of conditions to serve their ends. However, the misfortunes of the underclass were more readily apparent than in previous times because of the increase in population in urban centers, where privations could be more frequently observed and reported to a nation that was becoming increasingly concerned with such issues.

The lesser and greater "Captains of Industry," who typically did not come from the aristocracy, were able to sell large quantities of necessary and luxury products to all segments of society. As the Captains of Industry became rich, the whole society was enriched simultaneously. All benefited from it, in spite of what collectivists suggest.[25] While poverty was not eliminated by the Industrial Revolution, it was reduced significantly by the gains that were experienced, as seen in the increased standard of living (poverty was far more severe prior to industrialization where

_____

25   Collectivists cling to the seventeenth century mercantilist view that there is a static and unexpandable body of wealth in the economy, which we now know is a false assumption in a free market society. They are convinced that we live in a limited world in which one cannot gain wealth unless another's is taken. They are either ignorant or deceitful, since wealth is constantly growing in a healthy free nation as entrepreneurs create new wealth, which then spreads throughout the society. However, in a collectivist type of society, wealth creation is curtailed, a subsequent static economy emerges with increased poverty as the end result, and one cannot advance but at the expense of another. A self-fulfilling prophecy appears to be their goal.

women, for example, would have far fewer children because of malnutrition amongst other health issues). But the standard of living is an issue of perception by contemporaneous populations. They do not compare current conditions to past hardships or progress, but focus almost exclusively on current social status and material possessions in comparison to other people. The wealth accumulated by the Captains of Industry was a target of envy by unethical or ignorant people who saw themselves as deserving of such wealth, but didn't have the wherewithal to be as successful.[26] It is easy to demonize successful capitalists since they are a minority, and then after they've been marginalized, focus on justifying the extraction of their wealth and rights, given their "evilness" for having been successful. Envy, that human emotion that does great harm to those it touches, is the primary motivator for such diabolical tactics of theft. And the socialist sophists know how to use envy to manipulate the ignorant to garner their support for the transgression of constitutional law in order to acquire power.

The Industrial Revolution and capitalism had to be discredited as anarchical by collectivist leaders—who came from the socialist and statist ranks—in order to rally the poorer classes around their banner as the means to extract private wealth through the power of government. Earlier in the century, Taylor (1822) summarized the perspective of usurpers such as these through the following words: "We will gratify your avarice if you gratify our ambition."

The term *laissez faire* was manipulated into a negative connotation by this movement. The collectivists successfully couched the argument in extreme terms, as they typically do: Either you believe in *laissez faire*, i.e., anarchy with no government, or you believe in the State controlling the lives of all citizens, i.e. statism or socialism, through regulatory mandates, so that wealth and "privileges," as opposed to rights, can be distributed by an omnipotent government run by beneficent and angelic collectivists. As usual, there was no middle ground in their dogmatic argument.

Statism—a blend of German capitalism and socialism—vested sovereignty in the State, i.e., the politicians instead of the people,

---

26   "[I]n issues between the strong and the weak, the latter is by no means always the wronged party. On the contrary it often happens that in his very weakness he has an effective weapon for making the circumstances comply with his view. Not infrequently it is the weak who is the real tyrant. In his judgment of others he finds a compensation for his weakness," (Nygren, p. 445, 1949)

which in 1910, William Graham Sumner predicted would cause "The next generations ... to see war and social calamities," (Gabriel, 1956, p. 241). As the maxim goes, if we surrender liberty for security, both will be lost. We seem to have not yet learned this lesson. Many American politicians and jurists still hold to the statist philosophy, though they may not know it by that name. In the United States it was known by various names, but eventually the term "Progressivism" took hold in the early twentieth century. When that finally became unpopular, like all of its previous names, it hijacked the endearing title of "Liberalism," which traditionally had been a philosophy of enlightened self-interest, equality before the law (not equality of outcomes), and liberty. Of course, this was turned on its head by the Progressive movement in order to "save" humanity.

The new "Liberalism" was a political war against capitalism, with the expectation of replacing it with collectivism. The word socialism, Progressives/Liberals discovered, could not be used because of its unpopularity with the majority of Americans, so they deceitfully denied any affiliation with it.

Let us consider what Skousen (1962, pp. 259-62) informs us regarding what the collectivist tactics have entailed in the twentieth century:

> Let us go down a list of current strategy goals which the Communists and their fellow travelers are seeking to achieve. These are all part of the campaign to soften America for the final takeover. It should be kept in mind that many loyal Americans are working for these same objectives because they are not aware that these objectives are designed to destroy us.

- Provide American aid to all nations....
- Use technical decisions of the courts to weaken basic American institutions by claiming their activities violate civil rights.
- Get control of the schools. Use them as transmission belts for socialism and current Communist propaganda. Soften the curriculum. Get control of teachers' associations. Put the party line in textbooks.
- Infiltrate the press. Get control of book-review assignments, editorial writing, policy-making positions.
- Gain control of key positions in radio, TV and motion pictures.

- Continue discrediting American culture by degrading all forms of artistic expression. An American Communist cell was told to "eliminate all good sculpture from parks and buildings, substitute shapeless, awkward and meaningless forms."
- Control art critics and directors of art museums. "Our plan is to promote ugliness, repulsive, meaningless art."
- Eliminate all laws governing obscenity by calling them "censorship" and a violation of free speech and free press.
- Break down cultural standards of morality by promoting pornography and obscenity in books, magazines, motion pictures, radio and TV.
- Present homo-sexuality, degeneracy and promiscuity as "normal, natural, healthy."
- Infiltrate the churches and replace revealed religion with "social" religion. Discredit the Bible and emphasize the need for intellectual maturity which does not need a "religious crutch."
- Eliminate prayer or any phase of religious expression in the schools on the ground that it violates the principle of "separation of church and state."
- Discredit the American Constitution by calling it inadequate old-fashioned, out of step with modern needs, a hindrance to cooperation between nations on a world-wide basis.
- Discredit the American founding fathers. Present them as selfish aristocrats who had no concern for the "common man."
- Belittle all forms of American culture and discourage the teaching of American history....
- Support any socialist movement to give centralized control over any part of the culture—education, social agencies, welfare programs, mental health clinics, etc.
- Infiltrate and gain control of more unions.
- Infiltrate and gain control of big business.
- Discredit the family as an institution. Encourage promiscuity and easy divorce.
- Emphasize the need to raise children away from the negative influence of parents. Attribute prejudices ... of children to suppressive influence of parents.
- ... Give the World Court jurisdiction over nations and individuals alike.

Carson (1985, p. 68) points out that in the *Communist Manifesto*, Marx and Engels set forth a ten-point program by which countries would move [toward communism]:

1. Abolition of property in land and application of all rents of land to public purposes.
2. A heavy progressive or graduated income tax.
3. Abolition of all right of inheritance.
4. Confiscation of the property of all emigrants and rebels.
5. Centralization of credit in the hands of the State, by means of a national bank with State capital and an exclusive monopoly.
6. Centralization of the means of communication and transport in the hands of the State.
7. Extension of the number of State factories and instruments of production...
8. Equal obligation of all to work. Establishment of industrial armies, especially for agriculture.
9. Combination of agriculture with manufacturing industries; gradual abolition of the distinction between town and country, by a more equable distribution of the population over the country.
10. Free education for all children in public schools. Abolition of children's factory labour in its present form. Combination of education with industrial production, etc.

Much of this has already transpired, especially under FDR's reign, but subsequent presidents have reversed certain portions.

It is interesting to note that since our American system has adopted significant aspects of socialism, many contemporary Liberals are once again advocating and defending it—the ruse worked, and now they can come out of their closets.

The collectivist's *modus operandi* has been to tear apart the fabric of our culture and to reconstruct it with socialistic religious ideology,[27] as was observed in China, the Soviet Union, and to a limited extent in the United States. It is seen in our contemporary revisionist history books and in the subversive multicultural education teachers are expected to embrace; our Western culture is to be overthrown. Academia is dominated by collectivists (Maranto, Redding, & Hess, 2009, pp. 15-33), and they are attempting to indoctrinate our youth through their version of history and science, and to this day, many of them still speak disparagingly of *laissez faire* government. Perhaps this is due to the inability of many of them to compete in this environment. They demonize it since it is beyond their understanding, which reveals another human frailty—the inability to respect talents one does not possess or understand.

Of course, collectivists have adored sophistry and used it masterfully to manipulate a large segment of the population, especially through our educational system. However, *laissez faire* economists have always been steadfastly opposed to anarchical forms of government. Taylor (1822, p. 161) quotes the British economist, Thomas Malthus:

> In leaving the whole question of saving to the uninfluenced operation of individual interest and individual feelings, we shall best conform to that principle

27   Consider FDR's 1939 New Deal Court choice of Felix Frankfurter for the Supreme Court Justice position. Frankfurter was a Progressive and collectivist. Consider his own words in "Law and Order," *Yale Review* 10 (1920, 233-34), where he provides, "It is nothing but belated recognition of economic facts—that the era of romantic individualism is no more *[Whoever said individualism was romantic? Perhaps Frankfurter read to many romantic novels! Maybe this is the reason he lived in a fantasy world where he believed Utopia could be achieved.]*.... We are confronted with mass production and mass producers; the individual, in his industrial relations, but a cog in the great collectivity.... And it is through the collectivity, through enlisting its will and its wisdom, that the necessary increase in production alone will come," (Epstein, 2006, quoting Frankfurter, p. 94). Are we to take this individual's and other judicial collectivists' desire to rewrite the Constitution as precedent-setting and unalterable? Are future Supreme Court nominees to be held to standards established by such dangerous radicals as Frankfurter, who was mentored by another extreme and dangerous radical, Justice Oliver Wendell Holmes, Jr.? The individual being nothing but "a cog in the great collectivity" means that private property, private contracts, rights, etc., are worthless romantic notions no longer having a place under the new collective state leviathan—the very antithesis of our Constitution. For a Supreme Court Justice to assert this upon citizens would be nothing short of treason! And decisions based on statism/collectivism should be sought out and overturned with extreme prejudice–even by lower courts! Frankfurter et al. pursued saving humanity by extracting rights and liberties of individuals who are not of the collectivist religion and assigning them to the true believers. It appears the separation of church and State does not apply to collectivists, as evidenced by their holy crusade.

of political economy laid down by Adam Smith, which teaches us a general maxim, liable to very few exceptions, that the wealth of nations is best secured by allowing every person, **as long as he adheres to the rules of justice**, to pursue his own interest in his own way.

Malthus was also quoted (p. 160) as stating, "If a country can only be rich by running a successful race for low wages, I should be disposed to say at once—perish such riches." Malthus may be controversial for his theory on population dynamics, since it appeared cold and calculating, but he truly cared about the poor. After all, he researched the subject extensively because of his concerns for them. But he was a scientist attempting to answer difficult questions of the times, and scientists need to appear detached from emotions when analyzing phenomena, though, obviously, he was not completely detached given his concern for them. His population theories may have been proven erroneous, since he appeared to be unaware of the pace at which scientific advancements were progressing, but his concern was genuine.

Adam Smith (1776) was also very concerned about the poor, and sharply criticized powerful associations, politicians, and moneyed interests who were abusive of the weak (see Smith, p. 493-94, where he severely condemns monopolistic tendencies of both the moneyed interests and the craft guilds). England had a variety of laws and regulations favoring the moneyed interests and craft guilds at the expense of laborers. On behalf of the laborers, Smith pushed for the repeal of such government infringement.

He points out:

> Soldiers and seamen ... when discharged from the king's service, are at liberty to exercise any trade, within any town or place of Great Britain.... Let the same natural liberty of exercising what species of industry they please be restored to all his majesty's subjects, in the same manner...; that is, break down the exclusive privileges of corporations, and repeal the statute of apprenticeship [*which protected members of trade and craft guilds*], both which are real encroachments upon natural liberty, and add to these the repeal of the law of settlements, so that a poor workman, when thrown out of employment either in one trade or in one place, may seek for it in

another trade or in another place, without the fear either of a prosecution or of a removal, and neither the publick [sic] nor the individuals will suffer much more from the occasional disbanding some particular classes of manufacturers.... Our manufacturers [*referring to the owners*] have no doubt great merit with their country, but they cannot have more than those who defend it with their blood, nor deserve to be treated with more delicacy. (pp. 470-71)

It becomes obvious that the defenders of *laissez faire* were not the demons the collectivists have made them out to be. They have always been more concerned about the underclass than the collectivists. Their goal has consistently been to establish an environment where all may enrich themselves, though it may be challenging to get there because of unethical and greedy people from unions and from moneyed and collectivist interests (greed is not only measured in money and possessions; there is also lust for power, which no sector is immune from). The collectivists have always wanted to establish a divided society where they have the control and all others are to be pawns for the collectivists' self-aggrandizement, and many in the academic community lead this charge.

Epstein (2006, pp. ix-x) refers to Progressives' accusations against classical liberalism[28] as "overblown rhetoric" and provides: "We are often told that defenders of the pre-New Deal world order believe in an 'unregulated America'...[and] that all property rights are inviolable"—both of which Epstein points out are falsehoods. Of course, the greater part of American nineteenth century educated society that embraced *laissez faire* never pursued an anarchical form of government in which a completely unregulated society dictated social intercourse—that would have been suicidal, demonstrating the ridiculousness of this assertion. *Laissez faire* was a belief that minimal government intrusion—only the amount necessary to achieve social peace, harmony, safety, and security—is the best means of raising the standard of living for all, which has proven to be absolutely true when compared to all other economic systems. When we look at earlier republics,

---

28   Classical liberalism is based on Natural Law from the Enlightenment period, which the Founders relied upon in establishing our form of government. It is in no way to be confused with contemporary liberalism—a name hijacked from its traditional meaning because of its attractiveness to most Americans—which is grounded in statism and goes by the name of progressivism.

such as Rome (prior to Caesar of course), the Italian republics of the Renaissance period, Holland, industrialized England, and then the United States, we see a pattern of success emerge when liberty, property rights, and a free market economy are allowed to flourish, tempered, of course, by just and objective regulation.

Popular literature in the late nineteenth and early twentieth centuries, in part, demonized capitalism and subsequently influenced legislation. It is amazing how fiction dictated the course of American politics to the degree it did. Consider Upton Sinclair's fictional book, *The Jungle*, which Sinclair intended as an attack on capitalism. Instead, it influenced the enactment of the 1906 Pure Food and Drug Act and the Meat Inspection Act. We need to keep in mind that Sinclair and many of his colleagues were novelists and socialists, not scientists. He even stated in his gubernatorial bid in 1951, "The American People will take Socialism, but they won't take the label." This is the type of novelist that influenced politics in the free world. This is not to say that corrective action in some sectors wasn't warranted, but sound science and constitutional law must provide the guiding light rather than arbitrary emotional appeals by abstract romantic thinkers who were at war with logic and reason.[29] John Adams (1776) put it well when he said "poets read history to collect flowers not fruits—they attend to fanciful images, not the effects of social institutions."

An important point collectivist types miss is that the state of mind a population experiences under either depressed or affluent economic conditions determines their altruistic tendencies. When the majority of a population is in a depressed economic state, nearly everyone is looking out for their own survival and have little time to consider the needs of others. When a majority of the population is

---

29   As it relates to the environment, John Muir wrote literature based on abstract romantic and sentimental views of nature in this period, with religious overtones scattered throughout his works. The Romantic Movement, which began in the early nineteenth century, was still strong in the late nineteenth and early twentieth centuries, and Muir captured this perspective in his works on nature adventures. He influenced a swing in the country's view on nature from one of science and reason to romanticism and adventure. While this is fine for individuals to identify with, it was not appropriate for our Federal or State governments to do so. Of course, motivated citizens help drive legislation to serve their interests, so the dream of high wilderness adventure might be useful for motivating the electorate in pushing for environmental legislation where it is beneficial to society, but once legislators are involved, environmental laws MUST be based on reason and logic, not romantic fantasies conjured up by the imagination, which has come to dominate environmental law.

affluent, as industrialized England and America were in the period under discussion, the people have a sense of security; and being a social animal with compassionate tendencies, a significant portion will seek to help their fellow man[30] (the United States is by far the largest charitable contributor in the world, when private and public donations are combined). This behavior in itself demonstrates the success of capitalism, since we don't observe much philanthropy in nations that are not predominately capitalistic. Of course, such philanthropic tendencies can be taken to extreme levels in which everything possible must be done to "save" the poor, even to the point of destroying the very economic conditions that allow for compassion and philanthropy to flourish.

In addition to altruistic tendencies, the success of an economic system can be measured by the support of the arts, sciences, literature, crafts, technological advances, etc., which the American Captains of Industry were famous for. Under a depressed economic system, as seen in predominately socialist nations, we see little advancement in any of these areas of human endeavor, unless acquired through imitation, importation, or espionage, as we observed in the Soviet Union; whereas under affluent economic circumstances, we see a proliferation of such interests developed to the highest levels (Andrew Carnegie being perhaps the best example, though by collectivist standards he would have to be labeled as a "robber baron," since he created and accumulated so much wealth).

England was the origin of the Industrial Revolution because of its respect for the rule of law, private property rights, the reduction of class barriers, and the establishment of the fractional reserve banking system, which allowed for the financing of the Industrial Revolution (Quigley, 1961, p. 380). America adopted these attributes and took them to a higher level. Combining this with the *laissez faire* economic approach, American prosperity went through the roof, and the country became a magnet for foreigners who had no hope of wealth creation in their home countries, where factions/institutions had once again resurrected regulatory barriers to protect themselves. This created a serious problem for America, which brings us to the second major change that occurred here—the immigration flood.

---

30   Consider the eighteenth century French Philosophes who were dedicated to improving the lot of mankind based on Enlightenment principles.

The wave of millions of ill-equipped—in capital, skills, and education—poor immigrants coming to this country in the latter part of the nineteenth and early part of the twentieth centuries was unparalleled in history. This drastically increased the number of unemployed and underemployed, which expanded the underclass and our slums (a comparison that might put it into perspective is the conditions of refugee camps of the twentieth century, which were notoriously unhealthy and dangerous). The economy simply could not absorb such numbers of immigrants fast enough, and their huge numbers, some have referred to as a tidal wave, depressed wages for all in the laboring classes, including U.S. citizens, and thereby created a cycle of perpetual poverty as long as immigration went unchecked.[31] However, instead of checking immigration as conditions demanded, popular opinion turned on capitalism – the very engine that created the incentive to immigrate to this country – pushing for extensive regulations, and blaming business owners (who were compared to feudal aristocrats) for the plight of laborers (who were portrayed as feudal serfs). Of course, no such comparisons were justified, since historically, the interests of aristocrats demanded that they keep serfs in perpetual servitude, which was not the policy of the American capitalist system, since it would have damaged the system rather than helped it. Naturally, anti-capitalistic policies promoted by collectivists would simply inhibit economic growth and job creation, thereby harming the very population it was meant to help. See Carson (1985, pp. 58-63) for an in-depth look at the difficulties immigration created.

---

31   Even though this is after the immigration flood, *West Coast Hotel Co. v. Parrish*, 300 U.S. 379 at 399 (1937) demonstrates the evils of excessive amounts of available labor relative to the demand and the subsequent knee-jerk reaction of legislators and Courts attempting to address the problem in an unreasoned manner. The Court stated, "The Legislature was entitled to adopt measures to reduce the evils of the 'sweating system,' the exploiting of workers at wages so low as to be insufficient to meet the bare cost of living, thus making their very helplessness the occasion of a most injurious competition." Such injustices are the product of too much supply of labor relative to the demand. Immigration contributed to this problem in profound ways earlier in the century. Obviously, 1937 was the time of our Great Depression, the protracted length of which was due to very bad and un-American economic policies on the part of FDR. Regulation that ties the hands of capital in the name of helping the laboring class typically intensifies the economic problems; thereby causing more harm than good to the very class it claims to be helping. Neither West Coast Hotel Co. nor Parrish were at fault; poor government policies that created poor economic conditions and causing extensive unemployment (as well as underemployment and poor wages) with too many unskilled workers (demonstrating a serious problem with the educational system) was at fault. (See Epstein, 2006, pp. 92-93, for an analysis of improper labor regulation and the potential consequences).

Of course, the immigrant problem is not typically discussed, since it is not politically correct to point this out; and since most of us are descendants of immigrants, many feel they can't blame their ancestors. But before we can address problems, we must first identify them—as painful as it might be—even if it affects us individually.

The third change that brought about radical regulatory transformation in the United States was the expansion of regulations to the larger units of government, i.e., from the States to the Federal government (a trend that the anti-federalists, who argued against the proposed Constitution, predicted). Quigley informs us this is a natural progression in which power tends to devolve upon the core of a civilization at the expense of the periphery (this explains why the anti-federalists wanted major revisions to the proposed Constitution, in order to protect individuals and the States, before they would sign on to it). The Founders had provided for the broadest responsibilities to be vested in the more local units of government, and lesser amounts in the larger units as a check on this evolutionary tendency—though it proved to be inadequate. This principle was supported by utility, i.e., authority is to be vested in that level of government that best serves the needs of the people, or which cannot be adequately accomplished at another level. Where society's needs are capable of being accomplished at local levels, the authority MUST remain there in order to disperse power and minimize the concentration of it (a concentration of power creates an environment fertile for corruption since there is access to large sums of revenue, whereas dispersed power and revenue robs overly-ambitious men of incentive). Late nineteenth century American statist politicians wished to reverse this, and, to the detriment of the country, they were largely successful, which was due in large part to the Civil War marginalizing States' rights.

This has been an important ingredient in the debate between the polar political philosophies in America. One side wants most, if not all power in the hands of an omnipotent and beneficent Federal government (of course, power can be centralized, but beneficence will only be provided to those belonging to the political party, as we observed in China and the Soviet Union), the other side wants it dispersed only to the appropriate level, which depends on the current needs and circumstances.

The latter half of the nineteenth and the first half of the twentieth centuries was a period of political upheaval in America in which the pendulum swung away from liberty and toward authoritarianism, as it had in Europe. Quigley says that civil evolutionary forces advance from one of economic expansion—where prosperity dominates—to one of conflict, where domineering institutions and their irrational, defensive arguments rule. He refers to this period as an Age of Conflict, which he estimates our country entered into around 1890. Citizens began to organize in order to achieve

> all kinds of restrictive agreements, tacit or explicit, restricting new investment or entry of new enterprises into an activity. Increased pressure was put on governments … and business organizations were formed to fight labor demands for any larger share of the goods being produced.
>
> At the same time, labor and agriculture were reacting in a similar fashion, forming political pressure groups or even political parties, and seeking common action to raise prices, divide markets, exclude foreign competition, and to strike back at organized industry, finance, or transportation.
>
> While these activities were occurring as symptoms … of the growing class conflicts associated with an Age of Conflict, the other marks of such a period were no less obvious. Imperialist wars developed from epidemic to endemic status in our culture…. At the same time, on the intellectual level occurred a great upsurging of irrationality…. All the characteristics of an age of irrationality began to appear on all sides—increased gambling, increased smoking, the growing use of alcohol and narcotics, a growing obsession with sex and with perversions of sex, [etc.]; above all, perhaps, a growing tendency to regard violence as a solution for all problems, be they domestic, social, economic, ideological, or international….
>
> All these characteristics of any Age of Conflict are too obvious to require further comment. They arose, as is usual in an Age of Conflict, because the organizational patterns of our culture ceased to function as instruments but had become institutionalized. This process was evident on all levels of culture. Religious organizations no longer linked men to God but adopted diverse mundane purposes…. Our social patterns no longer satisfied our gregarious needs…. Our political organizations increased the burden

of their demands on our time, energy, and wealth but provided with growing ineffectiveness the justice, public order, education, protection, or incidental amenities we had come to expect from them. And, on the military level, costs rose at an astronomical rate without being able to catch up with our increasing danger. (Quigley, 1961, pp. 404-06)

Summary of the Evolution of our Regulatory Culture

This is the atmosphere in which changes in wildlife management took place, and the enactment of wildlife statutes and their subsequent regulations tended to be as extreme as the times. Change was certainly necessary as social conditions changed, but extreme radical change was not required to solve the problems of the day. Sensible and reasonable laws and regulations should have been enacted to address current problems—not corrosive policies injurious to liberty and the Constitution. In the future, citizens must elect representatives that have the vision to see where we deviated from sound principles, and who have the will to make our way back to them (the principles, not the times) in order to restore liberty to its proper place.

Given what has been provided above, this chapter may lead one to conclude this is more of a political treatise than a work addressing environmental law and wildlife management, and there would be some truth in this, since the two are intertwined to the point where law and regulation cannot be comprehended unless an understanding of political forces are grasped. This requires a historical review, brief as it may be in this work, in order to understand how we arrived where we now stand, and then to determine how best to make corrections for our deviations from sound law.

The Application of Regulation

Understanding the need for regulation provides us with a framework to decide what sort of regulations we should have, what level of government would best serve the regulatory ends, how broad or limited the regulations should be, and what level of punishment is adequate to accomplish deterrence of violations? Keep in mind that no matter how severe punishment may be, we will never achieve perfect compliance with the law. It always comes down to what the average level of delinquency is. The point of diminishing returns (i.e., where more severe punishment achieves little to no further deterrence) is a good gauge, however, it must be balanced with individual rights at all times. For without this fundamental understanding of justice, government power becomes a weapon to punish those of the unpopular political persuasions.

Novak (1996, p. 45) summarizes the purpose of regulation:

> By abating a nuisance or imprisoning a criminal, courts were not destroying liberties, they were defending the rights, actually expanding the liberty, of wronged citizens. The theorists of the well-regulated society, it is important to remember, saw themselves as champions, not critics, of liberty and rights. They merely pointed out that true freedom was always a product of **reciprocal** protection and respect. Liberty and the common good were not antagonistic in this formulation; they were mutually reinforcing. (Emphasis added)

This passage is the key to an understanding of our system of law. Unfortunately, most do not understand this principle. In particular, many in the academies do not understand it, yet they are responsible for educating our youth. Many academics believe liberties and rights must be marginalized, if not outright eliminated, in order to "save" humanity—the poor in particular, whom William Graham Sumner (1883, p. 107) classified as their "pets." What they fail to realize is that if there are no rights, individual liberties, and respect for property, what source of authority can they look to for justification in government helping the poor? Obviously there is none, since no one's life really matters under this misguided philosophy (the tens of millions that died in Nazi Germany, communist China, and the Soviet Union attest to this fact). The do-gooders do it because it gives them a sense of purpose and power. What they don't understand is, by destroying rights and liberties, they plant the seeds for the eventual abandonment of the poor. If government can be used to abuse the rich, e.g., through the present penal (i.e., illegal) graduated income tax system, it can also be used to abuse the poor. It is safer to treat everyone equitably, with a high regard for rights and liberties, so that all are protected from the extreme gyrations of fickle constituencies who can be easily swayed by masters of sophistry and specious rhetoric. Just because the "save humanity" faction is dominant today doesn't mean it will be tomorrow—this is a certainty. It is better to erect barriers against factional forces so that when a certain faction's power is out of favor, the interests of its members are still protected from the specious forces of the current dominant faction.

An extremely important figure, whose works substantially influenced the formation of our system of government, is John Locke—a true champion of free government. Locke (1690, page 234) states:

> So that, however it may be mistaken, the end of law is not to abolish or restrain, but to preserve and enlarge freedom ... for liberty is, to be free from restraint and violence from others ... but freedom is not, as we are told, a liberty for every man to do what he [likes]: (for who could be free, when every other man's humour might domineer over him?) but a liberty to dispose and order ... his actions ... and his whole property, within the allowance of [law], and therein not to be subject to the arbitrary will of another, but freely follow his own.

This defines the fundamental purpose of all law and regulation within a free society. In discussing rights and liberties based on Hugo Grotius's perspective (commonly considered the father of modern Natural Law), Haakonssen (1996, p. 26) provides that Natural Law sanctions "any action [by individuals] which is not injurious to others in such a way that social relations break down." Stealing from the rich to give to the poor is a breakdown of social relations. This is also the case when giving preferential rights to certain groups at the expense of others. Or, as it relates to wildlife management, extreme regulatory controls over a benign activity such as falconry also breaks down social relations, given the unjustified law enforcement encroachments falconers must contend with. Rights and liberties decay under these circumstances, and the progression of this decay is reinforced with each additional encroachment.

Chief Justice Shaw refined Grotius's and Locke's principles in a key decision in *Commonwealth v Alger*, Supreme Judicial

Court of Massachusetts, 61 Mass. 53 (1851), where he embraced common law principles and applied the term *police power*. While the principle expressed in this case was nothing new, the term was relatively new. Perhaps the eloquence of Shaw's words so impressed the legal establishment of that period that they decided to embrace the term *police power* as a symbol of the principle he expressed, rather than looking at it as an innovation of law, which it most certainly was not.[32]

One Cyrus Alger was indicted for erecting a wharf beyond established limits. In his decision, Shaw provides:

> We think it is a settled principle, growing out of the nature of well ordered civil society, that every holder of property, however absolute and unqualified may be his title, holds it under the implied liability that his use of it may be so regulated, that it shall not be injurious to the equal enjoyment of others having an equal right to the enjoyment of their property, nor injurious to the rights of the community. [*This expresses perfectly the principled reasoning of the need for regulation. Legal regulation is an* **objective** *pursuit of promoting civil behavior, which maintains a harmonious society. Illegal regulation, which is the pursuit of* **subjective** *behavior deemed appropriate by factions—the timeless enemies of liberty—is the cause of social strife.*]
>
> … The power we allude to is rather the police power, the power vested in the legislature by the [State] constitution, to … establish all manner of … reasonable laws, statutes and ordinances, either with penalties or without, **not repugnant to the constitution**…. [*This is a critical aspect of regulation. If a constitution, State or Federal, is inadequate to a need, then it can be amended before action can take place.*] (Emphasis added)
>
> [The prohibitions established by the legislature of noxious use of property,] a prohibition imposed because such use would be injurious to the public … is not an appropriation of the property to a public use [*i.e., a taking*], **but the restraint of an injurious private use by the owner**…. [*However, we must not be lured into the deceptive*

---

32   Epstein (2006, p. 9) states, "[T]he proper rendering of the police power—the ability of the state to act to advance health, safety, morals, or the general welfare—is one of the critical elements of constitutional law."

practice that is being employed by using the term "the public good" to regulate or prohibit the use of private property for any and all reasons a legislative body or bureaucratic agency may conjure up. A key litmus test is to determine if an owner is using his property in such a way that causes injury or is a nuisance to others. However, if his actions might indirectly affect society, such as using his land where an endangered species is found, then in order to mitigate a wrong to the owner, his right to use his land may be restrained for the necessary period of time. But he must be compensated by society so that the cost is not borne by individual citizens, but rather shared by all because the benefit is to all. (see Epstein, 1997)] (Emphasis added)

Wherever there is a general right on the part of the public, and a general duty on the part of a land owner, or any other person, to respect such right, we think it is competent for the legislature, by a specific enactment, to prescribe a precise, practical rule for ... securing such right, and enforcing respect for it."

Chief Justice Shaw's explanation of the need for regulation expresses perfectly the *laissez faire* perspective of governing in a free society. He adequately defends individual liberty and property rights, but conditions this perspective on the need for every citizen to respect the rights and interests of all other citizens—not just a few and not the majority, but all. In other words, no one may be allowed to infringe upon another. This is in stark contrast to the collectivist types, who infringe upon individual liberty and property rights in the name of "saving humanity," or in the case of environmental protectionists, in the name of "saving animals and the environment." The destruction of rights opens the door for totalitarian governments, where the "saving" of anything will be dependent upon the will of the dictators.

Goble and Freyfogle (2002, p. 412) describe the progression from our well-established common law understanding of our forefathers, grounded in principles of equity, to the social welfare philosophy grounded in the massive and illegal expansion of Federal powers that came to dominate the twentieth century:

The transition from the common-law vision of a "well-regulated society" to the police power[33] carried important implications in terms of the allocation of power among government branches.... At common law, judges hearing nuisance actions decided whether a particular activity did or did not cause undue harm, and hence whether it was consistent with the public good. As statutes became more widespread and specific [*and as elected representatives and jurists came to embrace statism*], the key issue in a judicial dispute increasingly was not whether the defendant's activity was a nuisance, but whether it complied with the governing statute [*i.e., a shift away from the concept of liberty under the rule of law, and the beginning of authoritarianism under the rule of legislators and jurists—based frequently on arbitrary, subjective agendas emanating from factions—in which individuals are sacrificed on the altar of the collective needs*]. Statutes could be more precise than the common law, and hence could give clearer guidance, as the court in *Alger* recognized [*although Alger followed common law reasoning perfectly*]. When legislatures updated statutes they changed the law in a more clear-cut, abrupt way than did common law courts with their characteristically ... precedent-tied style of decision writing [*since in America it is not the job of jurists to change law*]. Yet, once enacted, statutes also had a static quality that gave rise to potential problems of obsolescence. Moreover, statutes with all their detail often obscured the underlying principles— such as *sic utere tuo ut alienum non laedas* [use your own so as not to injure another] and *salus populi suprema lex est* [the welfare of the people is the supreme law]—which emerged so clearly in common law decisions.

These two maxims express the political philosophy our law rests upon. While liberty is understood as the greatest good, it is

---

33   This is not accurate. The transition was from the common law vision to the statist vision, where government is seen as the beneficent parent. The police power expressed in *Alger* was based on common law understanding, whereas statism, under the perspective of collectivists, was a policy of using government to extract liberties in order to "cure" society of all social evils. It appears in some circles the term *police power* is synonymous with *statism*. This is not to imply these authors were of the statist persuasion. However, there are many who use the police power as a synonym for statism, with many legal scholars not knowing the difference.

not boundless. Boundless liberty is anarchy, and would place us back in a state of nature in which, as Thomas Hobbes asserted, all would be at war with one another. These maxims state that individual actions must be in line with responsible behavior so as to avoid harm to others or to society. Law and regulations are the means to this end, and so long as they are understood as a means to protect *socially responsible liberty*, they are not a threat to individuals or society. However, once they no longer protect responsible liberty, they are no longer a mechanism for good, and therefore become the vehicle for abuse and tyranny. The nature of mankind defines this truth.

Under Enlightenment-era principles, there was a constant struggle to restrain the subjective values of factions (the checks and balances principle) while searching for objective values that fit all men under all circumstances, for the time man has on this earth. Hence the reason for studying history. Sir Matthew Hale, the preeminent seventeenth century English jurist and legal scholar, provides us with insight into this principle in his book, *The History of the Common Law of England* (1713). Hale makes it clear that the common law was to provide for "the common rule for the administration of common justice." (This is something we have deviated from because of factional influences asserting that the poor and minorities have one set of rights, while middle and upper class white males have a subservient set of rights—affirmative action being the perfect example.) Hale points out how the common law made corrections for "errors, distempers or iniquities of men or times," and that when "the peace of the kingdom, and right order of government, have received interruption, the common law [makes corrections for] those distempers, and reduce[s] the kingdom to its just state and temperament, as our present (and former) times can easily witness." Hale continues: "[The common law] is also, that which declares and asserts the rights and liberties, and the properties of the subject; and is the just, known, and common rule of justice and right between man and man, within this kingdom." In addition Hale provided, "[I]t is called the common law, because it is the common ... rule of justice in this kingdom ... [and is] that law which is common to the generality of all persons, things and causes." (pp. 30-31 & 37)

However, the new statist doctrine discards all of this, believing legislatures enacting statist oriented statutes are, for the most part, free from scrutiny. Jurists of the statist persuasion frequently believe they are not to analyze the legitimacy of statist statutes (Justice Frankfurter and his "judicial restraint" position exemplify this); they are simply to enforce them without question. They see the legislative power of liberal causes in a similar light as the archaic concept of the Divine Right of Kings, in which the law cannot be questioned because it is ordained by a higher power, which in the minds of liberals is the desire to save mankind collectively, as opposed to individually, and to create a utopia on Earth.

It becomes evident that our legal system has been experimenting with dangerously new legal innovations throughout the late nineteenth century and most of the twentieth century. Oliver Wendell Holmes, Jr. (a devout follower of skepticism) was at the pinnacle of legal experimentation in the early twentieth century, and admitted to his part in it. He inserted his relativistic perspective (which came to be known by the inappropriate name of *Legal Realism*—the idea that law is simply the arbitrary creation of men with no underlying fundamental principles) into judicial decision-making. Holmes came to be known as the patron saint of Legal Realism (Gabriel, 1956, pp. 411-12 & 419). (Frank (1930, p. 277) summarizes Holmes' thought: "Holmes has been telling us for fifty years that, in effect, the Golden Rule is that there is no Golden Rule.") Scientists and mathematicians could never come to any conclusions if this were to be embraced. Based on Holmes' relativistic "philosophical" assertions, a rocket could never have been sent to the moon because there is no reality and there are no truths. There are only emanations of relativistic "truths" from the minds of men who create their own reality (Carson, 1988, p. 20). This might make for entertaining metaphysical debates, but it creates chaos and ruin when applied to law and the governing of a civil society. For example, bureaucrats are unable to follow any stable pattern in applying regulations since law is a moving target; therefore, they make their own rules until some court tells them otherwise, and even then they may ignore it, knowing that another judge may very well rule differently.

Stability in law is a fundamental first principle for a prosperous society, and while we may not always fully comprehend the original causes of phenomena, we can understand the *effects* being either beneficial or detrimental to individuals and society. The Scottish Enlightenment taught us there are certain moral truths, discovered through our moral senses, that need to be followed if we expect to have peace, order, and harmony in society. Experimentation in social engineering, as Holmes and others played with, creates instability and chaos. If citizens are unsure of what the law will be from year to year, because of some arbitrary exertions by the ruling faction, which is what occurs under a relativistic system, they cannot make long-term commitments or investments. This is destructive to an economy because it tends to polarize economic conditions so that a very small minority holds all the wealth and power, while the majority becomes disenfranchised and ends up living in poverty. This will be the end result of relativism and skepticism.

A good example of the arbitrary experimentation of the Court is found in *Geer v. Connecticut*, 161 U.S. 519 (1896). In 1896, the Supreme Court was fumbling for answers to the serious problem of diminishing wildlife populations, which was blamed on excessive harvest of wildlife, but which was actually due primarily to the dramatic loss of habitat. Instead of searching for an answer within our Constitution—the only authority they had at their disposal—they searched outside our legal institutions and found something they believed could be force-fit into American jurisprudence. In *Geer*, the Court resurrected the antiquated feudalistic power the English King had over wildlife, thereby injecting a revised feudal system into our government,[34] which the Founding generation had utterly rejected over a century earlier. In addition, they seemed to have embraced statism, which had recently been imported from Germany. With eyes wide open, they invited the seeds of tyranny into our political system. Thankfully, future Supreme Courts resoundingly rejected this feudalistic/statist virus; however, we have yet to completely purge it from State institutions. In addition, some environmental law departments at universities recognize

---

34   As a side note: "[T]he Middle Ages had thought of society as an organism or a 'body' in which individuals were mere 'members'" (Strayer & Gatzke, 1979). (This is not unlike contemporary collectivists.) In contrast, under the Social Contract theory the Founders embraced, individual rights and independence (not unlimited rights and independence), which is grounded in civility and enlightened self-interest, come before society because the reason people belong to society is to protect their reciprocal and mutual interests. If their interests are not served, why belong to society? The majority in the *Geer* Court was either ignorant or dismissive of this fundamental principle in American governance. We merely need to look to the Soviet Union, which had an extensive underground black-market for many standard consumer products, to see what happens when government doesn't serve the interests of its people. Even though Soviet subjects lived within the nation, they were not really a part of it—they chose to live outside of it as much as they possibly could. They had no interest in contributing to the system; they simply weaved their way around it and through it in any way that served their selfish ends. This is the inevitable end result of collectivism. So one must ask which system of government promotes selfish behavior more—collectivism or capitalism? History unequivocally shows that collectivism does.

the opportunity the State Ownership Doctrine—initiated by *Geer*—offers them, and they are doing their very best to expand this Doctrine to provide more power to courts in order to extract more rights from citizens and to assert their protectionist agendas. More on *Geer* in the *Ownership* section of this work.

Twentieth Century America

What is the reason there is a viable market for wild fish and wild taken furs, but not for wild game birds? It is due to various sectors in the American political landscape that fought for dominance over wildlife access. Wealthy individuals—such as Theodore Roosevelt, who was a Progressive—in the nineteenth century attempted to import the European aristocratic perspective that sport hunting developed "noble" qualities in individuals and that it must be promoted as a gentlemanly sport. This perspective was warmly embraced by the first American practitioners of falconry in the early and mid-twentieth century, and there are still vestiges of this attitude amongst some in the falconry community.[35]

Sport hunting was one venue to develop these "noble" aristocratic attributes; conversely, market hunting was viewed with contempt as an example of the desperate lower classes' struggle to survive, and, further, of depleting the quarry that the aristocratic sportsman viewed as properly his—just as the English aristocrats saw it in Britain.

Goble and Freyfogle (2002, p. 33) provide some insight: "Beginning in the mid-nineteenth century, writers such as Henry William Herbert (writing as Frank Forester) began to extol the importance of sports hunting as a means for maintaining aristocratic vigor. Herbert's attempts to import an explicitly class-based approach to hunting … did not fare well [with citizens]." Of course, the lower class market hunter competed with middle and upper class sport hunters. Since sport hunters were limited in the amount of time they could spend in the field because of

---

35   McDonald, who was well acquainted with this early group of falconers, informs us of the reason: "I believe this was caused by a lack of any falconry background in the New World, with no other reason for practicing the activity other than recreational. The new practitioners of the art developed the attitude of the time as a defense against the killing of raptors important to the art and as a path to what was perceived as self-preservation. At that time, falconers were almost the only group of individuals who placed a positive value on birds of prey. This elitist perspective was fostered by the scarce and expensive falconry information available, lack of an American falconry history, poor communication between falconers in a very large country, and any true 'home grown' falconry traditions. Last but not least – small numbers 'spelled' ELITISM."

occupational responsibilities, they were also limited in the amount of game they could harvest. In comparison, the market hunter spent a great deal of time afield in order to harvest enough game to scrape a living off the land, or at least supplement his income. This was his occupation, if not the entire year, then at least seasonally, when his quarry was available. In the latter part of the nineteenth century, habitat was shrinking exponentially, mostly because of immigration, and market hunting was increasing simultaneously. The combination was devastating to many species. It appears that the loss of habitat, the primary cause of wildlife population declines, was not discussed much in the literature of the period. The primary blame was placed squarely upon the market hunter because he was vulnerable, but the expansion of agriculture could not be challenged.

The market hunter typically came from humble origins and lived a humble life (Smith, 1776, p. 118). He was usually not very well connected in political circles, was not well educated, and had little money to defend his rights. His hunting income would fluctuate wildly because of its seasonality. He had to scrape a living off the land one way or another, and when he came under attack by wealthy hunters, politicians, and manipulative scientists such as William Hornaday[36], he was powerless to ward off the demonization asserted against him by this powerful class of citizens.

Eventually, the upper class sportsmen joined forces with other factions and lobbied their representatives to enact statutes

---

36   Hornaday, W. (1913). *Our Vanishing Wild Life*, New York: Charles Scribner's Sons. Hornaday was a highly respected zoologist of his day and was very influential in establishing legal protections for wildlife. In this book, he viciously attacked market hunters for population declines of troubled wildlife species, while avoiding the primary issue of habitat loss (consider the demise of the Rocky Mountain locust). When market hunting was eliminated, many of those wildlife populations that were in decline continued their downward trend or simply maintained themselves at low levels, demonstrating that Hornaday either didn't understand ecology, or was a propagandist pushing his agenda. Based on the behavior of some segments of the scientific community, the latter is probably the case. This community has corrupt elements in it because of special interest agendas— consider its usefulness in the political arena—as well as competition amongst themselves for scarce funding in a large pool of interests, plus the desire for fame and prestige—not at all unlike "greedy capitalists" hording wealth. Consider the man-made global warming hoax as just one example: In the 1970s, scientists were asserting another ice age was coming (see Gwynne, P. (April 28, 1975). The cooling world. *Newsweek.* page 64). Climate change is a permanent part of our environment—it is not new and no proof has thus far been presented to correlate man's activities and climate fluctuations, but the assertions serve some scientists' careers very well.

and regulations that were advantageous to their own interests. By the 1920s, such management regulations were embraced by nearly every State. The competition—market hunting—was, for the most part, denied the access that the regulatory program offered (commercial fishing, fur trapping, and commerce in wild reptiles managed to survive, however, since these were either of lesser or of no interest to the wealthy sport hunter). This created a monopoly for sport hunters to have game birds to themselves. The propaganda worked, and we still embrace this perspective without ever questioning what really happened.[37]

It is interesting to note that for close to four thousand years, civilized man has been aware of the tendencies of the strong to oppress the weak; however, we have yet to provide sufficient instruction to citizens regarding the destructiveness of such behavior. Consider the code of Hammurabi. In their text *Western Heritage* (2010, p. 9), the history faculty of Hillsdale College provides, "According to its preface, the law code of Hammurabi (c. 1792-1750 BC) was given him by the gods 'to destroy the wicked and the evil, so that the strong may not oppress the weak.'" It is hoped that one day, civilized man may evolve to the point where oppressive behavior is recognized as completely unacceptable (and through this evolutionary process, "wicked" and "evil" behavior will be destroyed), that the weak may be free from fear of the strong, and that the strong will become the greatest defenders of the weak without the intervention of government. For when the weakest parts of society are defended, the interests and property of all is far more secure because of the underlying social principles being observed by all. Only then may we truly be called "civil."

For a more in depth explanation of the conflicting interests of sport versus market hunters see Tober (1981) pages 43-56.

Did market hunters harvest large numbers of wild birds? The answer is yes, and sport hunters contributed too. Population growth due to immigration and advances in technology provided for this. Are market hunters to blame for over-harvesting birds? The answer is no! Government is to blame for not responding to a problem with appropriate regulatory measures, taking into consideration

---

37   Henderson recognized the primary reason for the decline of so many bird species, i.e., loss of habitat: "The birds disappeared as people turned prairies into farms." No pointing the finger at market hunting as the primary or exclusive reason for population declines. Minnesota Public Radio, "Egg Collection Offers Lessons," Stephanie Hemphill interviewing Carrol Henderson of MN Dept. of Natural Resources, May 20, 2005.

all stakeholders. However, habitat loss was truly the primary cause for the reduction in numbers of most species. Even today we have this problem (consider prairie grouse), and there is no market hunting pressure, which unmasks the deceit perpetrated by sport hunters early in the twentieth century. Goble and Freyfogle (2002, p. 72) provide, "Most declining species are at risk, not because of overharvesting, but because of habitat loss and degradation." On page 133, Goble and Freyfogle, in trying to explain the reason for the extinction of the Carolina parakeet, state, "The volume of land cleared is noteworthy: while land clearing was relatively modest until 1800, almost 114,000,000 acres had been cleared by 1850; in the next decade, almost 40,000,000 more acres were cleared for agriculture." In spite of such habitat destruction, market hunters were blamed for the decline of all bird species and then executed, figuratively speaking of course, and a way of life was thus eliminated. This is a story of a weak minority being squashed by a very powerful minority. Any who have read *The Federalist Papers* of Madison, Hamilton, and Jay know that any sector of our society—minority or majority—infringing upon another is against the fundamental principles of our system of government. But this lesson seems to have been forgotten by most.

Is it desirable that we no longer have market hunting of game birds? Perhaps, but we need to take into consideration that we are able to manage fur trapping, commercial fishing, and commerce in reptiles, so it may have been possible to successfully manage market hunting. It would compete with sport hunters, so this sector would surely oppose it. However, it is possible that, with an industry dedicated to the pursuit of wildlife, they may contribute substantially to habitat restoration via commercial license fees, since they would have a real stake in wildlife populations (farming subsidies could be eliminated, allowing for cheaper land that could easily be turned into wildlife habitat for all sectors to enjoy). One thing is certain, the return of market hunting would not be well received by many Americans, and most wildlife officials would oppose it with every fiber of their being. At this point in time, it is a good academic debate to consider political forces, the rule of law, rights and liberties, and the effects of immigration, amongst other social forces, to better understand human nature as it relates to the abuse of government power.

Conservationism

The late nineteenth century movement to protect natural resources from over-harvest came to be known as conservationism. It was not, however, a movement to protect natural resources from any and all harvest—i.e., protectionism. It was meant to establish sensible and manageable harvest for sustainable take of natural resources in perpetuity. Dorsey (1998) explains the circumstances leading up to the passage of Federal wildlife statutes.

> As a movement, conservationism arose in opposition to the myth of superabundance widely held in American society.... For centuries, Americans had found more resources whenever the need arose....
>
> Improved transportation and technology, inseparable from industrialization and population growth, compounded the problems caused by the belief in unlimited resources. Railroad expansion opened ... wilderness to economic activity and hunting.... Better firearms and fishing apparatus allowed people to take more resources for the same effort....
>
> Fish, seals, birds, and many other types of natural resources are [commonly available]—a resource used by many but owned by no one until killed, captured, or extracted. Because there is no [ownership of wildlife, there are] many users. These users have no economic incentive to show forbearance in their harvesting.

Like Hornaday, Dorsey proceeds to blame only market hunting for the demise of these species. In addition, newly introduced European competitive species and the new diseases they brought with them contributed to wildlife problems. Sport and subsistence hunters also contributed to the problem. Efforts to destroy species that competed with man's interests added to the difficulty. All of these issues and more played major roles in the demise of many North American native species. This is not to say that market hunting didn't play a role in the demise of some species, but given the fact that no one performed any research at the time to determine the extent of all the contributing factors, it is irresponsible and unscientific to blame one source for everything. This marginalizes those who assert this position since it demonstrates a bias and a factional agenda. A single "evil" is frequently cited as the culprit, and a war must be waged against this evil in order to enflame emotions and unite the troops against a common enemy (think of Hitler attacking the Jews or FDR blaming the rich for all of our problems as examples of this behavior). Subsequent generations blindly follow the contemporaneous mob's beliefs, unknowingly preserving the deception in perpetuity, and never questioning how the mob came to its conclusions in the first place. This is a human frailty that must be recognized, which John Stuart Mill expounded upon in his 1859 classic, *On Liberty*. He emphasized that every generation must question preceding generations' conclusions so that they may understand the good in established norms or discover errors in them, and make the necessary corrections when needed.

Dorsey continues:

> In a culture that **enriched**[38] [resource users who had no incentive to conserve], the only recourse for conservationists was government action. Beginning in the 1880s, a small group of dedicated people lobbied state legislatures to protect wildlife, but for a variety of reasons they gradually concluded that only the federal government could do an adequate job.... [I]n order to get complete, uniform coverage throughout the United States, conservationists had to pound laws through more than forty state legislatures instead of one Congress.... [*Using the Federal government in this way had the potential of violating States' rights.*] (Emphasis added)
>
> The next step, then, was to legitimize federal control over those species that, because of their range, migratory movements, or economic value, the states could not protect.... [C]onservationists wanted Washington's intervention into traditional states' rights areas [*which could potentially be a violation of the Tenth Amendment*]. The first step in this direction was the Lacey Act of 1900, which justifiably used federal police powers to regulate interstate commerce in game birds. From that point on, conservationists waged a steady battle to broaden federal

---

38   The author demonstrates his bias and perpetuates the propaganda here by implying that market hunters as a class became rich because of hunting. It is probable that the middlemen, who bought game from the hunters and sold it to the market, may have been "enriched" by the trade, but it is highly unlikely that any individual hunter became wealthy by his efforts, given the economic forces that surrounded market hunting.

authority [*i.e., to eliminate State boundaries in favor of a single national government, with the power to override even the Constitution when it would serve their purposes, which is the very issue the Founders were most concerned about*].

It is perfectly appropriate to utilize the Federal government for issues that States cannot individually handle. This, of course, is the very reason the Founders established a central government in the Federal scheme. However, where States are adequate for addressing the task, our system demands that such issues be left to them. In the case of migratory birds, States were inadequate to the task, and therefore the Federal legislature was the appropriate body to provide a remedy, but only to address the issues of over-harvest and the protection of endangered species. Certainly not to be used as a legal/political tool to further a subjective policy.

Restraining representatives, jurists, and bureaucrats from overstepping their bounds is the challenge of checking the power of government. Madison's famous words in *Federalist* No. 51 are instructive here:

> If men were angels, no government would be necessary.... In framing a government which is to be administered by men over men, the great difficulty lies in this: you must first enable the government to control the governed; and in the next place oblige it to control itself.

A tall order, to be sure, and one we have yet to come to terms with. Madison concludes, "A dependence on the people is, no doubt, the primary control on the government." In other words, citizens must assert their authority over every aspect of government in order to keep it within the bounds established in the Constitution.

This chapter has taken us from Roman law, to British, and finally to American law. In America we can see a transition from a completely unregulated environment to an excessively regulated system. Pendulums swing from one extreme to another and we can see this in our wildlife management regime. We need to move the pendulum toward the middle, where sensibility rules and factions are marginalized. The twentieth century was the century of statism, and we now have the luxury of looking back over this period and seeing it as a time of tremendous failure—in Europe, Asia, and America—regarding the protection of individuals and their rights. There were a few victories for rights, but far more losses than gains. We must learn from the mistakes of this period and recover much of our founding principles. The Founders were not perfect, nor is the system of government they implemented, but it has proven to be the best yet devised by man. The system they designed needs amending, as the concentration of Federal power in the hands of a minority has demonstrated, but minor tweaking is all that is required. Certainly not radical alterations, which the collectivists have been successfully and deviously implementing throughout much of the twentieth century.

We must push hard to educate citizens of the dangers inherent in statism. However, our public education institutions typically embrace the statist movement, so we can expect no assistance from this quarter. We must find alternative means of informing the citizenry of the precipice we face. This is a battle we can ill afford to lose if we hope liberty may yet endure.

Gyrfalcon.

U.S. Wildlife Laws and Regulations

Let us begin with State regulations.

State Regulatory Structures

States vary considerably in the application of natural resource laws and wildlife regulation; the scope of which is beyond the intent of this work. A thorough analysis of this subject can be acquired in *State Wildlife Laws Handbook,* Musgrave and Stein, Government Institutes, 1993.

A quick summary of State regulatory structures is provided by Goble and Freyfogle (2002, p. 762) where they provide the following explanations regarding State game laws:

[S]tates have … power to protect wildlife. States commonly exercise this power by enacting fish and game codes. Although these vary widely in detail, they generally
(a) create an agency: Each state has established an agency … with the power to manage the state's wildlife resources. The structure of these agencies vary widely as do the powers delegated to them….
(b) adopt a classification scheme for wildlife: … Frequently, this involves enumerating a list of game animals and another of 'vermin'—with a residual, "everything else" category.
(c) mandate a regulatory scheme: The code often provides that game may be taken subject to specified conditions, that vermin may be killed at anytime, and that the species in the residual category are protected.

Game laws can be categorized in a variety of ways. For example, Thomas Harelson [*Streamlining Waterfowl Enforcement,* Proceedings of the International Conference on Improving Hunter Compliance with Wildlife Law, 153 (1992)], a game warden, divided his state's statutes into three groups:

(a) *social* statutes such as those prohibiting hunting on Sunday [*This is where the greatest abuses occur. The Sunday prohibition is a perfect example. Sunday is a Christian day in which one is supposed to dedicate the day to God. This has no place in civil law. It enables a majority to infringe upon a minority based on their subjective values. This would, perhaps, be more acceptable at the county level, but certainly not at the State.*];

(b) *traditional* laws such as the rule against hunting waterfowl with a shotgun that has too many shells in the chamber [*Technology provides for efficient and excessive harvests that can quickly deplete populations*]; and

(c) resource protection statutes such as bag limits. [*Quotas are to allow for sustainable harvest.*] (pp. 804-05)

Alternatively, the *State Wildlife Laws Handbook* notes that there are several common types of statutes:

(a) *taking restrictions,* including closed seasons, bag limits, gear restrictions, baiting prohibitions;

(b) *waste statutes* generally prohibit permitting game to go to waste once it has been taken;

(c) *spotlighting laws* prohibit hunting at night with artificial lights;

(d) *commercial transactions* are often restricted, although there is substantial variance among the states;

(e) *transportation restrictions* may apply to individual hunters or to common carriers; and

(f) *regulation of businesses* such as guides, outfitters, fur dealers, and taxidermists.[39]

Federal Wildlife Statutes

A reminder of the fundamental Federal authority, and the subsequent power derived from this authority, is necessary prior

---

39   Goble & Freyfogle, 2002 (summarizing Musgrave et al. *State Wildlife Laws Handbook*) p. 805.

to discussing Federal laws and subsequent regulations. Congress' authority to manage wildlife and natural resources in general derives from the General Welfare Clause of the Constitution. Without this authority, or some other enumerated Constitutional authority, Congress would be powerless to act since the Constitution defines the limits of government. It limits what the government can do, which is something many Americans, including many academics, bureaucrats, and representatives, have completely lost sight of. Therefore, without an enumeration of power (which citizens have selectively assigned to government) provided in the Constitution, Congress is prohibited to act, and all powers not enumerated remain with the people or the States (see the Ninth and Tenth Amendments), where citizens assign further powers through their individual State constitutions.

Counties and municipalities have the broadest latitude in experimenting with new ideas, so long as they do not conflict with State or Federal constitutions or with constitutionally grounded statutes. A town can establish a communistic community if it so chooses, which has indeed occurred in our past (the Amana Colonies of Iowa for example, amongst others) and is perfectly legal. However, without radically altering the Federal Constitution, communism and socialism are illegal as it relates to Federal statutes and policy. Therefore, those who believe in communism are free to practice it amongst themselves, but are prohibited from forcing it upon the rest. This is true of many beliefs that factions hold dear, such as animal rights and protectionism, which attempts to prohibit others from pursuing legitimate natural resource use. Government is powerless to prohibit those endeavors if there are no health, safety, or welfare issues at stake. This was thoroughly covered in the section *The Beginning of a Culture of Regulation* earlier in this work.

Let us now analyze the progression of Federal wildlife law and its relation to American culture.

The Lacey Act

The Lacey Act of 1900 ... was the first federal wildlife conservation statute with a national scope. The Act prohibited specific categories of interstate commerce in wildlife.... As originally enacted, the Act contained three types of provisions. First, it added federal criminal penalties to interstate shipments of wildlife that violated state law; second, it imposed labeling requirements on interstate shipments of wildlife; and, third, it created an affirmative federal duty to conserve wildlife. (Goble & Freyfogle, 2002, p. 833)

This Act has felony provisions for certain violations. This is arguably a violation of the Eighth Amendment's Excessive Fines and Cruel and Unusual Punishment clauses.

The Migratory Bird Treaty Act (MBTA) of 1918

The Lacey Act did not supply wildlife sufficient protection because it applied only to illegal possession of wildlife under State law. With the Migratory Bird Treaty Act of 1918, Congress decided to directly involve the Federal government in wildlife conservation.

Earlier, Congress had enacted the Weeks-McLean Migratory Bird Act in 1913. It was challenged and declared unconstitutional. See *United States v Shauver,* 214 F. 154 (E.D. Ark. 1914); *United States v McCullagh,* 221 F. 288 (D. Kan. 1915). In 1916, the United States and Great Britain signed the Convention for the Protection of Migratory Birds. After its ratification, Congress enacted the Migratory Bird Treaty Act in 1918. The MBTA was challenged, but this time it was upheld by the Supreme Court in *Missouri v Holland,* 252 U.S. 416 (1920), based on the treaty making power of the Federal government joined with the public welfare concern of what the loss of many species would result in. The general welfare aspect provided the constitutional authority for the treaty making power to protect declining species and to manage harvest, but there was no power to outright prohibit harvest of birds unless there was a compelling public welfare issue at stake.

> The agreement with [Britain] established three categories of migratory birds: migratory game birds, migratory insectivorous birds, and migratory nongame birds.... The Convention established closed seasons on birds in each category. For the final two categories, the closed season is year round [*which is unconstitutional since there is no compelling public interest at stake to do so year round*]—effectively prohibiting any killing of such species except pursuant to a scientific permit [*which is unconstitutional if limited to only degreed scientists, because*

it establishes a title of nobility of sorts, not unlike England's qualification statutes].... For migratory game birds, the closed season is between March 10 and September 1, with "the High Contracting Powers" further agreeing that the actual open season will be for no more than three and one-half months as each party "may severally deem appropriate and define by law or regulation."

The combined coverage of the various treaties is such that all migratory species—except the European Starling (*Sturnus vulgaris*) and the House Sparrow (*Passer domesticus*) [as well as other non-indigenous species]—are protected under the Act. Non-migratory species such as quail, grouse, ptarmigan, and pheasant are not covered by the conventions or the Act.

Despite the additional treaties, the MBTA has remained largely unchanged since 1918—in part because the 1918 Act was broadly drafted.... **The basic structure of the Act ... is somewhat unusual: rather than prohibiting specific conduct, the MBTA prohibits all killing or possession and all commercial activity in migratory birds and authorizes the Secretary to promulgate regulations exempting conduct from this general prohibition.** [*This is constitutionally acceptable for endangered species, based on the General Welfare Clause, but not for healthy species, since there is no public welfare issue at stake. This, in effect, asserts that there are no boundaries on Congressional authority.*] (Emphasis added)

The Act initially provided only misdemeanor penalties [for violations]. In 1960, [however], Congress amended the Act, adding a provision making the sale of protected species a felony. The objective, Congress stated, was to impose "heavier penalties" on "commercial hunters" who "slaughte[r] these wildfowl for commercial purposes." (Goble & Freyfogle, 2002, pp. 855-56)

The sale of wildlife being placed in the extreme category of felony is an outrage, unless one belongs to the environmental religion, since convictions would then deny constitutional rights to citizens. This provision most assuredly needs to be repealed. It should be no more than a misdemeanor, with sufficient punishments that achieve deterrence. The punishment must fit the crime, and a felony is an excessive punishment, which violates the Eighth Amendment. Such offensive punishments are reminiscent of religious persecutions, and in fact are grounded in environmental religious views, which violates the separation of church and State doctrine.

If we consider Bracton's three levels of law—natural, human, and civil—we can see that the use of wildlife does not violate natural or human law because it is only natural to do so. As it relates to civil law, we then need to consider if a society has the authority to deny the use of natural resources (it most certainly cannot be based on the subjective and arbitrary will of the faction in power), and if so, under what circumstances and to what extent is this authority applicable, and what level of punishment will deter the activity in a sensible and unbiased manner? Such prohibitions must be deemed objectively good for all to be considered just. To do otherwise is to admit we have no system of justice; we only have a system of manmade laws based on the arbitrary will of those who possess the reins of power. This begs the question, is this any better than a monarchy? Some political philosophers of the past argued that such a condition is worse than a monarchy. As we saw in democratic Greece, the tyranny of the many is far more dangerous than the tyranny of one or of a few, who can be held accountable when they go too far.

"Since the inception of the MBTA …, misdemeanor violations of the MBTA … have been interpreted by the majority of the courts as strict liability crimes, not requiring the government to prove any intent element." (Goble & Freyfogle, 2002, p. 858)

Sayre (1933) provides insight into what "strict liability" encompasses:

> Although most criminal statutes require that a person's acts be accompanied by some degree of fault— such as intent, willfulness, or knowledge [i.e., *mens rea* or *scienter*]—legislatures in the early nineteenth century began to enact a new type of criminal statute that regulated natural resources, business practices, and similar problems. These new offenses differed from traditional crimes (such as murder, rape, burglary, and the like) that involved immoral conduct. The new public welfare offenses were not, according to the then-prevailing perspective,

inherently immoral [*However, in time, those convicted of wildlife offenses did indeed become ostracized by society as any other criminal would be. Conviction of any offense carries with it a stigma that is detrimental to those convicted. A faction within the North American Falconers' Association implemented a policy of marginalizing those convicted of wildlife offenses. Such offenders were unable to hold office in the club, and were therefore silenced from political participation. So these laws did indeed become "moral" issues.*]; they could, however, be performed improperly and it was this that the new statutes sought to prohibit. The enactment of these offenses thus reflected a shift of emphasis from protection of individual interests to the protection of public and social interests. [*Which defines statism!*]

This last sentence speaks of the shift away from individual liberty to one based on an omnipotent government. There was never a time when our government was uninterested in the protection of public and social interests. It was the intent of the Founders to balance individual and public interests so they would be equally protected. However, in the latter part of the nineteenth century, there was certainly a shift away from individual rights and liberties in favor of collective interests, as expressed in the statist movement. This is an extremely dangerous road to go down. Hitler, Mussolini, Stalin, and Mao all asserted the protection of public and social interests in the name of the common good, as have all tyrants throughout the centuries. This allows for individual rights and liberties to be ignored or even destroyed. When this occurs, no one is safe, as these tyrants have demonstrated, and it is through the destruction of individual liberty that such tyrants acquire their power.

The strict liability principle is antithetical to liberty and the presumption of innocence, unless reckless conduct, grossly negligent conduct, or a public hazard is involved (e.g., storing a large volume of explosives in a residential neighborhood, which any reasonable person would know is unsafe and exposes the community to extreme risk – hence the reason citizens can possess firearms but not bombs for self-defense). The presumption of innocence is a right destroyed, it is claimed, to protect wildlife populations or to dictate some arbitrary social behavior. We cannot allow subjective values to dictate objective legal principles.

If the MBTA cannot be interpreted in any other way than as a strict liability statute, then it is unconstitutional as written because of the absence of any public hazard or reckless or negligent conduct, and language needs to be added in order to make it constitutional like the Bald & Golden Eagle Protection Act where it provides for *scienter*, i.e. with guilty knowledge.

Another aspect of the MBTA that is unconstitutional is the outright prohibition of take of migratory birds. Some would say that a treaty with another nation provides for the power, but a treaty cannot trump the authority of the Constitution or the underlying principles of our government. If a treaty is in conflict with the Constitution, the treaty, or the offensive portion, is null and void. The offensive language in the MBTA is, "Unless and except as permitted by regulations … it shall be unlawful at any time … to pursue … [or] possess … any migratory bird." The MBTA was enacted as an early form of endangered species act. Many bird populations were in serious trouble in 1916-18, requiring strong protections, and the *Missouri* Court, in defending the constitutionality of the Act, made its decision based on this position. However, those species that were not in trouble or those species that had recovered could not be protected by outright prohibitions (now that we have the Endangered Species Act (ESA), we no longer need to use the MBTA in this manner), though they should have been protected by harvest quotas like any other game bird. Congress does not have the authority to outright ban an activity based on prejudices or without a solid justification steeped deeply in general welfare principles—i.e., some social threat or mischief is at stake. Therefore, the treaty-making power cannot be used in this manner since it conflicts with the rights of citizens to have access to natural resource harvest.

Harvesting of any species of wildlife not threatened or endangered with extinction does not threaten the nation in any way. It causes no harm and infringes upon no one. This is therefore off limits to Congress, and the MBTA needs to be rewritten by first removing the prohibition and possession provisions (if a migratory bird or its parts were taken legally, FWS has no authority to dictate possession parameters), and then adding a provision that **requires** FWS to establish harvest parameters for every species listed in the MBTA (those listed in the ESA should be allowed to be taken for breeding purposes by any who are so inclined, since it leads to securing the species' survival). Whether or not anyone harvests any of these species is irrelevant. It is the right of Americans to have access to all of our natural resources so long as they do no harm to the environment or wildlife populations or to fellow citizens, which expresses the very purpose of regulations. Anything beyond this allows one sector of society to harm another, which is antithetical to the purpose of regulations. In other words, if a statute and its regulations are to prevent one sector of society (e.g., a user group) from damaging the interests of another, how can it be acceptable for the protected group to damage the interests of the user group when the activity is benign? It is utterly nonsensical, unless the projection of religion or the subjective interest of some faction comes into play. Then we can see that dogmas are dictating law. Taylor (1822, p. 13) addresses this when he offers,

> Enmities among men are produced by a clashing of interests, and the intention of republican governments is not to promote, but to prevent this clashing, by a just and equal distribution of civil or legal rights.

In addition, Section 704 of the MBTA possesses more offensive language: "[T]he Secretary of the Interior is authorized and directed ... to determine ... [if] it is compatible with the terms of the conventions **to allow** hunting, taking, [or] capture ... of any [migratory] bird." It should actually state that the Secretary **must** provide for take of migratory birds by citizens, in conjunction with appropriate limitations to ensure the health of species' populations, i.e., sustainable use. Again, access to all of our natural resources is a right with conditions attached, which is the case for all rights. (Emphasis added)

Epstein (2006, p. 11) explains a principled explanation of how legislation should be scrutinized when there appears to be a constitutional conflict. In analyzing Progressive-era legislation, Epstein references

> Holmes's famous dissent in *Lochner v. New York* [198 U.S. 45, 76 (1905)], which indicated that courts should bend over backward not to upset the considered judgment of the legislature. At the opposite extreme is the standard of "strict scrutiny," which says that a statute that touches on a protected constitutional right is necessarily unconstitutional unless the end it serves rises to the level

of a "compelling state interest" and the means chosen are "narrowly tailored" to achieve that well defined objective.

This is a more reasoned approach in scrutinizing legislation so that rights and liberties may be defended while simultaneously protecting the well-being of the country. The protection of rights and liberties, properly understood, is synonymous with the well-being of the country.

Section 710 of the MBTA, "Partial invalidity," provides for the means to sever the offensive language. It states,

> If any clause, sentence, paragraph, or part of this subchapter ... shall, for any reason, be adjudged by any court of competent jurisdiction to be invalid, such judgment shall not affect ... the remainder thereof, but shall be confined in its operation to the clause, ... or part thereof directly involved in the controversy in which such judgment shall have been rendered.

Congress knew the MBTA had problems when it was enacted, and decided to provide a severance clause to allow for a redress of the constitutional conflicts without destroying the Act. If it was constitutionally sound, there would have been no need for this clause. Therefore, the suggested revisions would not invalidate it; they would simply align it with the Constitution, which, after all, is in the best interest of the country.

Hybrid Raptors Excluded from MBTA

Though not precedent-setting, the FWS withdrew charges in the California case *U.S. v. Kerster* after having read the brief written by Counsel William Horn. The court provided:

> The statute at issue in this case is 16 U.S.C. § 703, which prohibits the killing of native, migratory birds. ... 16 U.S.C. § 703(b) limits the application of this statute, and states:
>
> (1) In general. **This Act applies only to migratory bird species that are native to the United States** or its territories.
> (2) Native to the United States defined.
> (A) In general. Subject to subparagraph (B), in this

Prairie falcon.

Frank L Beebe

subsection the term "native to the United States or its territories" means **occurring in the United States or its territories as the result of natural biological or ecological processes.**

(B) Treatment of introduced species. For purposes of paragraph (1), **a migratory bird species that occurs in the United States or its territories solely as a result of intentional or unintentional human-assisted introduction shall not be considered native** to the United States or its territories. (Emphasis added)

Also relevant to this case are sections 10.12 and 10.13 of Title 50 of the Code of Federal Regulations. Section 10.12 purports to define "migratory bird" as any bird, "which is a mutation or a hybrid" of two native species. 50 C.F.R. 10.12. …

Prior to 2004, the Migratory Bird Treaty Act ("MBTA") contained no provision exempting non-native birds from the terms of the Act. In 2001, the circuit court for the District of Columbia interpreted the MBTA as it existed at the time. *Hill v. Norton,* 275 F.3d 98 (D.C. Cir. 2001), concerned a plan by the state of Maryland to reduce the population of the mute swan.… A Maryland property owner … brought suit to oppose the plan. The Court held that the terms of the MBTA as it existed at the time were clear, and that the Act did protect mute swans. Although the Secretary of the Interior argued that mute swans were a non-native species and therefore not protected by the Act, the Court found this argument unconvincing, stating that there was, "nothing in the statute, applicable treaties, or administrative record" supporting an exclusion for non-native species.

In 2004, in response to *Hill,* Congress amended the MBTA, adding section (b) and explicitly excluding non-native species from the protections of the Act. The amendment further defined the term "native" to mean, "occurring in the United States or its territories as the result of natural biological or ecological processes." 16 U.S.C. § 703(b)(2)(A).

Finally, the amended Act stated that, "a migratory bird species that occurs in the United States or its territories **solely as a result of intentional or unintentional human-assisted introduction shall not be considered native....**" Id. at 703(b)(2)(B) (emphasis supplied).

As a result of Congress' action, the D.C. Circuit found itself revisiting the plight of the mute swan. In *Fund for Animals, Inc. v. Kempthorne,* 472 F.3d 872 (D.C. Cir. 2006), the Court again analyzed a challenge to Maryland's swan reduction plan. However, because of the intervening Congressional action, the outcome was very different from that in *Hill.* The Secretary of the Interior argued that scientific and historical evidence indicated that the mute swan was not native to the United States. The Court agreed, and stated that the plain text of the amended Act, "clearly and unambiguously provide[s] that the Migratory Bird Treaty Act does not protect non-native species such as the mute swan."

In this case, the bird at issue—a Gyrfalcon/Prairie falcon hybrid—is non-native because it does not occur "as the result of natural biological or ecological processes," but rather "solely as the result of intentional or unintentional human-assisted introduction." 16 U.S.C. § 703(b).... The hybrid is entirely the product of human-controlled processes, specifically artificial insemination.... Because the Gyrfalcon/Prairie falcon hybrid occurs solely as the result of intentional human acts, this hybrid falcon clearly falls within the 16 U.S.C. § 703(b) limitation to the MBTA.

To the extent that the definition of "migratory bird" in 50 CFR 10.12, 10.13 includes hybrids which do not occur "as the result of natural biological or ecological processes," but rather "solely as the result of intentional or unintentional human-assisted introduction," this regulation is in conflict with the subsequently enacted amended MBTA, which overrides the CFR....

In the present case there is no ambiguity and the intent of Congress is clear. "Title I of S.2547 clarifies that the Migratory Bird Treaty Act's prohibition on taking, killing, or possessing migratory birds applies only to native migratory bird species whose occurrence in the United States results from natural biological or ecological conditions." S. REP. 101-313, 2004 WL 1909561 (Leg.Hist.)

Indeed, the plain text of the MBTA explicitly excludes species which occur "solely as a result of intentional or unintentional human-assisted introduction." 16 U.S.C. § 703(b). Because the Gyrfalcon/Prairie falcon hybrid does not occur without human intervention, it is a non-native species as defined by the amended MBTA. The agency's inclusion of this bird on the list of birds protected by the MBTA is in conflict with the statute, and is therefore impermissible.

CONCLUSION: Because the Gyrfalcon/Prairie falcon hybrid does not occur as the result of natural biological or ecological processes, but rather solely as the result of intentional or unintentional human-assisted introduction, it is non-native as defined by 16 U.S.C. § 702, and therefore not protected by the MBTA. To the extent that 50 C.F.R. 10.12 defines this non-native Gyrfalcon/Prairie falcon hybrid as a bird protected by the MBTA, it impermissibly conflicts with 16 U.S.C. § 702. For these reasons, the euthanization of this bird by Mr. Kerster was lawful. The government has, therefore, failed to allege a violation of federal law by Mr. Kerster, and the court must dismiss the charge against him.

Dated: February 22, 2008

Bald and Golden Eagle Protection Act (BGEPA)

Goble & Freyfogle summarize the BGEPA:

The genesis of the Bald and Golden Eagle Protection Act … is in the Bald Eagle Protection Act, adopted by Congress in 1940 to protect the "symbol of American ideals of freedom" by making it illegal to "take …" the protected species…. The Act criminalized the taking or possession of the species, its parts, nests, or eggs. Unlike the MBTA, the Act defined "take" as "[t]o pursue, shoot, shoot at, wound, kill, capture, trap, collect, or otherwise *willfully* molest or disturb," …; scienter [i.e., criminal intent or guilty knowledge] thus is an element of the crime [*whereas scienter is absent in the MBTA*]. The Act granted the Secretary of the Interior discretion to permit the taking and possession of eagles "for scientific or exhibition purposes" and "for the protection of wildlife or agricultural or other interests in any particular locality" if, "after investigation," the Secretary determines that the taking "is compatible with the preservation of the bald eagle."

In 1962, Congress added golden eagles to the Act's prohibitions.... The amendment added two additional exceptions. First, the Secretary was authorized to permit takings of bald and golden eagles "for the religious purposes of Indian tribes." Second, when requested by the governor of any state, the Secretary "shall authorize" taking golden eagles "for the purpose of seasonally protecting domesticated flocks and herds ... in such part or parts of such State and for such periods as the Secretary determines to be necessary to protect such interests." (2002, pp. 875-76)

This Act also conflicts with the Constitution. As with the MBTA, Congress needs to amend this Act to provide for harvest by those interested in taking eagles. It is another resource that citizens have a right to access. The religious symbol it has inherited from protectionist types is inappropriate given our doctrine of

Golden eagle.

separation of church and State. Individuals and groups are free to see wildlife as religious symbols, but they are not allowed to project those beliefs upon others through government enforcement. This is yet another example of a faction infringing upon citizens.

However, rather than amending this Act, it would make more sense to repeal it and include golden and bald eagles in the MBTA. When the eagle act was enacted in 1940, and then amended in 1962, raptors had no protection. Since raptors were brought under the protection of the MBTA in 1972, eagle protection should follow suit since they too are raptors.

The Convention on International Trade in Endangered Species of Wild Fauna and Flora (CITES) of 1973 states:

> The contracting States of this Convention agreed to the following:
> *Recognizing* that wild fauna and flora … are an irreplaceable part of the natural systems of the earth which must be protected for this and the generations to come;
> *Conscious* of the ever-growing value of wild fauna and flora …;
> *Recognizing* that peoples and States are and should be the best protectors of their own wild fauna and flora;
> *Recognizing,* in addition, that international co-operation is essential for the protection of certain species of wild fauna and flora against over-exploitation through international trade;
> *Convinced* of the urgency of taking appropriate measures to this end; *Have agreed* as follows:
> … 1. Appendix I shall include all species threatened with extinction which are or may be affected by trade. Trade in specimens of these species must be subject to particularly strict regulation in order not to endanger further their survival and must only be authorized in exceptional circumstances.
> 2. Appendix II shall include:
> (a) all species which although not necessarily now threatened with extinction may become so unless trade in specimens of such species is subject to strict regulation in order to avoid utilization incompatible with their survival [*one can argue that this provision could be used mischievously for any species*]; and

(b) other species which must be subject to regulation in order that trade in specimens of certain species referred to in sub-paragraph (a) of this paragraph may be brought under effective control. [*This too can be used mischievously due to its vagueness.*]

3. Appendix III shall include all species which any Party identifies as being subject to regulation within its jurisdiction for the purpose of preventing or restricting exploitation, and as needing the co-operation of other Parties in the control of trade. [*However, we cannot allow one party to dictate how other members are to manage their resources or their trade with other parties, since this would be a means to circumvent our sovereignty and our Constitution. This would cause the Convention to be null and void in the United States.*]

4. The Parties shall not allow trade in specimens of species included in Appendices I, II and III except in accordance with the provisions of the present Convention. [*This must be monitored very carefully, since it too may be a means to circumvent our sovereignty, which would be utterly unacceptable. We must jealously guard our autonomy since there will always be those who will attempt to tear down our defenses in order to benefit by our losses. And frequently, bureaucratic positions are highly prized by those with factional agendas because of the power those positions wield.*]

The CITES text then continues to provide the parameters of this agreement. For the most part, CITES is implemented fairly in most countries. In the last few years however, FWS has changed its interpretation and has deviated from the common understanding found in the rest of the world (It has become the common opinion of many raptor breeders that this is due to a particular breeder who leads a raptor breeding organization that serves his own protectionist agenda, but does not share his FWS communications with the membership). It uses the text's language to interpret the agreement in order to place barriers around importers and exporters. FWS has effectively cut off most U.S. trade in raptors with most nations.[40] The animal rights activists have infiltrated FWS and assert tremendous

---

40   Bill Meeker, President, American Falconry Conservancy, personal communication, 2010

influence over the Management Authority office as it relates to CITES permitting.

Most of the raptors used in falconry are neither threatened nor endangered, and therefore should be excluded from CITES' oversight.

Endangered Species Act (ESA) of 1973

Basically, the Act provides the following:

Findings. The Congress finds and declares that: various species ... [of] wildlife ... in the United States have been rendered extinct as a consequence of economic growth and development untempered by adequate concern and conservation; other species of ... wildlife ... have been so depleted in numbers that they are in danger of or threatened with extinction; ... [*This closely resembles the language of USC Chap. 7 Subchapter I, sec. 701 where is states, "...The object and purpose of this Act is to aid in the **restoration** of such birds in those parts of the United States adapted thereto where the same have become **scarce or extinct** ...," which primarily falls under the "preservation" clause and which provides the general intent of the MBTA of subchapter II. This creates redundancy; therefore the MBTA can be amended to reflect a harvest management regime rather than a prohibitory regime since the protection of threatened species is now thoroughly covered under the ESA. This will clarify law enforcement efforts under the MBTA, which are presently vague and confusing, causing conflicts between law enforcement and citizens, which is not a matter to be taken lightly. (Emphasis added)*]

Purposes. The purposes of this Act are to provide a means whereby the ecosystems upon which endangered species and threatened species depend may be conserved, to provide a program for the conservation of such endangered species and threatened species....

Prohibited Acts
General. Except as provided [by] this Act, with respect to any endangered species of ... wildlife listed ... it is unlawful for any person subject to the jurisdiction of the United

States to: import any such species into, or export any such species from the United States; take any such species within the United States ...; possess, [or] sell ..., any such species taken in violation of [this Act] *[This "possession" provision in the ESA reflects the same intent as the "possession" provision in the MBTA, i.e. the MBTA provision relates to possession of migratory birds taken in violation of the Act, not possession as it relates to use of migratory birds, as the FWS presently asserts its authority is derived from to regulate falconry. The word "use" is not included in the MBTA; therefore FWS cannot regulate use. Endangered species management being of greater urgency than management of healthy populations clearly demonstrates the truth of this position.];* ... sell ... in interstate or foreign commerce any such species; or violate any regulation pertaining to such species....

When ESA authority is used to prohibit the use of private property because of the presence of a threatened or endangered species, this is a takings, and affected citizens must be compensated based on Fifth Amendment standards. Otherwise, individual citizens are forced to bear the burden of providing costly benefits for the public good. This is unacceptable and is contrary to our founding principles. Jurists who have ignored the Fifth in such cases should be impeached for their callous disregard of the Constitution.

Restrictions on import and/or export of raptors should be linked with the ESA. CITES and the ESA must be coupled for there to be authority to restrict trade in North American raptors. As for non-indigenous raptors, there must be evidence of a threatened or endangered status for there to be authority to restrict trade. This is important because of the fact that there are international organizations conspiring to eliminate all trade in wildlife, including the pet trade, and they use conventions and treaties to accomplish this goal. They use manipulative tactics and then plant their own kind in wildlife management positions.

The civil and criminal penalties are severe for ESA violations— up to $50,000 and/or one year in prison—which violates the Eighth Amendment of the Constitution in regards to excessive fines and cruel and unusual punishment. While the protection of endangered species is a social good, when taken too far it becomes a tyrannical club with which to beat citizens into submission. Great care must be taken to balance the interests of society with the rights of individuals, which, of course, is something statists and religious environmentalists would like to completely ignore.

Many argue that the application of the ESA is out of control and it is now used in abusive ways that are in severe conflict with civil liberties. If this is true, and there is ample evidence to support this claim, the ESA may itself be threatened with extinction once citizens have had enough. This would be unfortunate, but it is an expected and justifiable outcome when power is abused.

Wild Bird Conservation Act of 1992

Goble & Freyfogle offer some insight into the purpose of the Wild Bird Conservation Act (WBCA):

> The MBTA and the BGEPA protect birds that are indigenous to the United States. The Wild Bird Conservation Act, on the other hand, protects "exotic birds"; that is birds that are not naturally found within this country or non-indigenous.
>
> Congress found that "[p]opulations of many species of exotic wild birds ... have declined dramatically due to habitat loss [*now that market hunting is out of the picture, we don't hear it being blamed anymore; instead we here the real reason for declines in wildlife populations*] and the public's demand for pet birds." H.R. Rep. No. 102-749 (II), 102d Cong., 2d Sess. 7 (1992).... Enactment of the WBCA also reflected congressional recognition that the Convention on International Trade in Endangered Species of Fauna and Flora (CITES) had proven ineffective, in part because many exporting countries "lack the means to develop or effectively implement scientifically based management plans." Id. sec. 4901 (7). (2002, pp. 883-84)

One can observe a progression of statutes and conventions being enacted to tighten the noose around the neck of wildlife users. They are being used insidiously to achieve complete prohibition of access to wildlife. If this cannot be accomplished through the statutes themselves, then it can be accomplished through the planting of protectionists in FWS bureaucratic positions who will interpret the statutes and write the regulations in ways that serve the protectionist agenda.

Raptors could have and should have been exempted from the WBCA, as many other animals were – achieved through the efforts of various stakeholders – since most populations of falconry raptors are not declining and they are not pets in the traditional sense of the word. But unfortunately they were not. Those who held the responsible positions in the then-dominant national falconry organization stated, "They dropped the ball." Some have speculated that certain factions within the falconry community desired the inclusion of raptors in the Act because of the increased value restrictive regulations tend to have on highly regulated animals. A thorough study of the Congressional hearing records may reveal whether or not a particular faction of falconers had anything to do with raptors' inclusion. Perhaps these findings may lead to the exemption of raptors when the Act is eventually amended.

We must be as vigilant as we can in monitoring the implementation of this Act and the previously mentioned Acts. The protectionist groups will undoubtedly attempt to use these Acts as a means to restrict movement of birds—and ultimately their possession—through bureaucratic positions. Heavy prison terms should be applied when such abuses of power are detected and conviction is secured. Such deterrence for this type of illegal behavior is a necessity. Up to this point, offenders have been immune from being held accountable. A break of the public trust through the abuse of government power is a very serious matter. If we expect the citizenry to have respect for law and order, such corruption must be weeded out. If citizens are required to comply with the law, government officials must be held to even higher standards, otherwise the system will break down and anarchy, as subtle as it may start off, will begin to deteriorate our system of government.

Ownership of Wildlife

This section on falconers' property rights in their raptors is necessary because of FWS's assertion in the proposed raptor propagation regulations (Federal Register/Vol. 70 No. 198 Oct. 14, 2005, 60052-58) and in the *2007 Final Environmental Assessment: Take of Raptors from the Wild Under the Falconry Regulations and the Raptor Propagation Regulations* (page 35), that falconers do not own their raptors. They sought to frame the relationship between raptor, FWS, and falconer as one where tamed – *mansueta naturae* – raptors are always kept in the category of wildlife – *ferae naturae* – in order to keep them in perpetual, free-roaming status, claiming FWS always maintains stewardship over our raptors and that we could never own them. This is an absurd assertion, but they felt emboldened to make such a claim in written regulation because they believed they had this stewardship authority since the implementation of the interim federal falconry regulations in 1972.[41] FWS withdrew this assertion because of the efforts of American Falconry Conservancy,[42] through their legal counsel, William Horn, but there are those in the wildlife management community who won't let go of this unjustified position. Therefore, it is necessary to present the legal issues at stake to the falconry community so that all falconers will be armed with the law if and

---

[41] Between 1972, when raptors were classified as federally protected migratory birds under the MBTA, and 1978, our community practiced falconry under interim Federal regulations—see *1988 Final Environmental Assessment: Falconry & Raptor Propagation Regulations.*

[42] At that time, the name of the organization was Wild Raptor Take Conservancy (WRTC).

when some wildlife official illegally attempts to deny falconers their property rights.

Let us start with a paper that Counsels William Horn and David Lampp wrote for American Falconry Conservancy. Highlights from this work provide insight into what is at stake.

> Since property is a "bundle of rights," the falconry community needs to be alert to attempts to take away rights from the bundle. Incremental efforts to take away one right at a time are the most likely line of attack. It is important to be watchful and maintain a robust claim of ownership to avoid erosion of falconers' property interests.
>
> ... Falconers' ownership of their birds ... is important because it is a protection against governmental overreaching and intrusive law enforcement tactics. The Fourth Amendment's limitations on the FWS's *seizure* of birds relates directly to the issue of ownership. The Fourth Amendment's protections against government seizure apply, at their base, to *property*. Accordingly, to benefit from the protections of the Fourth Amendment, it is important for falconers to maintain that their raptors are their private property.
>
> The Fifth Amendment provides, in relevant part, "No person shall be ... deprived of life, liberty, or property, without due process of law; nor shall private property be taken for public use, without just compensation." The U.S. Supreme Court has recognized that this language protects private citizens from being arbitrarily deprived of their property by the government for any reason other than a "public use." Furthermore, even when a public use is at issue, the government must provide due process of law, including provision for "just compensation" for the taken property....
>
> The plain language of the Fifth Amendment, and U.S. Supreme Court opinions interpreting the Amendment, are clear that it applies to *property only*. At its most basic, the Fifth Amendment is designed to protect citizens' interests in their private property from government intrusion or appropriation. For the Fifth Amendment to protect falconers' interests in their raptors, raptors must

be falconers' property, not merely animals 'on loan' from the government, as the FWS attempted to assert....

The Fifth Amendment applies not only where the government has taken possession of private property, but also where regulation is so burdensome that it severely impacts a property owner's rights with regard to that property. As the U.S. Supreme Court recognized in 1922, "if regulation goes too far it will be recognized as a taking."[43]

The prohibitions on taking without due process and just compensation serve as a further check on overreaching by regulators. Regulations that are sufficiently pervasive and burdensome may be subject to a claim that they are, in fact, a taking of private property. The remedy in such circumstances is compensation to the property owner for the "taking" or removal of the regulations.... Falconers' ownership of their raptors serves as another check on government overreaching by allowing them a basis to potentially invoke the Fifth Amendment against overreaching regulations.

In addition to protecting against governmental taking, ownership of raptors may confer on falconers the legal standing to seek damages or other civil remedies against private parties who deprive them of their birds. A falconer whose raptor is killed or otherwise taken, intentionally or otherwise, by a private party may be able to seek monetary damages against that party, or a court order against that party to return the raptor, or, in some circumstances, both. However, such civil remedies may not be available if the falconer does not "own" the raptor at issue. If the government is allowed to assert its ownership of falconers' raptors, a court may find that it is the government who is entitled to pursue damages for loss of a raptor, not the falconer. (Horn & Lampp, 2008)

Let us lay out the progression of court cases to learn how we have deviated so far from the protection of our property rights and infected our system with a virus that has been labeled the State Ownership Doctrine, in which it is claimed that the State "owns" wildlife. To begin, let's consider four nineteenth century

---

43   *Pennsylvania Coal Co. v. Mahon*, 260 U.S. 393, 415 (1922)

Supreme Court decisions that exemplify citizens' rights to natural resources.

In *Martin v. Waddell*, 41 U.S. 367, 1842, (the case that established the Public Trust Doctrine in the United States) the Court provided that waterways were held by the sovereign, i.e., the people, for the public benefit and use and that this right could not be destroyed.

The Court quoted the renowned legal scholar and jurist of seventeenth century England, Sir Matthew Hale. Hale provides:

> [A]lthough the king is the owner of this great coast, ... the common people of England have, regularly, a liberty of fishing in the sea, or creeks ... **as a public common of [fishing], and may not, without injury to their right, be restrained of it,** unless in such places ... where either the king or some particular subject hath gained a propriety exclusive [i.e., a privilege] of that common liberty. (41 U.S. 412) (Emphasis added)

The Court pointed out that this common right to this natural resource had been a fixed policy for over six hundred years "to be freely used by all ... and how carefully it has preserved this common right for the benefit of the public." (41 U.S. 412, 413) Therefore, the Court asserted the State's authority to protect its citizens' access to natural resources by protecting that property that provides free people with opportunities to enrich their lives. In other words, the Court was validating general welfare principles. In *McCready v. Virginia*, 94 U.S. 391, 1876, the Court provided that the fisheries

> remain under the ... control of the state, which has consequently the right, in its discretion, to appropriate its tide-waters and their beds to be used by its people as a common for taking and cultivating fish.... Such an appropriation is in effect nothing more than a regulation of the use by the people of their common property. **The right** which the people of the state thus acquire comes not from their citizenship alone, but from their citizenship and property combined. It is, in fact, a property right, and **not a mere privilege or immunity of citizenship.** 94 U.S. 395 (Emphasis added)

This dispels the assertion that hunting, trapping and fishing are privileges. The property the Court speaks of is the waterways where fish are to be found, not the fish themselves.

In his dissenting opinion in the Supreme Court decision *Spring Valley Waterworks v. Schottler*, 110 U.S. 347, 374 (1884), Justice Stephen Field—an eminent Justice who truly respected the rule of law regarding wildlife—expressed his view on ownership of wildlife, which became the basis for twentieth century Supreme Court decisions on this subject. He stated:

> The wild bird in the air belongs to no one, but when the fowler brings it to the earth and takes it into his possession it is his property. He has reduced it to his control by his own labor, and the law of nature and the law of society recognize his exclusive right to it.... So the trapper on the plains and the hunter in the north have a property in the furs they have gathered, though the animals from which they were taken roamed at large and belonged to no one.

In *Manchester v. Massachusetts*, 139 U.S. 240, 1891, the Court recognized the right of the State to regulate the fisheries within the boundaries of the State. This Court cited *Smith v. Maryland*, which provided: "[T]his soil is held by the state, not only subject to, but in some sense in trust for, the enjoyment to certain public rights, among which is the **common liberty of taking fish**." (139 U.S. 260) There is no conflict with citizens possessing rights and liberties as it relates to access of natural resources, and government managing that harvest for citizens' common access and use in perpetuity. In fact, this is a perfect example of the need for government regulation. (Emphasis added)

It is interesting to note that in the three cases related to fishing, the Court makes it clear that harvest of these resources is an undisputed **right**—not a "privilege." It can be seen that the State Ownership Doctrine is not required to manage wildlife. By avoiding this doctrine, citizens' rights to natural resource use remains secure, with no denial of States' regulatory authority to manage resources for sustainable-use harvest principles. It seems clear that while some earlier Courts may have tried to alter our understanding of property rights, it was not mistaken in citizens' rights to natural resource access.

Now that we've provided language from four Court decisions that support and defend our rights, we turn to the decision that attempted to reverse this settled law principle.

Geer v. Connecticut, (1896) is the U.S. Supreme Court case that asserted the sovereign "ownership" of wildlife—as opposed to proprietary ownership—by States on behalf of their citizens. It initiated the State Ownership Doctrine. Fundamentally, it established that wildlife is the property of the State in perpetuity and that citizens have no rights, other than what the State dictates, in possession of wildlife. This case, of a narrow 5 to 4 margin, established the mistaken notion that hunting, fishing, and trapping are privileges and not rights. It is an assertion that privileges can be taken away and that rights cannot. Of course, anyone with an elementary understanding of law knows that rights can indeed be taken away when a citizen transgresses the law and is convicted of a felony. Even misdemeanor convictions affect rights, as do citations, as in cases involving the **right**—not privilege, as many would assert—to operate a motor vehicle when a driver has demonstrated substantially irresponsible behavior. An activity doesn't need to be a privilege to prohibit an individual from practicing it if he has demonstrated he is a nuisance or menace to society. His proven anti-social or irresponsible behavior is sufficient to bar his participation in it. After all, the fundamental purpose of society is to protect our life, liberty, and property from those who would infringe upon these interests, whether intentionally or not.

The "privileges" notion also asserts that with the State's generosity of "allowing" citizens to take wildlife, citizens must be grateful to their beneficent master and be indebted for the limited opportunities government bestows upon them. Government grants certain "privileges" in the use of wildlife and can just as easily extract them depending on the mood and biases of the bureaucratic class or judiciary. This explanation is a perfect example of the arbitrary use of power, and arbitrary power is the antithesis of liberty.

The *Geer* Court held, "The common ownership imports the right to keep the property, if the sovereign so chooses, always within its jurisdiction for every purpose." (161 U.S. at 530) The majority in this case implied that sovereignty resides in the government, which is not true in this country. Sovereignty resides in the people (see James Monroe, 1867).

One can imagine that the *Geer* decision was influenced by the contemporaneous statist movement, which had been imported from Germany only a couple of decades earlier by American students studying abroad who had, by 1896, become dominant in academia and amongst the so-called "intellectual elite."[44] This movement followed Germany's approach to a beneficent and utopian State, under Chancellor Bismarck, that provided for the needs of the masses at the expense of property rights, individualism, and liberty. The individual is to be subservient to the State, and *Geer* reflects this perspective. It was the statist philosophy that provided the fertile ground, which led to the terrors of both world wars. We were fortunate not to have had such violent leaders in North America, but the statist foundation was here nonetheless.

The *Geer* Court appears to have favored the collectivist perspective—identifying the sovereign power in the State—at the expense of the individual in claiming that the State owns wildlife. This is a key point in that it demonstrates the political leaning of these five justices. They certainly were free to believe in whatever political view they favored, and one can certainly push for collectivism or statism if one desires, but until our system of government has been amended to provide for this sort of authority, courts are not free to make law from the bench, such as the *Geer* majority was attempting to accomplish. If we were to have the full

---

44   It is quite obvious the statist movement was dangerous to mankind's very existence, as the first half of the twentieth century demonstrated. Nations attempted to apply these principles, and the results were loss of individual rights, world wars, genocide, development and use of weapons of mass destruction, establishment of concentration camps, etc., all of which are directly attributable to statism. With the abandonment of Enlightenment and Natural Law principles (i.e., Classical Liberalism), respect for human life and individualism was, for the most part, lost, with terror taking its place. See lectures, Liulevicius (2003). *Utopia & Terror in the 20th Century*. The Teaching Co. Univ. of TN. Also, see *The Origins of Totalitarianism*, Hannah Arendt, Harcourt Books, 1968, pp. 267-69. I leave it to the reader to research the philosophies that were imported to the U.S. from Germany in the late nineteenth century that obviously influenced the *Geer* decision. Please look into: the Historical School of Economics, founded in Germany and which dominated American and central European academia until around 1900; statism, where individual rights and private property are sacrificed in the name of the public welfare; Welfare Capitalism, the blending of socialism and capitalism; plus the influence of Otto von Bismarck, Chancellor of Germany from 1867-90, who created the Reich and saw the State as the means to solve all social problems and whose policies American Progressives embraced and eventually implemented. Also, research the Religion of Humanity and the Social Gospel to better understand the origins of contemporary Liberalism based on these branches of its religious roots, which espouse the way to salvation is not through the individual, but rather through collective efforts; i.e. either we get there together, or not at all.

measure of checks and balances in this country, those justices in concurrence with the *Geer* decision should have been impeached and then tried for their dismissal of Constitutional principles, which they had vowed to uphold. These issues are not a matter of opinion, they are a matter of law,[45] and those five justices ignored the law and followed their preferences, and therefore attempted to make their own law, which is usurpation. Have we traded the concept of *the divine right of kings for the divine right of justices*? Do justices receive their inspiration from Mount Statism? Are justices above the law, and their decisions untouchable except by other justices as though they were the high priests—the intermediaries between the vulgar masses and whatever higher power they genuflect to?

The position of the majority in the *Geer* decision is a treasonable offense, and if we are to prevent an oligarchy from ruling our country from the bench, we must deter such behavior like any other high crime, with commensurate punishments. But let us always remember the Eighth Amendment's protections. Even though usurpation by powerful government officials is the greatest offense there is, we must respect their rights even if they don't respect ours. It is the greatest offense because it does the greatest damage to our system of government, other than by an invasion of foreign forces or insurrection by factions that attempt to overthrow the government. A spy does terrible damage to society, but it is not permanent in that our system remains intact and unaltered. Terrorists do tremendous physical damage, but they strengthen the resolve of the people to eliminate them. However, government officials can do the most damage, with the embellishments of law surrounding them, by extracting individual nuts and bolts that hold our system together. The removal of too many fasteners will eventually cause the entire system to come crashing down—which has been the plan of socialists within this country. Because of the insidiously slow manner in which this takes place, no one will be able to identify what really caused the downfall, just as historians still argue over the fall of Rome.

The *Geer* decision demonstrates a Court bankrupt of constitutional understanding, and   informs   us   that   their

---

45   "The judges, both of the supreme and inferior courts, shall hold their offices during good behavior...." Article Three, Section One, U.S. Constitution. If justices ignore the Constitution or attempt to change it, they are violating their oath and the law.

assertion of State ownership must be dismissed with extreme prejudice because of its offensiveness to liberty and to free government.

What all subsequent Courts established after the *Geer* decision was an ancient principle found in all good governments and which had been provided for in our Constitution: government must provide for the general welfare of society. The health of our environment is at the very base of all responsibilities. If the air is unbreathable, if the water is undrinkable, if the natural resources are unusable or unavailable, then government has failed its people and condemned them to ruin. For how can a people survive without access and use of natural resources? It is an utter impossibility, which is the reason access and use are **fundamental rights** for citizens. It is the reason government must ensure that natural resources will be managed in such a way that citizens will have a generous access in perpetuity, which requires adequate managerial authority.

Epstein (2006, p. 17) reflects on the founding position when addressing such issues:

> [T]he classical liberal position accepts the proposition that certain forms of market failure require, or at least allow, some form of government intervention. Thus, government may restrict the acquisition ... of forms of wildlife and natural resources that are subject to premature dissipation through the standard common-pool problem: the party who takes fish or wildlife gets all the gain, but suffers only a tiny fraction of the long-term losses. State regulation of some form is needed to counter the potential for overconsumption.

The General Welfare Clause is the only source of governmental authority that the *Geer* Court required (not, for example, the twisted interpretation used by FDR to redistribute wealth), but it eluded them, and now we must reverse all subsequent precedent established by lower court decisions and purge subsequent legislation and regulation of the viral infection *Geer* introduced. This demonstrates the importance of the Supreme Court and the need to choose judicial candidates who respect the rule of law and the strict interpretation of the Constitution.

The Supreme Court case *Missouri v. Holland*, 252 U.S. 416, 1920, essentially overruled *Geer* when it provided:

> The State [of Missouri] ... founds its claim of exclusive authority [over wildlife] upon an assertion of title to migratory birds, an assertion that is embodied in statute. No doubt it is true that, as between a State and its inhabitants, the State may regulate the killing and sale of such birds, but it does not follow that its authority is exclusive of paramount powers. **To put the claim of the State upon title [of ownership] is to lean upon a slender reed. Wild birds are not in the possession of anyone, and possession is the beginning of ownership.** (252 U.S. 416, 434) (Emphasis added)

It is evident that "wild birds" means birds not in anyone's possession, i.e. free roaming; the corollary is, wild birds brought into possession, and therefore owned, would need to be re-designated as "tamed"—*mansueta naturae*. *Missouri's* provision that "possession is the beginning of ownership" makes it unmistakably clear that all migratory birds, including raptors that are legally taken, are the exclusive property of the possessor. But, as in all cases in civil society, property is conditioned by a bundle of rights. In other words, our liberty to do what we will with our property has legal boundaries and may be subject to regulatory limits based upon legitimate objective public interests—not subjective agendas of factions represented by ignorant or scheming legislators, jurists and bureaucrats.

Missouri, in a seven to two decision, was the first Supreme Court case to constructively overturn *Geer's* claim of State ownership. However, the *Missouri* Court did not overturn the principle *Geer* affirmed regarding States' obligation to manage wildlife in a manner consistent with the legitimate needs of its citizens. This is now undoubtedly a settled law principle. The ownership issue, first articulated in Rome and rediscovered through trial and error (which is to be expected when we ignore history), is also settled law, i.e., wildlife belongs to no one until possession takes place.

In *Toomer v. Witsell*, 334 U.S. 385 (1948) the Court articulated the settled law principle:

The whole ownership theory, in fact, is now generally regarded as but a fiction expressive in legal shorthand of the importance to its people that a State have power to preserve and regulate the exploitation of an important resource. (334 U.S. 402)

In *Douglas v. Seacoast Products*, 431 U.S. 265, 284 (1977), the Court cited the dissenting opinion in *Geer*, where Justice Field stated, "A State does not stand in the same position as the owner of a private game preserve and it is pure fantasy to talk of 'owning' wild fish, birds, or animals. Neither the States nor the Federal Government, any more than a hopeful fisherman or hunter, has title to these creatures until they are reduced to possession by skillful capture." (161 U.S. 519, 539-540) The dissenting opinions of Justices Field and Harlan in *Geer* became the basis of future decisions that constructively overturned *Geer*, which eventually lead to *Hughes*. The *Douglas* Court continued, "The 'ownership' language of cases such as those cited by appellant must be understood as no more than a 19th-century legal fiction expressing 'the importance to its people that a State have power to preserve and regulate the exploitation of an important resource.' *Toomer v. Witsell*, 334 U.S at 402."

The Court in *Hughes v. Oklahoma*, 441 U.S. 322 (1979) (a seven to two decision) found an "Oklahoma statute … repugnant to the Commerce Clause." The Court held: "*Geer v. Connecticut* is overruled. Time has revealed the error of the result reached in *Geer* through its application of the 19th-century legal fiction of State ownership of wild animals." There are many environmental law professors who are not willing to admit that this decision once and for all destroyed the State Ownership Doctrine. Some States' legal counsel for their wildlife agencies also hold tight to this now obsolete and archaic doctrine that never had a place in our system of law. The *Hughes* Court provided:

States may promote the legitimate purpose of protecting and conserving wild animal life within their borders only in ways consistent with the basic principle that the pertinent economic unit is the Nation [*if the State owned wildlife, this would not be possible*]. 441 U.S. 338 … The cases defining the scope of permissible State regulation in areas of congressional silence reflect an often controversial evolution of rules to accommodate Federal and State interests. *Geer v. Connecticut* was decided relatively early in that evolutionary process. We hold that time has revealed the error of the early resolution reached in that case, and accordingly, *Geer* is today overruled. 441 U.S. 326

... [The *Geer*] conclusion followed ... the view that the State had the power, as representative for its citizens, who "owned" in common all wild animals within the State, to control not only the *taking* of game but also the *ownership* of game that had been lawfully reduced to possession [*"common ownership" of resources is a socialistic doctrine antithetical to our system*]. 441 U.S. 327 ... Mr. Justice Field and ... Mr. Justice Harlan dissented, rejecting as artificial ... the Court's analysis of "ownership" and "commerce" in wild game. 441 U.S. 328 ... The view of the *Geer* dissenters increasingly prevailed in subsequent cases.... The erosion of *Geer* began only 15 years after it was decided. 441 U.S. 329 ... **The *Geer* analysis has also been eroded to the point of virtual extinction in cases involving regulation of wild animals.** The first challenge to *Geer's* theory of a State's power over wild animals came in *Missouri v. Holland*, 252 U.S. 416 (1920). 441 U.S. 331 ... *Foster-Fountain Packing Co. v Haydel*, 278 U.S. 1 (1928), undermined Geer even more directly. 441 U.S. 332 Foster-Fountain Packing's implicit shift away from *Geer's* formalistic "ownership" analysis became explicit in *Toomer v. Witsell*, 334 U.S. 402 (1948). 441 U.S. 333 (Emphasis added)

If the States owned wildlife, FWS would have absolutely no authority to regulate migratory birds, and therefore migratory birds, including raptors, would be under the exclusive authority of the States, as was argued and defeated in *Missouri*. This demonstrates that both the Federal and State governments have regulatory authority over migratory birds within their delegated powers, but neither owns these birds.

Even the dissenters in *Hughes* rejected the State Ownership Doctrine, making this aspect of the decision unanimous:

Admittedly, **a State does not "own" the wild creatures within its borders** in any conventional sense of the word.

441 U.S. 341 … This Court long has recognized that the ownership language of *Geer* and similar cases is simply a shorthand way of describing a State's substantial interest in preserving and regulating the exploitation of the fish and game and other natural resources within its boundaries for the benefit of its citizens. 441 U.S. 343 (Emphasis added)

It is to *Hughes'* dissenters that loyalists of the State Ownership Doctrine reach for that last gasp of air as their world closes in around them. These two dissenters state:

To be sure, a State's power to preserve and regulate wildlife within its borders is not absolute. But the State is accorded wide latitude [*it would be better to state "sufficient latitude within Federal and State constitutional constraints"*] in fashioning regulations appropriate for protection of its wildlife. Unless the regulation directly conflicts with a federal statute or treaty …; allocates access in a manner that violates the Fourteenth Amendment …; or represents a naked attempt to discriminate against out-of-state enterprises in favor of in-state businesses unrelated to any purpose of conservation [*why are these two dissenters ignoring the rest of the Constitution and asserting that only the treaty-making power, the Fourteenth Amendment, the Privileges and Immunities Clause, and the Commerce Clause apply to the States?*]…, the State's special interest in preserving its wildlife should prevail. (441 U.S. 342)

This is simply asserting that the States Right's Doctrine is grounded in the Tenth Amendment, which, per se, is absolutely true. Where the U.S. Constitution is silent, the States' authority prevails; and where the States' constitutions are silent, individual liberties prevail. However, there is no provision in State constitutions providing unconditional authority to deny property rights to citizens. If the States did have such authority, there would be no property rights at all. Therefore, citizens' property rights are paramount. States can deny property rights only when there are compelling and justifiable public welfare interests at stake.

The whole purpose of Federal and State constitutions is to protect the property and liberty of citizens, so how can it be used to destroy these rights without some very compelling public interest to justify such an infringement? Unless of course we've surrendered these rights and now have an entirely new system of government. Was there a silent revolution that was never ratified by the people? If so, words that describe this are *subversion* and *usurpation*, and such insidious tactics, and the resultant changes, are to be condemned with extreme prejudice!

It is State Ownership loyalists' belief that the meaning of *Hughes* is to be found in the above dissenting paragraph, and they interpret the decision to mean that the overturning of the State Ownership Doctrine is applicable **only** when a State statute infringes upon Federal constitutional authority as it relates to interstate commerce, equal protection, and privileges and immunities. They believe *Hughes* does not control outside of these constitutional provisions—e.g., see *State v. Fertterer*, Supreme Court of Montana, 841 P.2d 467 (1992)—which demonstrates a complete lack of understanding of our system of limited government and that sovereignty resides in citizens, not in government. Their mistake is confronting the issue as one that can only be resolved based on proprietary interests rather than general welfare interests.

It is interesting how they cling to *Geer*, a rogue decision based on statism and perhaps elements of feudalism, yet ignore a sound decision rooted in the rule of law, constitutional government, and fundamental principles of liberty, as seen in *Hughes*! This is an excellent demonstration of the historic tendency for power to be accumulated by government at the expense of citizens' freedoms, and the unwillingness to surrender the acquired power, even when proven wrong. In the name of one cause—i.e., conservationism—all wildlife related liberties must be sacrificed. Even the Fourth Amendment's protection from unreasonable search and seizure is asserted to be of little consequence whenever wildlife is at issue. The pendulum swung from unregulated liberty to an over-regulated management system that tends to ignore citizens' rights and at times has terrorized citizens, as Operation Falcon demonstrates—more on this later.

We need to start referring to State authority over natural resources as "jurisdiction," which is rooted in general welfare parameters, over common resources for common access and use.

Is Poaching Theft?

A couple of State court cases provide some insight into what has been attempted by protectionists when they've tried to assert that poaching is theft from the State.

In *State v. Bartee*, TX Court of Appeals, 894 S.W.2d 34 (1994), the State prosecutor attempted to charge a citizen with theft and criminal mischief involving the poaching of deer, based on the proposition that Texas "owned" wild deer.

> In Texas ... the common law provides that ... no individual property rights exist as long as the animal remains wild, unconfined, and undomesticated.... Unqualified property rights in wild animals can arise when they are legally removed from their natural liberty and made the subjects of man's dominion.

In concluding this case, the *Bartee* court instructs:

> A white-tailed deer in its natural state of liberty cannot be the subject of the theft and criminal mischief statutes.... The prosecutor in charging theft or criminal mischief involving a white-tailed deer must be extremely careful in choosing the proper allegations in the State's pleadings, but also keenly aware of the facts which will support those allegations. Otherwise, the prosecutor may be up the creek without the proverbial paddle. (Goble & Freyfogle, 2002, p. 154)

Runnels v. State (Tex. Crim. App. 1948) is another case demonstrating States do not own wildlife since States do not possess wild animals. In this case

> the Court of Criminal Appeals discussed when wild animals became subject to theft. The Court wrote: 'Wild animals are not subject to theft until they become the property of an owner. This they do immediately upon being reduced to possession. ... This seems to be the **settled law** in all jurisdictions,' (Goble & Freyfogle, 2002, p. 156; Emphasis added).

In a letter dated July 7, 2010, Warren Buhl, Assistant Special Agent in Charge, FWS, Office of Law Enforcement, Fort Snelling, MN, provided the following to William Wegner, Pace University School of Law (Wegner had not received payment for a gyrfalcon/Barbary falcon hybrid and was inquiring what authority FWS had over such issues):

> There are no theft provisions within the Migratory Bird Treaty Act or the Lacey Act. While the purchase or sale of wildlife which were taken, possessed, transported, or sold in violation of Federal or Tribal law may constitute a crime under the Lacey Act, the predicate law must have wildlife protection as its purpose. Theft violations are crimes committed against persons, not wildlife.

And as pointed out above, theft violations involving wildlife are not crimes committed against States.

Admission by a Protectionist of our Property Rights

The Pragmatic Migratory Bird Treaty Act: Protecting "Property" by Hye-Jong Linda Lee, is a research paper written by an animal rights advocate to analyze property interests as they relate to migratory birds. In her abstract she provides, "This Note explores America's attachment to wildlife as property under the terms of the conventions, the statutory language, the history, and the case law pertaining to the MBTA, with specific focus on the curious distinction between wild and captive-bred mallard ducks." Her Introduction provides, "The Migratory Bird Treaty Act (MBTA) was enacted in 1916 to protect migratory birds from unrestrained killing. The MBTA, however, treats migratory birds as human property that is deserving of protection only to the extent that they continue to serve human interests."

In the section titled *Judicial Challenges to the Applicability to the MBTA to Captive Raised Birds*, Lee provides

> In *United States v. Conners*, the court held that the MBTA applied only to wild mallard ducks and not to those which were captively-bred. In reaching this conclusion, the court examined the MBTA and the Mexican and Japanese Conventions to determine whether the MBTA contemplated captive-reared, in addition to wild, mallards.

The court noted that two of the three treaties referred specifically to "wild ducks," including the operative Canadian Convention giving rise to the MBTA. Therefore, **since criminal statutes had to be strictly construed**, the MBTA did not apply to the killing of captive-reared ducks. Thus, should it be found that the ducks killed were "wild," the defendant's conviction under the MBTA would be sustained, whereas if they were captive-bred, the charges would have to be dismissed. (Emphasis added) [*The falconry community needs to analyze this further regarding captive-raised, native raptors.*]

If birds are now worth protecting, they are worth protecting because humans find them useful.

The very language of the MBTA's regulatory scheme suggests that it is designed to protect birds only to the extent necessary to preserve their value or utility to humans.... It is their value as a useful commodity that earns migratory birds significant protection under the Canadian Convention. [*Compare this to the Rocky Mountain Locust, which not only had no value to humans, but was considered a pest (but then, so were raptors, until falconers lobbied for their protection under the MBTA), which caused great economic loss. Are we to accept the proposition that on the one hand we can annihilate species that are pests (even though these "pests" may be critical to the survival of species we find valuable, such as prairie grouse), but on the other hand, animals with value must be regulated under draconian regulations from the depravations of "greedy men"? Such extremes demonstrate hypocrisy.*]

Similarly, the Mexican Convention also declares it necessary to "employ adequate measures which will permit a rational *utilization* of migratory birds...." The Convention acknowledges the recreational and economic values of migratory birds and affords them protection on that basis, "[i]n order that the species may not be exterminated ... it is right and proper to protect birds ... for the purposes of sport, ... commerce and industry."

The Japanese and Russian Conventions likewise extended protection on the basis of recreational value, establishing open hunting seasons.... **This language reveals that migratory birds were not placed off-limits under the**

conventions; their uses were simply limited to ensure that their value as food and sport would be protected for years to come. (Emphasis added)

Additionally, the legacy of viewing wildlife as property to be owned and controlled is apparent in the MBTA's exemption for migratory birds raised in captivity. The Act provides that, "[n]othing in this subchapter shall be construed to prevent the ... sale of birds so bred [on farms and preserves] ... for the purpose of increasing the food supply." **This language suggests that captive-bred migratory birds are property subject to the control and disposal of breeders, not to be tampered with by the Act.** (Emphasis added)

The legislative history of the MBTA boldly suggests the role property rights and interests played in shaping the vision of MBTA's protectionism and rationale. Congress clearly saw in migratory birds food, sport, and aesthetic enjoyment.... **Indeed, many congressmen either suggested or wanted confirmation that the true purpose of the MBTA was to preserve the sport of hunting for generations to come....** What was common to this discourse and debate about the MBTA was that it was not extending help to birds for their sake, but for people's sake. (Emphasis added) [*Enlightened self-interest dictates this to be the only logical course that we can take that will ensure proper protections for species.*]

Curiously, the FWS allows **any person to take "captive-reared" mallard ducks and other captive-reared migratory waterfowl without a permit....** [*The fact that raptors are managed differently demonstrates falconers are regulated in an arbitrary manner.*] Similarly, **any person may lawfully acquire, possess,** and transport **captive-reared and properly marked migratory waterfowl without a permit....** Thus, the distinction between captive and wild mallard ducks suggests the modesty of the MBTA. (Emphasis added)

[In *Koop v. United States*, for example, the Court provided,] "[i]t is common knowledge that ducks, and particularly mallard ducks, lend themselves to being tamed or domesticated and that ducks generally found in most farmyards trace their ancestry back to the wild and untamed ducks with whose protection and care the Migratory Bird Treaties and regulations were concerned. Concededly, however, **the law was not meant for, nor may it regulate or control <u>the use of</u>, such tamed or domesticated ducks.**" (Emphasis added) [*This applies to raptors used in falconry as well. However, FWS ignores this fact.*]

Rather, once persons exercised possession and control, birds became property; indeed, **"[i]n determining when ... 'wild' birds are no longer considered 'wild,' courts and writers have made the major consideration one of possession and control.**" (Emphasis added)

The court explained that "[t]here is no property in wild animals until they have been subjected to the control of man. If one secures and tames them, they are his property; if he does not tame them, they are still his, so long as they are kept confined and under his control."

... [O]nce people exercise control over wildlife, this possession marks the "beginning of ownership," and **thereafter the MBTA has limited application**. (Emphasis added)

In an email dated September 26, 2008, Dr. George Allen, Chief, Branch of Permits and Regulations, Div. of Migratory Bird Management, FWS, retracted the previous FWS assertion that falconers did not own their raptors. He stated:

I'd ... like to try to clarify an ongoing issue involving possession of falconry birds. I should not have put the statement in the proposed propagation regulations stating the birds held under the permit are not private property.... MBTA falconry and propagation raptors are private property.... In short, I've been corrected— and we won't say falconry raptors are not private property.

To be fair to Dr. Allen, he had previously taken legal advice from a particular attorney within the Solicitor's Office for the Department of the Interior. This attorney obviously had a protectionist agenda and asserted an illegal position, which Dr. Allen did not feel qualified to refute since he is a biologist and not an attorney.

Beebe and Webster[46] argued long and hard regarding the property rights falconers have in their birds. They had lost a lot of friends because of their insistence that the government did not own either wild taken or domestic bred raptors. Because of Webster's involvement with American Falconry Conservancy as a Director, he was able to raise the funds necessary to retain the legal services of Counsel Horn and overcome that faction within FWS that attempted to deny property rights.[47] Beebe and Webster have been vindicated, and their detractors will go down in falconry history as having exposed falconers to the possibility—some would argue the probability—of losing this outstanding art and sport because of capitulation to those who are no friends of falconry. For it would simply have been a matter of time before the animal rights faction would demand falconers relinquish their "privilege" to practice falconry and surrender the State's "property." The falconry community, having previously accepted these illegitimate assertions based on what they had been told by the controlling faction, would have surrendered both, not unlike the Jews walking through the gates of Auschwitz—without hesitation and without question, and having been well-trained by public education to be subservient to the State.

This may seem like a stretch, but those who know history understand the characteristic progression of tyranny—insidiously slow and methodical. Once the populace is sufficiently indoctrinated, it is an easy next step to demand unconditional obedience. This is why it is important to continue educating our citizens about the progression of Nazism, how it indoctrinated the citizenry into obedience for the "good of the State," and how the obedience of the populace could be twisted to evil ends. Societies are especially vulnerable to such manipulation during crises, as the Germans were faced with after WWI. Just like contemporary

---

46   Founders of North American Falconers' Association and authors of the "bible" of North American falconry: *North American Falconry and Hunting Hawks*, the first instructional book on falconry in America. In addition, Beebe was the first to breed peregrine falcons in captivity in North America.

47   McDonald wishes to point out that "although Counsel William Horn and Hal Webster certainly deserve a great deal of credit for the private ownership aspect, recognition must also be given to all of the falconers who, between 1970 and 2009, fought to make significant changes in falconry regulations, both Federal and State. Some of those deserving of recognition besides Frank Beebe and Hal Webster are Jim Fritz, Alva Nye, Jim Ruos, Brian McDonald, Willston Shor, Bill Lauer, Gerald Richards, James Doyle, Jeff Peters, Eric Awender, Stephen Gatti and Steve Chitty." McDonald mentions there are others, but these are the primary individuals who fought for our rights.

Liberalism in the United States, Nazism's parent was statism, which was based on Chancellor Bismarck's late nineteenth century system of government that was taught in German universities of that period. Liberalism and Nazism were siblings—not identical twins—that simply took different roads. The former took an evolutionary approach to gain control of the domestic population primarily through government, manipulative science, and the academe; the latter took a revolutionary, militaristic, and expansionist approach to control mankind. I highly recommend the reader research German statism and its importation into the United States by academics in the latter half of the nineteenth century to discover the origins of the Progressive/Liberal movement and how, in Germany, the statist movement laid the groundwok for the Nazis. A suggested starting point might be Gabriel (1956), pages 246-48, who was himself a liberal history professor at Yale. Understanding these roots prepares us to combat their attacks on liberty and property rights.

The Public Trust Doctrine

The chief legal counsel for Montana Fish, Wildlife & Parks, Bob Lane, states, "[The Public Trust Doctrine is] a concept, not a legal imperative," (Dickson, 2005). Sax (1970, p. 521) offers: "The 'public trust' has no life of its own and no intrinsic content. It is no more—and no less—than a name courts give to their concerns about the insufficiencies of the democratic process."

The underlying principal behind this American doctrine originated in Rome as a general welfare rule, was bent to the will of the Norman monarchy of feudal England, and was tailored to the American political system approximately a century and a half ago. The term "Public Trust Doctrine" (trust) was established under American common law jurisprudence in order to provide full recognition of the age-old protection of public access of waterways (first advanced by the New Jersey Supreme Court in *Arnold v. Mundy*, 1821, and firmly established by the U.S. Supreme Court in *Martin v. Waddell*, 41 U.S. 367, (1842)). It is a doctrine that ensures access for navigation, commerce, and harvest of our common water resources. Such access is an absolute must for a free people to reap the bounty of liberty. Without it, wealth will unjustly be accumulated in the hands of a few, thereby centralizing regional power with the subsequent diminishment of liberty and wealth to the many. The court cases that established the trust exemplify the truth of this statement. Private entities that attempted to monopolize waterways would have been able to exclude the public from their use or charged fees for passage through them. This would have unjustly enriched the few and alienated the masses from the potential opportunities and wealth that scarce waterways provide. While such wealth cannot be distributed equitably through government mandates without great harm to the economy and liberty, it can be made available to all who have the will to utilize it, which is the most effective and efficient means to distribute wealth—i.e., through the natural process of human economic intercourse with just regulations to ensure the rule of law is being observed by all. No unjust barriers can be allowed to stand in the way of a free people if prosperity is expected to endure, as Quigley (1961) explains. Unjust barriers are erected in the name of individuals as well as in the name of public interests—either can be used to harm the other and neither have a monopoly in causing injuries.

Unlike feudal Europe, in the United States, sovereignty resides in the people, not the State (see James Monroe, 1867). This is why free-roaming wildlife can belong neither to landowners nor to the State. It would be like "owning" air, sunlight, and rain. Who can claim ownership of these transitory things? Americans will not tolerate a class of people denying them the right of access to natural resources—including the bureaucratic class. And since the people have not relinquished all of their rights as of yet, government cannot deny this right of access to wildlife.

If the State were to own our resources, as is the case under socialistic governments, then the State could dictate who would get the resources and for what purposes. Those who hold the power will determine the outcome, and since authority and responsibility to manage wildlife is vested in State wildlife agencies, whoever controls these agencies possesses the power to dictate the conditions. Therefore, protectionists have been slowly moving into wildlife agency positions for the last few decades in an attempt to dictate how statutes and policy will be interpreted and how regulations will be written for wildlife management. It is quite common for bureaucrats to take a statute and twist it out of shape to serve their agendas when writing regulations.

There have been many papers written by extreme environmentalist types in law schools (e.g., Sax, 1970, and his followers) and wildlife agencies (e.g., *The Value of the North American Model of Fish & Wildlife Conservation*, by Prukop and Regan, International Association of Fish & Wildlife Agencies, 2002 White Paper), who wish to broaden the authority of the trust doctrine to incorporate all natural resources, including wildlife. They cite various governmental powers and interests to justify the expansion of the trust's use in judicial intervention, i.e., legislate from the bench. Huffman (2007) states, "The possibilities [of the application of the trust], it seems, are only limited by the imagination," which, of course, is how the Commerce Clause has been interpreted by extreme and dangerous elements of the Supreme Court (*Wickard v. Filburn*, 317 U.S. 111 (1942), for example, which provided for massive expansion of the Federal government; the consenting justices should have been impeached because of their contempt for and treasonous disregard of the Constitution). This removes government restraints and exposes free citizens to the arbitrary whims of lawmakers, and in particular, to the bureaucratic class, which is incrementally expanding its powers when it writes regulations that are directly at odds with statutes.

Once wildlife has been incorporated into the trust, the protectionists will then manipulate it to deny the use of wildlife (including raptors) by citizens. Thankfully, as Huffman (2007) informs us, so far "there has not been widespread application of the doctrine beyond the waters and submerged lands to which it originally applied.... But the drumbeat continues in the academy and among environmental groups ... to 'liberate' the doctrine by applying it to non-navigable waters.... I examined several possible theoretical foundations for the public trust doctrine and concluded that it is best understood as an aspect of property law."[48] Applying a principle based on a public interest grounded in a constant, like waterways, and transferring this principle onto transient objects like animals, is mischievous.

As previously stated, if we need to apply a doctrine in order to provide authority to managing wildlife, it must fall under the General Welfare Clause of the Constitution (again, not like the distorted and abusive use of it by FDR) as well as State public welfare constitutional provisions. The interests of wildlife management on behalf of the people are well served by this principle. It fits it like a glove.

The true purpose of the trust can be understood with a brief explanation by the U.S. National Oceanic & Atmospheric Administration (NOAA).

---

48   He was referring to an earlier paper of his, "A fish out of water: The public trust doctrine in a constitutional democracy," (19 Envtl. Law 527, 1989)

The Public Trust Doctrine is a common-law doctrine of property law, customized by each state, which establishes public rights in navigable waters and on their shores. The doctrine is premised on the fact that such waters and shores have been used as common areas for food, travel, and commerce since time immemorial.... The legal interest of the public is determined by balancing public and private rights and interests.

NOAA uses a formula to demonstrate the doctrine: "A Legal Interest + Held by States + Tidal & Navigable Waters + For the Benefit of the Public = Public Trust Doctrine"
NOAA continues:

The concepts presented in the Public Trust Doctrine date back at least to the Roman Empire. English common law recognized public rights in navigable waters and on their shores. American colonial courts followed English common law. Each state has since further refined the doctrine through its courts and legislatures to best fit the unique circumstances and societal needs of the state.
    The Public Trust Doctrine exists because historically the use of navigable waters and their shores for navigation, commerce and fishing has been a mark of a free society. The public nature of navigable waters as highways for navigation and commerce is self-evident.

In his paper, Sax (1970, p. 556) explains the narrowness of the application of the trust:

It is clear that the historical scope of public trust law is quite narrow. Its coverage includes ... that aspect of the public domain below the low-water mark on the margin of the sea and the great lakes, the waters over those lands, and the waters within rivers and streams of any consequence.

Sax (1970, p. 477) informs us:

Three types of restrictions ... are often thought to be imposed by the public trust: first, the property subject to the trust must not only be used for a public purpose, but it must be held available for use by the general public [*a harvested duck cannot be shared in this manner*]; second, the property may not be sold, even for a fair cash equivalent [*which automatically excludes wildlife—consider commercial fishing, commerce in reptiles, and the fur trade*]; and third, the property must be maintained for particular types of uses [*will the government dictate how to use the fish I caught or the pelt I tanned, excluding commercial considerations?*].

This makes it quite clear that the trust encompasses principles that are fundamentally land and water related—not wildlife in particular or renewable resources in general. Since wildlife belongs to no one, trust principles may be related, like a relative, but it is not a doctrine that can be directly applied to wildlife.
Sax (1970, p. 509) referenced the public trust in Wisconsin since, as he explains, "The Supreme Court of Wisconsin has probably made a more conscientious effort to rise above rhetoric and to work out a reasonable meaning for the public trust doctrine than have the courts of any other state." When considering a trust question, the Wisconsin Court considers whether a use conflicts with or is compatible with the public's interests. If it conflicts, they will restrain or prohibit the activity. Obviously, ownership and personal use of harvested wildlife, including raptors, is not in conflict with the principles of the trust.
    Sax (1970, p. 527) analyzes California's trust cases and points out that these "cases stand for the more limited proposition that the state cannot give to private parties such title that those private interests will be empowered to delimit or modify public uses." Of course, ownership of harvested wildlife does not fall within this test. Property rights in wild taken animals do not modify public uses, since they are a highly transitory resource, i.e., they grow and then perish either by age or by consumption. Whereas public lands have greater permanency and provide access to renewable resources that can be used for recreational or economic purposes in perpetuity.
    Sax (1970, p. 531) continues:

Any action which will adversely affect traditional public rights in trust lands is a matter of general public interest and should therefore be made only if there has been full consideration of the state's public interest in the matter;

such actions should not be taken in some fragmentary and publicly invisible way. Only with such a safeguard can there be any assurance that the public interest will get adequate public attention.... Consistency with this principle would require that decisions likely to inhibit public uses be made in a public forum. [*Though this deviates from the present discussion, what Sax provides here should be taken into consideration when discussing eminent domain issues, which also need to be made in a public forum for the whole community to decide upon.*]

Conversely, any action that will adversely affect private property rights is a matter of general interest. If there are to be any changes in property rights of harvested wildlife, the same principle would apply. Remove the words "public rights in trust lands" in the first line of the above quotation and insert "private rights in harvested wildlife," and we begin to see a larger picture in which both public and private interests must be safeguarded.

Sax (1970, p. 534) points out that governmental bodies "may interfere with the public trust in the same manner as private profit-oriented interests; many aspects of local self-interest are as inconsonant with the broad public interest as are the projects of private enterprises." This indicates that all segments of society, including the government, can abuse some portion of our common interest. Therefore, reins need to be applied to all because none can be completely trusted. It's the difference between liberty and anarchy: liberty is tempered with socially responsible restraints embraced by the individual, whereas anarchy knows no restraint.

Therefore, as Sax (1970, p. 552) explains

Indeed, if there is any lesson to be learned from the cases which have been examined in this Article, it is that a much more sophisticated examination into the manipulations of legislative and administrative processes is required if the public interest is to be promoted.... [*Private interests have also been manipulated by legislative and administrative processes that are of equal importance.*] The very fact that ... courts perceive a need to reorient administrative conduct in this fashion suggests how insulated such agencies may be from the relevant constituencies.

Frequently, legal counsel is required to navigate through the maze of bureaucracy in order to protect the interests of citizens. To place wildlife in the hands of bureaucrats under the trust is to lose the **right** of use through the slow process of attrition. Use will be considered a "privilege," in the disparaging sense, that can be withdrawn at the whim of an agency.

Sax (1970, pp. 559-60) points out how courts attempt to push public trust questions onto "a truly representative body" in order to minimize special interest influence. He states:

> Certainly even the most representative legislature may act in highly unsatisfactory ways when dealing with minority rights, for then it confronts the problem of majority tyranny. But that problem is not the one which arises in public resource litigation. Indeed, it is the opposite problem that frequently arises in public trust cases— that is, a diffuse majority is made subject to the will of a concerted minority. [*Besides private enterprises, such as developers, animal rights activists and environmental religious protectionists also exert undue influence.*] For self-interested and powerful minorities often have an undue influence on the public resource decisions of legislative and administrative bodies and cause those bodies to ignore broadly based public interests. Thus the function which the courts must perform, and have been performing, is to promote equality of political power for a disorganized and diffuse majority by remanding appropriate cases to the legislature after public opinion has been aroused. [*This paragraph addresses Madison's concerns about factions— minority and majority—and their destructive tendencies to both public and private interests.*]

While the trust has attributes that bear a resemblance to sustainable-use principles as it relates to wildlife, they are not grounded in the same rule. They serve different purposes, yet they can complement each other when they meet. Trust principles guarantee us and posterity continued access and use of *trust* property. Sustainable-use principles, empowered by general/public welfare principles, guarantee us and posterity continued use of renewable resources located on or off trust property for our human needs. Any attempt to fuse the two doctrines into one will certainly destroy our right to access and use of wildlife.[49]

The Alienation of State Property is Impermissible

When the Public Trust Doctrine is applied to wildlife, it becomes linked to the State Ownership Doctrine and will be used by protectionists to further their agenda. The primary reason the State Ownership Doctrine is dangerous is that it provides regulators with broad powers to infringe upon citizens' rights and to be arbitrary in applying those powers, which is the antithesis of liberty. Some courts have asserted that wildlife agencies have broad powers to interpret statutes based on their own agendas and against citizens' constitutional rights, giving the appearance that the rights of citizens and the interests of the environment are mutually exclusive. There is an environmental religious undercurrent in this way of thinking, and since animal rights activists and protectionists have infiltrated wildlife agencies, regulatory interpretation has been steering away from the rights of citizens and more toward the "rights" of animals.

With the attempt by some in protectionist circles to include wildlife under the trust, it's simply a matter of time before the trust is used to deny all access to wildlife, given the legal principle that trust property cannot be alienated from the public. In other words, if wildlife belongs to the people collectively, why should an individual benefit exclusively from the use of public "property"? For example, if I legally harvest a duck or pheasant, what right do I have to consume public property? Those who are attempting to overshadow natural resources with the trust umbrella know this to be the case and are deviously manipulating public perception to accomplish this end. Once legislatures and courts have embraced this idea, it is a simple matter to claim that all natural resources, including wildlife, belong to the public and therefore are no longer accessible for individual use. Hunting, fishing, and trapping will then be outlawed, and to reverse this would take Herculean efforts or a drastic political shift away from collectivism

---

49   For a more honest approach to the underlying principles of the trust, see MacGrady, G. (1975), The navigability concept in the civil and common law: Historical development, current importance, and some doctrines that don't hold water, 3 Fl. St. *U. L. Rev.* 513; Deveney, P. (1970), Title, *jus publicum*, and the public trust: An historical analysis, 1 *Sea Grant L. J.* 13, 37; Huffman, J. (2007), Speaking of inconvenient truths–A history of the public trust doctrine, Lewis & Clark Law School; and Epstein, R. (Fall, 1987), The Public Trust Doctrine, *Cato Journal* Vol. 7, No. 2.

and back to our founding first-principles of individual rights and liberty—a seismic paradigm shift, to be sure.

Huffman (2007) explains the Roman understanding of wildlife law, which fits ours like a glove:

> Wild creatures were owned by no one, not because they were thought to be owned by everyone, but because establishing private ownership required special rules adapted to their wild nature. **If there was a right held in common it was the right to acquire private ownership of wild animals by capturing them.**" (Huffman, 2007; Emphasis added)

This last sentence expresses the principle of what the common right really means—not common "ownership," but rather common access and use for private purposes.

Huffman (2007) warns us of protectionists' designs:

> To the extent that state laws do not have differential impacts on non-residents, do not conflict with legitimate federal laws and do not violate the federal constitutional rights of the state's own citizens, state legislatures can do what they like, **subject only to any limits imposed by their own state constitution** and courts. It is such limits that advocates for extension of the public trust doctrine to wildlife seek to establish. Although they have relied on the state ownership rhetoric of Supreme Court cases and on the Roman and English references to common property in wildlife, their objective is to justify court imposed limits on the legislative power or to justify legislative actions that might limit the property rights claims of state citizens. Rather than accept that wildlife conservation and management is one among a multitude of competing interests in the give and take of the state legislatures, **they seek a trump in the political game. State ownership theory has been the hoped for trump card**. (Emphasis added)

Goble and Freyfogle (2002, p. 961) reveal a viewpoint circulating amongst protectionists that supports Huffman's words regarding the use of the Public Trust Doctrine as it relates to the taking of wildlife. They rhetorically ask, "Can public trust resources be alienated [*the authors were referring to fish which are not under the trust but were attempting to make it so*]? If so, should they be?"

Falconers, as well as all outdoorsmen, had best be well aware of this view and be prepared to fight this effort at every turn if they hope to maintain the right to practice falconry and to hunt, fish, and trap.

Warrantless Administrative Inspections

The right of the people to be secure in their persons, houses, papers, and effects, against unreasonable searches and seizures, shall not be violated, and no Warrants shall issue, but upon probable cause, supported by Oath or affirmation, and particularly describing the place to be searched, and the persons or things to be seized. Fourth Amendment, U.S. Constitution.

U.S. Fish & Wildlife Service (FWS) asserts it has the authority to require warrantless administrative searches—referred to as "inspections"—of curtilage (homes and their surrounding property) of citizens who possess raptors for personal use under falconry regulations in order to ensure compliance with these regulations. They assert this authority is derived from the Migratory Bird Treaty Act (MBTA). The Act provides under USC Title 16, Chapter 7, Subchapter II, Section 706 Arrests; search warrants:

Any employee of the Department of the Interior authorized by the Secretary of the Interior to enforce the provisions of this subchapter shall have power, **without warrant, to arrest any person committing a violation of this subchapter in his presence or view** and to take such person immediately for examination or trial before an officer or court of competent jurisdiction; shall have power to **execute any warrant** or other process issued by an officer or court of competent jurisdiction for the enforcement of the provisions of this subchapter; **and shall have authority, with a search warrant, to search any place**. The several judges of the courts established under the laws of the United States, and United States magistrate judges may, within their respective jurisdictions, upon proper oath or affirmation **showing probable cause, issue warrants in all such cases**. All birds ... possessed contrary to the provisions of this subchapter or of any regulation prescribed thereunder[50] shall, when found, be seized and, upon conviction of the offender or upon judgment of a court of the United States that the same were ... possessed contrary to the provisions of this subchapter or of any regulation prescribed thereunder, shall be forfeited to the United States and disposed of by the Secretary of the Interior in such manner as he deems appropriate. (Emphasis added)

This makes it quite clear that a warrant is required to "inspect," i.e. search, any falconer's facilities unless an illegal act is occurring in plain view of an officer.

Under 18 USC Chapter 109—Searches and Seizures (1/8/08) Section 2236 Searches without warrant, it provides:

-STATUTE-
Whoever, being an officer, agent, or employee of the United States or any department or agency thereof, engaged in the enforcement of any law of the United States, searches any private dwelling used and occupied as such dwelling without a warrant directing such search, or maliciously and without reasonable cause searches any other building or property without a search warrant, shall be fined under this title for a first offense; and, for a subsequent offense, shall be fined under this title or imprisoned not more than one year, or both.

This section shall not apply to any person -

---

50   Given the fact that the current falconry regulations have numerous unconstitutional provisions in them, and since there is no provision for regulating activities such as falconry, this provision of seizure and prosecution for violating MBTA regulations would not apply to falconry should a falconer violate falconry regulations, since the MBTA's legitimate regulations applies to wild migratory birds taken and/or traded illegally, not legally taken raptors used in ways FWS has a prejudice against.

(a) serving a warrant of arrest; or
(b) arresting or attempting to arrest a person committing or attempting to commit an offense in his presence, or who has committed or is suspected on reasonable grounds of having committed a felony; or
(c) making a search at the request or invitation or with the consent of the occupant of the premises.

This precludes FWS from requiring States to provide for warrantless inspections, for how can they require States to perform acts FWS is prohibited from performing?
Definition of Administrative Search:

[A]n inspection or search carried out under a regulatory or statutory scheme esp. in **public or commercial premises** and usu. to enforce compliance with regulations or laws **pertaining to health, safety, or security**—one of the fundamental principles of *administrative searches* is that the government may not use an administrative inspection scheme as a pretext to search for evidence of criminal violations. *People v. Madison*, 520 N.E.2d 374 (1988)[51]

There are different interests at stake between administrative searches and searches involving criminal activity. However, administrative searches require justifiable public welfare issues to authorize their use. Kozinski (2000) provides some insight:

The Supreme Court has placed fewer checks on government searches pursuant to administrative schemes (health and safety inspections, for example) than it has placed on searches aimed at gathering evidence of criminal wrong-doing. Moreover, under current doctrine, **government officials are less likely to need a SEARCH WARRANT for administrative searches of businesses than for similar searches of homes**. (Emphasis added)

The Service's claim of authority to require warrantless inspections of falconers' curtilage, at the State or Federal level, as a condition of the falconry permit, is ungrounded in that

---

51   http://research.lawyers.com/glossary/administrative-search.html

there is no provision in the MBTA authorizing it; and it being a strict liability statute, this is an absolute necessity. There can be no statutory justification in it, and further, it violates Fourth Amendment protections guaranteed by the Federal Constitution. Therefore, FWS asserts their warrantless inspection requirement without sanction of law. This will be aptly demonstrated by U.S. Supreme Court decisions.

In *Marron v. United States*, 275 U.S. 192 (1927), the Court states,

> The requirement of the Fourth Amendment that warrants shall particularly describe the things to be seized makes general searches under them impossible.... As to what is to be taken, nothing is left to the discretion of the officer executing the warrant. ... It has long been settled that the Fifth Amendment protects every person against incrimination by the use of evidence obtained through search or seizure made in violation of his rights under the Fourth Amendment.

In *McDonald v. United States*, 335 U.S. 451 (1948), the Court clarifies the purpose of the Fourth:

> Where, as here, officers are not responding to an emergency, there must be compelling reasons to justify the absence of a search warrant. A search without a warrant demands exceptional circumstances.... The right of privacy was deemed too precious to entrust to the discretion of those whose job is the detection of crime.... Power is a heady thing, and history shows that the police acting on their own cannot be trusted. And so the Constitution requires a magistrate to pass on the desires of the police before they violate the privacy of the home.

In *Henry v. United States*, 361 U.S. 98 (1959), the Court provides, "It is better, so the Fourth Amendment teaches, that the guilty sometimes go free than that citizens be subject to easy arrest."

In the dissenting opinion in *Abel v. United States*, 362 U.S. 217 (1960), the Justices provide:

Some things in our protective scheme of civil rights are entrusted to the judiciary. Those controls are not always congenial to the police. Yet, if we are to preserve our system of checks and balances and keep the police from being all-powerful, these judicial controls should be meticulously respected. When we read them out of the Bill of Rights by allowing shortcuts, as we do today ..., police and administrative officials in the Executive Branch acquire powers incompatible with the Bill of Rights.

In *Silverman v. United States*, 365 U.S. 505 (1961), the Court provides

The Fourth Amendment, and the personal rights which it secures, have a long history. At the very core stands the right of a man to retreat into his own home and there be free from unreasonable governmental intrusion. What the Court said long ago bears repeating now: "It may be that it is the obnoxious thing in its mildest and least repulsive form; but illegitimate and unconstitutional practices get their first footing in that way, namely, by silent approaches and slight deviations from legal modes of procedure." *Boyd*

In *Rogers v. Richmond*, 365 U.S. 534 (1961), the Court states,

[O]urs is an accusatorial, and not an inquisitorial, system—a system in which the State must establish guilt by evidence independently and freely secured, and may not, by coercion, prove its charge against an accused out of his own mouth.

Warrantless inspections are coercive and demand that the accused provide evidence that can be used against him—i.e., "out of his own mouth." The warrantless inspection approach is very much like an inquisition, indiscriminately searching falconers' curtilage for evidence of wrongdoing, and then using that evidence against them so that the agency may flex its muscles and demonstrate the need for further law enforcement efforts. Heaven help us should a bath pan be momentarily missing or improper jesses (leather fetters around the raptor's legs) be used! Based on FWS's interpretation of the MBTA provision that "[a]ll birds ... possessed contrary to the provisions of this subchapter or of any regulation prescribed thereunder shall, when found, be seized," a missing scale for weighing raptors, or any minor infraction such as this, is cause for a falconer's bird to be seized and for the permit to be revoked. (Emphasis added)

In *Griswold v. Connecticut*, 381 U.S. 479 (1965), the Court describes the right to privacy:

> The association of people is not mentioned in the Constitution nor in the Bill of Rights. The right to educate a child in a school of the parents' choice—whether public or private or parochial—is also not mentioned. Nor is the right to study any particular subject or any foreign language. Yet the First Amendment has been construed to include certain of those rights.... Without those peripheral rights, the specific rights would be less secure.... The foregoing cases suggest that specific guarantees in the Bill of Rights have penumbras, formed by emanations from those guarantees that help give them life and substance.... The Fifth Amendment, in its Self-Incrimination Clause, **enables the citizen to create a zone of privacy which government may not force him to surrender to his detriment....** [T]he Framers did not intend that the first eight amendments be construed to exhaust the basic and fundamental rights which the Constitution guaranteed to the people.... Mr. Justice Brandeis, dissenting in *Olmstead v. United States*, 277 U.S. 438, 277 U.S. 478, comprehensively summarized the principles underlying the Constitution's guarantees of privacy: "The protection guaranteed by the [Fourth and Fifth] Amendments is much broader in scope. The makers of our Constitution ... conferred, as against the Government, the right to be let alone—the most comprehensive of rights and the right most valued by civilized men."

This quote summarizes the reason why falconers have a right to practice their art and sport unmolested by government intrusion.

Camara v. Municipal Court, 387 U.S. 523 (1967), is a landmark Fourth Amendment case addressing a warrantless code-enforcement inspection of a personal residence, which is related to falconry inspections. The Court states,

> With certain carefully defined exceptions [*which do not exist under the MBTA*], an unconsented warrantless search of private property is "unreasonable."… Warrantless administrative searches cannot be justified on the grounds that they make minimal demands on occupants; that warrants in such cases are unfeasible; or that area inspection programs could not function under reasonable search-warrant requirements.… In the nonemergency situation here, appellant had a right to insist that the inspectors obtain a search warrant.… Appellant has argued throughout this litigation that [San Francisco Housing Code] 503 is contrary to the Fourth and Fourteenth Amendments in that it authorizes municipal officials to enter a private dwelling without a search warrant and without probable cause.

The Court agreed with appellant and reversed the lower court's decision. The *Camara* Court further provides:

> In cases in which the Fourth Amendment requires that a warrant to search be obtained, "probable cause" is the standard by which a particular decision to search is tested against the constitutional mandate of reasonableness. To apply this standard, it is obviously necessary first to focus upon the governmental interest which allegedly justifies official intrusion upon the constitutionally protected interests of the private citizen. For example, in a criminal investigation, the police may undertake to recover specific stolen or contraband goods. But that public interest would hardly justify a sweeping search of an entire city conducted in the hope that these goods might be found [*yet FWS asserts they can do a nationwide sweep of all falconers' curtilage if they wish in order to discover if falconers, in general, are complying with regulations that are not even sanctioned by the MBTA*]. Consequently, a search for these goods, even with a warrant, is "reasonable" only

when there is "probable cause" to believe that they will be uncovered in a particular dwelling.

The *Camara* Court points to circumstances where warrantless inspections are justified:

> Since our holding emphasizes the controlling standard of reasonableness, nothing we say today is intended to foreclose prompt inspections, even without a warrant, that the law has traditionally upheld in emergency situations.

For example, seizure of unwholesome food, compulsory smallpox vaccination, health quarantine, and summary destruction of tubercular cattle fall within justified warrantless inspections. All of these cases demonstrate a serious public issue at stake, which is obviously absent from the art and sport of falconry.

Justice Douglas' dissent in *Warden v. Hayden*, 387 U.S. 294 (1967), provides some insight into the Fourth Amendment that further clarifies when warrants are needed. He states,

> This constitutional guarantee ... has been thought ... to have two faces of privacy:
>
> (1) One creates a zone of privacy that may not be invaded by the police through raids, by the legislators through laws, or by magistrates through the issuance of warrants.
>
> (2) A second creates a zone of privacy that may be invaded either by the police in hot pursuit or by a search incident to arrest or by a warrant issued by a magistrate on a showing of probable cause.

Bumper v. North Carolina, 391 U.S. 543 (1968), was a rape and attempted murder case in which evidence was acquired under the false pretense of a warrant. The conviction was reversed based on the stated principle,

> When a law enforcement officer claims authority to search a home under a warrant, he announces in effect that the occupant has no right to resist the search. The situation is instinct with coercion – albeit colorably lawful coercion. Where there is coercion, there cannot be consent.

The same principle applies when an agency claims power to search property under an unauthorized (i.e., no legitimate statutory authority) inspection—it is coercion without consent, and therefore illegal.

In *Marshall v. Barlow's, Inc.*, 436 U.S. 307 (1978), the

Appellee brought this action to obtain injunctive relief against a warrantless inspection of its business premises pursuant to § 8(a) of the Occupational Safety and Health Act of 1970 (OSHA), which empowers agents of the Secretary of Labor to search the work area of any employment facility within OSHA's jurisdiction for safety hazards and violations of OSHA regulations. A three-judge District Court ruled in appellee's favor, concluding, ... that the Fourth Amendment required a warrant for the type of search involved and that the statutory authorization for warrantless inspections was unconstitutional.

Unlike the MBTA, OSHA had a legislative provision for warrantless inspections, and yet the Court affirmed the District Court's ruling, which proves that even Congress' authority has constitutional limits. OSHA's purpose is to establish health and safety regulations and uncover violations of businesses, and yet they need a warrant to search premises to ensure compliance. Given this fact, how can FWS claim such a power for homes when there isn't even any health, safety, or other public welfare issue at stake? It is utterly nonsensical.

The *Marshall* Court continues:

The authority to make warrantless searches devolves almost unbridled discretion upon executive and administrative officers, particularly those in the field, as to when to search and whom to search. A warrant, by contrast, would provide assurances from a neutral officer that the inspection is reasonable under the Constitution, is authorized by statute, and is pursuant to an administrative plan containing specific neutral criteria.... We conclude that the concerns expressed by the Secretary do not suffice to justify warrantless inspections under OSHA or vitiate the general constitutional requirement that for a search to be reasonable a warrant must be obtained.

There are a number of valid statutes (i.e., not repugnant to constitutional principles) that provide for warrantless inspections, but these cover compelling interests of real substance to the nation's health, safety and security. These issues include the sale of liquor, the sale of firearms, the safety of mines, and the sobriety of train conductors.

In *Michigan v. Tyler*, 436 U.S. 499 (1978), the Court states, "Searches for administrative purposes, like searches for evidence of crime, are encompassed by the Fourth Amendment." Therefore, for an administrative search of falconers' curtilage to be lawful, a warrant is required.

In *Donovan v. Dewey*, 452 U.S. 594 (1981), the Court provides

> **Unlike searches of private homes, which generally must be conducted pursuant to a warrant in order to be reasonable under the Fourth Amendment**, legislative schemes authorizing warrantless administrative searches of commercial property do not necessarily violate that Amendment. A warrant may not be constitutionally required when Congress has reasonably determined that warrantless searches are necessary to further a regulatory scheme…. Inspections of commercial property may be unreasonable **if they are not authorized by law or are unnecessary for the furtherance of federal interests.** (Emphasis added)

FWS appears to have confused commercial property with the curtilage of a home; however, the MBTA does not even provide for inspections of commercial property, such as commercial raptor breeding facilities, which certainly are unnecessary for the furtherance of Federal or general welfare interests.

A couple of court cases provide insight into law and regulation and help us envision a clearer understanding of the role of government.

> However much in a particular case insistence upon such rules may appear as a technicality that inures to the benefit of a guilty person, the history of … law proves that tolerance of shortcut methods in law enforcement impairs its enduring effectiveness," *Mapp v. Ohio*, 367 U.S. 643 (1961).

For there to be confidence in law enforcement, citizens must perceive officers as symbols of justice and equity, as being above avarice, power, and ambition. In fact, it is these very evils that law enforcement is meant to check in order to secure liberty, protect property, and maintain peace and harmony. If agencies and officers are as depraved or corrupt as those they are empowered to arrest, citizens will then perceive them as a threat to their liberties; for even the innocent are not safe within such a treacherous culture. In a free society that respects law, citizens participate in fighting crime. In an authoritarian society where government agents are above the law or make law based on their arbitrary will, citizens band together to frustrate law enforcement efforts. They perceive government as a greater threat than criminals under such conditions. Consider it the Robin Hood syndrome.

"An overbroad statute is one that is designed to punish conduct which the state may rightfully punish, but which includes within its sweep constitutionally protected conduct," *Arkansas Game & Fish Commission v Murders*, Arkansas Supreme Court, 938 S.W.2d 854 (1997). This same reasoning is applicable to regulations that rightfully address a legitimate conservation interest, but sweeps into constitutionally protected areas. The Open Fields Doctrine, and the warrantless inspection of falconry facilities are perfect examples of such inspections sweeping into Fourth and Fifth Amendment protections in the name of ensuring that wildlife, in the present case raptors, are being treated humanely. In other words, the possibility of a raptor being treated inhumanely is of greater consequence than the protected rights of citizens.

The Fourth Amendment should be liberally construed in favor of protecting individual rights, not the interests of law enforcement officers. If this is not true, then we live in a police state and the Fourth Amendment no longer has any meaning.

Merlin.

Open Fields Doctrine

The Open Fields Doctrine, established by the U.S. Supreme Court case *Hester v. United States*, 265 U.S. 57 (1924), was a case that attempted to lift Fourth Amendment search and seizure restraints on law enforcement in open, outdoor areas. It has been interpreted by State wildlife agencies to mean that wildlife law enforcement officers can stop citizens, ask for their permit, search private property, and use any evidence obtained under this supposed authority to cite and convict citizens of any wildlife violation regardless of Fourth Amendment Search and Seizure protections, Fifth Amendment Self-Incrimination protections, or Fourteenth Amendment Equal Protection and Due Process protections. While the *Hester* decision did erode some of the fundamental protections the Fourth was designed to defend, it did not give a blanket pass for law enforcement officials to disregard all protections in "open fields" as States, in some cases, have interpreted this decision to mean. It declared that a warrant was unnecessary in "open fields" to search for evidence of wrongdoing. However, contrary to the opinion wildlife law enforcement agencies have asserted, it does not provide officials free reign to trespass without some suspicion that an illegal activity is taking place (in *Hester*, there was a report that illegal activity was occurring). In other words, some justification is required, i.e. reasonable suspicion, probable cause, or an illegal act is taking place in plain view of an officer (granted, *Hester* attempted to lower the bar for law enforcement efforts to conduct a search); the latter of which has come to be known as the Plain View Doctrine which, in the minds of jurists who respect the Constitution and the rule of law, has displaced the offensive Open Fields Doctrine.

Supreme Court Justice Oliver Wendell Holmes—who served on the Court from 1902-32 and, as previously mentioned, was a legal relativist and skeptic who injudiciously believed in experimenting with law (Gabriel, 1956)—delivered the decision for the *Hester* case and provides the following: "[T]he special protection accorded by the Fourth Amendment to the people in their 'persons, houses, papers and effects' is not extended to the open fields." Holmes, in this decision, attempted to marginalize Fourth Amendment protections from unreasonable searches and seizures without a warrant. This was beyond legislating from the bench; it was unabashed usurpation in an attempt to reshape the Constitution, which demonstrated disdain for the checks and balances of our system of government.[52] Contrast this with *Weeks v. United States*, 232 U.S. 383 (1914), a search and seizure case in which Justice Day delivered the opinion for the Court:

> To sanction such proceedings would be to affirm by judicial decision a manifest neglect, if not an open defiance, of the prohibitions of the Constitution, intended for the protection of the people against such unauthorized action.

---

52   Perhaps the most egregious example of Holmes' contempt for individual liberty is a eugenics case *Buck v. Bell*, 274 U.S. 200 (1927), where one Carrie Buck, "a helpless woman of normal intelligence and poor background" (Epstein, 2006, p. 107) who had been raped by a foster family member, was sent to a State epileptic and feeble-minded institution. One Dr. Priddy, an enthusiastic social engineer, wanted to sterilize Ms. Buck. The case was taken to the Supreme Court by Priddy and others hoping to set a precedent so they could continue their mass sterilization work of those they deemed "shiftless, ignorant, [and a] worthless class of antisocial" citizens. Holmes concurred. He believed it was constitutional to sterilize those the State deemed eugenically inferior, which was a social movement of the Progressive doctrine of the time. He continued, "The principle that sustains compulsory vaccination is broad enough to cover cutting the fallopian tubes. Three generations of imbeciles are enough." He believed that the interests of society are above the rights of individuals, which again turns our system of government on its head! This is a man whose every word in any court decision must be scrutinized with a microscope in search of any viral infection from such blatant relativism. Something that must not be forgotten: The Nazis commended the eugenic work done in the U.S. during the 1920s and 30s (when 60,000 U.S. citizens were sterilized), which provided some justification in the minds of Nazis to pursue genocide of the Jews. Thank you Progressives for handing Hitler the justification he needed, which allowed for the greatest terror the world has ever known. How one can admit to being a Progressive given their history is beyond comprehension. It's like being proud to be a KKK member.

This earlier case conceptually expresses the objection to Holmes' words in *Hester*, which were indeed defiant of the Constitution and which must be rejected with extreme prejudice because of their blatant subversion of the Fourth Amendment. Inside or outside of a building is irrelevant. If an illegal act is occurring in the plain view of an officer, or if an officer has justifiable suspicion to believe an illegal act has or is about to occur, then the Fourth Amendment is not a barrier to an officer's duty to enforce the law. Absent such circumstances, law officers are prohibited by the Fourth Amendment from stopping or searching any citizen of this country regardless of the difficulties they will experience in enforcing laws. If this is not an understood truism, then the Fourth has been subverted by the Court and is merely awaiting burial.

The offensiveness of Holmes' language is even more outrageous when we consider there was no need to use those words to uphold the lower court's decision. The person who was convicted had been illegally selling moonshine, and when law officers were spotted during an illicit exchange in front of his home, the bootlegger ran and then dropped his bottle of moonshine. All of this occurred on the property – curtilage – of the bootlegger's father, so the question that needed to be answered was, did the law officers need a warrant to take the discarded bottle of moonshine that was in their plain view, and arrest the bootlegger on private property? Let's consider the circumstances: The officers were approaching the house to inquire about "suspicious occurrences in that vicinity at the time of their visit." Officers certainly have every right to approach a person's home in the customary manner in which anyone approaches a house. But when the officers observed the approach of a vehicle, they quickly concealed themselves so as to observe what might transpire (this may be considered a gray area since they were on the property). When the exchange occurred, an alarm was given and the chase ensued. There is no Fourth Amendment violation here: The officers were not trespassing per se, they had reasonable suspicion to believe illegal activities might have been taking place, a suspicious exchange *did* take place, an alarm was sounded, Hester and his customer fled, the article of exchange was discarded, and all of this was in plain view of the officers. If the officers had not confiscated the evidence and arrested the defendants, they may have been disciplined for dereliction of duty.

Over the next several decades, a long train of Supreme Court decisions constructively overturned *Hester.* Some of these were: *Carroll v. United States,* 267 U.S. 132, at 149 (1925); *Henry v. United States,* 361 U.S. 98 (1959); *Katz v. United States,* 389 U.S. 347 (1967); and Adams v. Williams, 407 U.S. 143 (1972).

An important case was *Terry v. Ohio,* 392 U.S. 1 (1968). In it the Court provides:

> The Fourth Amendment right against unreasonable searches and seizures ... **"protects people, not places,"** and therefore applies as much to the citizen on the streets [*a form of open field*] as well as at home or elsewhere.... The Fourth Amendment applies to "stop and frisk" procedures such as those followed here. Whenever a police officer accosts an individual and restrains his freedom to walk away, he has "seized" that person within the meaning of the Fourth Amendment. (Emphasis added)

This constructively overturned (*sub silentio* – overruled silently) the Open Fields Doctrine established in Hester.

Another important case that constructively overturns *Hester* is *Delaware v. Prouse,* 440 U.S. 648 (1979). The Court states:

> Except where there is at least articulable and reasonable suspicion that a motorist is unlicensed or that an automobile is not registered, or that either the vehicle or an occupant is otherwise subject to seizure for violation of law, stopping an automobile and detaining the driver in order to check his driver's license and the registration of the automobile are unreasonable under the Fourth Amendment. Stopping an automobile and detaining its occupants constitute a "seizure" within the meaning of the Fourth ... Amendment.... The permissibility of a particular law enforcement practice is judged by balancing its intrusion on the individual's Fourth Amendment interests against its promotion of legitimate governmental interests. The State's interest in discretionary spot checks as a means of ensuring the safety of its roadways does not outweigh the resulting intrusion on the privacy and security of the persons detained. Given the physical and psychological intrusion visited upon the occupants

of a vehicle by a random stop to check documents, the marginal contribution to roadway safety possibly resulting from a system of spot checks cannot justify subjecting every occupant of every vehicle on the roads to a seizure at the unbridled discretion of law enforcement officials. **An individual operating or traveling in an automobile does not lose all reasonable expectation of privacy simply because the automobile and its use are subject to government regulation** [*The same can be said of falconry*]. People are not shorn of all Fourth Amendment protection when they step from their homes onto the public sidewalk [*i.e., an open field*]; nor are they shorn of those interests when they step from the sidewalks into their automobiles [*roads are also open fields*]. (Emphasis added)

This same reasoning applies to hunters, fisherman, and trappers in the field, especially when we consider that motor safety is of far greater public concern than outdoor sports. If too much poaching was to occur and it affected game populations, it is easy to cut back on bag limits or the length of seasons. Speed limits on roads are held back based upon the understanding that drivers will typically exceed the established limits. No comparable health or safety issues are at stake in harvesting wildlife as there is in driving, therefore, there is absolutely no justification in continuing this highly illegal allowance of warrantless search and seizure of citizens simply because they are practicing their **right** to harvest wildlife.

The Plain View Doctrine remedies the offensiveness of the Open Fields Doctrine. It is understood to mean that when a law officer can observe activities from a neutral location—unless a warrant is in hand to do otherwise—any illegal activity taking place or about to take place in plain view is exempt from Fourth Amendment constraints. The officer is free to act on the situation without hesitation and without magisterial authorization. This balances the needs of legitimate enforcement interests with the protections of innocent citizens.

Unfortunately, in 1984, the Supreme Court ignored much of this precedent and reestablished *Hester's* Open Fields Doctrine in *Oliver v. United States*, 466 U.S. 170, which was a marihuana conviction. However, this did not involve a random stop of a citizen, so it does not offer wildlife law enforcement cover for random stops. The officers in *Oliver* were given reports of marihuana being grown on the land of the defendant (this was a lead that should have provided law enforcement with probable cause and the opportunity to seek a warrant, which would have justified all subsequent actions. If a warrant were unattainable, the use of an aircraft along with the use of binoculars would have confirmed the suspicion, which would then have justified a warrant). They trespassed without a warrant and discovered the plants. They then acquired a warrant—which wildlife agencies believe they are immune from needing—and made the arrest. The Court affirmed the conviction, dismissing Fourth Amendment protections as not being applicable to open fields—but then there would have been no need for the warrant to make an arrest if this were true.

There may be a way to satisfy the concern of State wildlife agencies and protect individual rights simultaneously. Name badges, used at every type of convention, to identify individuals and to prove they have paid entrance fees, hangs in front of a person's chest. This can easily be incorporated as a hunting license and displayed on the outside of a person's clothing whenever they go afield. It's not unlike a license plate being required to be displayed on an automobile. This will allow wildlife officers to see, from a distance, that the person has in fact purchased a hunting license, thereby satisfying States' concerns regarding poaching while simultaneously protecting the individual from Fourth and Fifth Amendment violations by officers. Counterfeiting can be prevented by using the various security features now being offered in the plastic card market. Desktop dye-sublimation printers used at universities for student IDs (e.g., Fargo Printers) could be incorporated into the program and the costs would be passed on to hunters, who would be happy to incur the additional expense for the sake of constitutional protections.

Hopefully, in the future we will see confirmation of Supreme Court justices who have greater respect for the Constitution and individual rights and are opposed to the idea of an oligarchy legislating from the bench. Until then, citizens will be exposed to arbitrary use of power with no remedy at their disposal.

The erosion of the Constitution must be halted. Bit by bit we need to put it back together, not unlike a jigsaw puzzle where pieces that had been removed can be put back in their rightful place. Perhaps overturning *Hester* is a good place to begin.

The Role Religious Environmentalism Plays in Wildlife Management

Nagel (2005) raises an important issue when considering how wildlife and environmental laws evolved in this country. He examines the discussion that took place when the Wilderness Act was being discussed in Congress in 1964, and how religion became part of the legislative debate. He provides:

> The text of the Wilderness Act gives little indication of the crucial role of religious conceptions in forming our understanding of wilderness. "We live in a secular age," wrote one geographer, "so the religious essence of the wilderness ethic tends to be overshadowed by attempts to justify wilderness preservation on secular grounds, be they scientific, aesthetic, nationalistic, or hygienic." Yet wilderness is a profoundly spiritual concept.... The twentieth century push for wilderness preservation relied upon other ethical insights and the utilitarian concerns stated in the Act. But the spiritual values of wilderness played an important, albeit overlooked, role in the support for the Wilderness Act, and the years since 1964 have produced theological writings that have gleaned new insights ... to wilderness.

Nagle references famous naturalist authors such as Thoreau, Muir, and Leopold as expressing religious sentiments regarding nature and the frequent reference to these men's views in the promotion of the Wilderness Act.

Religious arguments appear throughout the legislative history of the Wilderness Act....

Only a few witnesses objected to this religious language. Warwick Downing criticized wilderness proponents "who seem to regard the wilderness system as something special, something different ... a holy of holies, as it were."

Spiritual arguments have continued to appear in the debates concerning the creation of wilderness areas since 1964. Sigurd Olson, the director of the National Park Service, told the 1965 Wilderness Conference that "the spiritual values of wilderness" are "the real reason for all the practical things we must do to save wilderness."

Taylor (2011)—Professor of Religion and Nature at the University of Florida, specializing in environmental and social ethics/religion—wrote a book, *Dark Green Religion: Nature Spirituality and the Planetary Future*, where he informs us how environmentalism has truly become a religion. He wrote an article in *Phi Kappa Phi Forum* summarizing his book. He explains:

[N]ature-based spiritualities are becoming an increasingly important global social force.... For more than two decades I have studied environmental mobilization around the world, focusing on the ... religious variables contributing to it. My earliest case studies explored radical environmental movements birthed in North America.... [T]hese activists generally perceived nature as sacred ... and ... these movements were significantly influencing environmental politics and growing globally.... Participants in [the mix] include environmentalists and scientists, politicians and diplomats, artists, writers, and film-makers, business people, professors, and museum curators, as well as mountaineers, surfers ..., gardeners, and many others. Among these far-flung individuals and groups I continued to see, despite significant differences, sufficient continuities to group them under the label "dark green religion." And not only do they share an affinity for dark green religion, they also effectively promote it within their own spheres of influence.... Dark green religion (which some call dark green spirituality) involves perceptions that nature is sacred....

A few years ago, in a presentation about the globalization of nature spirituality at Hamilton College in Upstate New York, I focused on how Gaian[53] spirituality was expressed and promoted through some TV and film.... [*The author then goes on to enumerate these renowned films and TV series.*] The most powerful recent example of dark green spirituality is the 2009 film *Avatar*, the highest-grossing movie of all time [*because of advances in film technology, not necessarily the subject matter*].

... [D]ark green religion is gaining cultural traction and may profoundly influence the planetary and religious future. But my hypothesis is based on a great deal of evidence, including an analysis of historical sources and recent trends, including the rise of nature-related romanticism; ... nature spiritualities; and the impact of, and on, educational institutions.

Many of us who love nature have what can be described as highly emotional sentiments bordering on spiritual experiences when we are pursuing our outdoor activities (perhaps making this a protected First Amendment area with regard to freedom of religion). This is an issue that belongs to the individual or with others he chooses to share it with. It may influence our desire to protect nature with the assistance of government, but if we are to maintain the separation of church and State, we must not allow religious positions to be used in political discussion to decide an issue. If we cross that line, then all other religions have every right to utilize their political influence to assert their will upon the rest of us, and we would have no right to object because of our own guilt in this regard.

Nagle and Taylor make it clear that much of twentieth century environmental legislation is rooted in religion, and it is the moral dimension of the environmental religion that has provided legislators with the hubris to enact unconstitutional wildlife laws and regulations in the name of some form of worldly salvation and Utopia. Besides the demands of statism, the environmental religion asserts the belief that harvest of wildlife is a privilege and not a right because of the religious sanctity wilderness represents (any act that is perceived by the environmental religious

---

53   The author provides that Gaian or Gaia is the modern nature god, demonstrating just how far this religion has gone in its formation.

doctrinaires as harmful to nature in any way, shape, or form is evil, and the miscreant must be damned to Hell. Therefore, assigning "privileges" to citizens is appropriate in their minds, since access must be controlled with draconian regulations). This would mean that it can be withdrawn for whatever reasons the government, or the powerful faction possessing the reins of government, might conjure up based on a religious dogma. Those bureaucrats of this faith have been pushing this concept in order to acquire the power of managing access and use, and to set policy based on their subjective religious views.

Nagel and Taylor's summaries demonstrate that when it comes to wildlife issues, religion has trumped law, and those who enter the realm of wildlife and nature-related activities are exposed to factional forces that will crush them if they do not accept the religious dogma of the new environmental religion – a form of religious persecution is presently in play. This is a very insecure situation, and it is simply a matter of time before enough rights have been encroached upon for them to be re-awakened from their hibernation and reestablished in their proper place in law.

Let us consider what Tucker (1803) provided in his treatise on our Constitution. Keep in mind that Tucker was intimately familiar with the structure of our system because of his close association with the Founders from Virginia and his studies under George Wythe of William and Mary College. Tucker, quoting the June 27, 1788 Virginia Ratifying Convention's provisions that were "to be recommended to the consideration of the [Federal] congress which shall first assemble under the said constitution," included the list of articles the Virginia Convention provided for. The twentieth article stated that

> religion ... and the manner of discharging it, can be directed only by reason and conviction, not by force or violence, and therefore all men have an equal, natural, and unalienable right to the free exercise of religion according to the dictates of conscience, and that no particular religious sect or society ought to be favored or established by law in preference to others" (p. 114-15).

This principle has certainly been violated as it relates to the environmental religion, which has insidiously crept into our bureaucratic, legislative, and judicial halls.

Tucker also provided, "The pretext of religion, and the pretenses of sanctity and humility, have been employed throughout the world, as the most direct means of gaining influence and power," (p. 235). We can observe these same old tactics being used by the environmentalists.

In analyzing religion and freedom of conscience, Tucker (1803) explains the abusive and arbitrary behavior of powerful religions over the course of history:

> Even in countries where the crucifix, the rack, and the flames have ceased to be the engines of proselytism, civil incapacities have been invariably attached to a dissent from the national religion…. [Superiority of a dogma in a nation] can take place only where there is a civil establishment of a particular mode of religion; that is, where a predominant sect enjoys exclusive advantages, and makes the encouragement of its own mode of faith and worship a part of the constitution of the state (p. 372).

While our government has not explicitly established a national religion, it has done so implicitly through numerous statutes that, in effect, create a national religion of environmentalism, and has placed bureaucrats—who are empowered as high priests—in powerful positions to support it. The qualification for such an office requires a test that is passed by acquiring an advanced degree from a university that provides instruction in environmentalism of one sort or another (most in academia either embrace the environmental religion or do not object to it), which, one might argue, is a violation of Article VI of the U.S. Constitution.[54] Story (1840, p. 253) explains why no test should be administered for public office.

> The remaining part of the clause declares, that "no religious test shall ever be required as a qualification to any office or public trust under the United States." This clause is recommended by its tendency to satisfy the minds of many delicate and scrupulous persons, who entertain great repugnance to religious tests, as a qualification for civil

---

54   "[N]o religious test shall ever be required as a qualification to any office or public trust under the United States."

power or honor. But it has a higher aim in the Constitution. It is designed to cut off every pretence of an alliance between the Church and the State, in the administration of the National Government. The American people were too well read in the history of other countries, and had suffered too much in their colonial state, not to dread the abuses of authority resulting from religious bigotry, intolerance, and persecution. They knew but too well, that no sect could be safely trusted with power on such a subject; for all had in turns wielded it to the injury, and sometimes to the destruction, of their inoffensive, but, in their judgement [sic], erring neighbors.

Then, on page 259, Story continues this line of reasoning:

The same policy, which introduced into the Constitution the prohibition of any religious test, led to this more extended prohibition of the interference of Congress in religious concerns. We are not to attribute this prohibition of a national religious establishment to an indifference to religion in general ... but to a dread by the people of the influence of ecclesiastical power in matters of government; a dread, which their ancestors brought with them from the parent country, and which, unhappily for human infirmity, their own conduct, after their emigration, had not, in any just degree, tended to diminish. It was also obvious, from the numerous and powerful sects existing in the United States, that there would be perpetual temptations to struggles for ascendency in the National councils, if any one might thereby hope to found a permanent and exclusive national establishment of its own, and religious persecutions might thus be introduced, to an extent utterly subversive of the true interests and good order of the Republic. The most effectual mode of suppressing the evil, in the view of the people, was, to strike down the temptations to its introduction.

We have lost sight of the principle *freedom of and from religion*; the Christian faith has been alienated and marginalized to the point where it is considered evil by the collectivist types (all other faiths have been given greater latitude in influencing our culture) because of it being the primary competing faith with the religion of socialism. Socialists have laid out plans to destroy capitalism, and Christianity is one of the primary targets on the socialist's hit list, which is something so well documented by socialists themselves that no citations are required.

Given the legislative history of unconstitutional provisions in environmental statutes, draconian bureaucratic regulatory interpretation of environmental statutes, and the judiciary's support of these misguided laws, we are not free from religion and religious persecution. It has simply taken a new form with too short a history to have developed extensive baggage that we can identify as a social evil as other religions may have in their past. We must revisit the discussion that took place when the Founders established the First Amendment—as it relates to religion—so that we may learn from history, as they did.

Parsons (1948, p. 35-36) references Madison in attempting to discover the intent of the Framers regarding the First Amendment and the freedom of religion clause. He takes us to the discussion of the matter in the House of Representatives in 1789, when the amendments were being formulated. Madison spoke before Congress and provided what he "really had in mind in introducing what became the First Amendment." Madison stated:

> Whether the words are necessary or not, … they had been required by some of the State Conventions, who seemed to entertain an opinion that the clause of the Constitution, and the laws made under it, which gave Congress power to make all laws necessary and proper to carry into execution the Constitution, enabled them to make laws of such a nature as might infringe the rights of conscience and establish a national religion…. [*One can argue this holds true for all rights that might be infringed upon, based on the expansion of the Necessary and Proper Clause to unlimited proportions.*]
>
> … [T]he people feared that one sect might obtain a pre-eminence, or two combine together, and establish a religion to which they would compel others to conform.

The final words agreed upon by this first Congress, which was the sixth version of the proposed First Amendment regarding religion, were, "Congress shall make no law respecting an establishment of religion, or prohibiting the free exercise thereof." Parsons (1948, p. 41) attempts to clarify the intent and purpose of this clause:

> It is abundantly clear from this authentic history of the adoption of the First Amendment on religious liberty that all that both branches had in mind to propose to the States for amendment was a limitation on the Federal Government against imposing a national religion on the States and using its power to enforce any specific profession of belief on any citizen.

With a firm understanding of the First Amendment, along with its evolution in constitutional law, one can see that we have deviated far from its purpose and the limitations that were placed upon the Federal government. Legislators and jurists need to familiarize themselves with the pitfalls this will expose the country to so other religions cannot jealously pursue their own agendas with the use of government power since the cat has been let out of the proverbial bag.

Privileges versus Rights

The *dispensation-of-privileges-by-government* position, which is held by many bureaucrats in a variety of agencies, is another demonstration of tremendous hubris in which government divvies out privileges, as though privileges belong to government to distribute or withhold at its pleasure. This is another hangover from British law when monarchs held sway. Perhaps an additional source of this mistaken dispensation-of-privileges assertion derives from the misunderstanding of the contemporary definition of *privilege*. I offer two basic definitions provided by the Oxford English Dictionary:

First Definition: "A right, advantage, or immunity granted to or enjoyed by a person, or a body or class of persons, beyond the common advantages of others." When used in our Constitution, the meaning of "privilege" is: The rights, advantages, and immunities possessed by all U.S. citizens derived from Natural Law authority (as expressed in the Enlightenment), i.e., liberties derived from the laws of nature that formed this earth and shaped mankind's behavior. In addition, since the early period of our nation was steeped deeply in the Christian faith, privileges would have been understood to be derived from the Creator, not from men, i.e. government. Another way to express privileges under this perspective is to understand them as blessings. In other words, Americans are blessed with liberty or are privileged with liberty, which has been bestowed upon them by a beneficent Creator. Whether one believes in a creator or not is irrelevant to the case. All self-determined animals on this earth are born free; it is only through social organizations that we limit these freedoms. This is as true of mankind as it is for wolves and primates, for example. Wolves and primates are free to leave their groups, but then survival would be more precarious. In the American system, it is understood that citizens have surrendered only certain freedoms—primarily the freedom to infringe upon others—so that the important and fundamental ones are secured. But should these freedoms be threatened, say, by the assertion that they are privileges bestowed upon citizens by an arbitrary government, citizens then have the right to take action to subdue the encroaching power. This includes fighting back through elections, through the judiciary, or should these prove ineffective, then the final form of resistance is through the use of force, as the Founders asserted; hence the primary and final reason for the Second Amendment. Those who do not understand this do not believe in liberty and therefore must be marginalized as usurpers, or enablers of usurpers, of our system of government. For if we do not marginalize these usurpers, in essence, we are saying we have no right to resist an encroaching power, but those in government have every right to encroach upon us, and we must therefore submit to their arbitrary will—the very antithesis of a free government. It is through the right to armed resistance that government is held at bay; for if this right were surrendered, government would know no restraint. In his dissent in *Silveira*, judge Kozinski informs us, "The Second Amendment is a doomsday provision, one designed for those exceptionally rare circumstances where all other rights have failed."[55]

Second Definition: "A privileged position; the possession of an advantage over others or another." This is only allowable in this country when no other means are available to accomplish a necessary end for the good of the whole community, not just a portion thereof. Law enforcement, the judiciary, and elected and bureaucratic government positions are privileges of this sort, but it needs to be understood that this is divvied out to them at the pleasure of the people who are the sovereign. Examples of temporary privileges are the protections a patent affords an inventor or a copyright affords an author.

Arendt (1948, p. 290) provides an example of where rights versus privileges lead a free people. She discusses the European "rightless" Displaced People (DPs)—who were refugees without citizenship and without a nation—after World War I:

---

55   See *Silveira v. Lockyer*, Ninth Circuit Court of Appeals, May 2003, at 5983

Without ... legal equality, which originally was destined to replace the older laws and orders of the feudal society, the nation dissolves into an anarchic mass of over- and underprivileged individuals. Laws that are not equal for all revert to ... privileges, something contradictory to the very nature of nation-states.

In the United States, we have provisions in the Constitution that were designed as barriers against privileges. Article 1, § 9 states, "No title of nobility shall be granted...." Nobility truly is an individual or family privilege, and this type of privilege is prohibited. Monopolies—another important form of specially granted privilege typically bestowed by a monarch—are also prohibited in this country (except temporary and explicitly defined privileges such as patents, which promote the good for all because they encourage innovation). Specially granted privileges are abhorrent to most Americans (except perhaps the recipients of them), so how is it that some bureaucrats believe they have this sort of power?

Taylor (1822) considered the monetary policies, protective tariffs, and bounties (a hangover from mercantilism) of the early nineteenth century a privileged system whereby the manufacturing, commercial, and financial classes benefited at the expense of the agrarians and the common citizens. He argued strongly against them because he considered them unconstitutional, and in 1822 he predicted disunion if republican principles of limited government weren't adhered to (this is a few years before the slavery issue began to heat up and before Southerners asserted that slavery was a social good rather than an inherited curse). The acceptance of a privilege-based system enforced by a Northern dominated government power, as the protective tariffs and bounties provided for, was understood to be divisive and destructive of the Republic. In the end, he was correct; disunion did occur primarily because of the privilege-based system, and it took military force to hold the Union together and demand the South's acceptance of Northern economic dominance (no, the Civil War was not exclusively nor primarily about slavery—it was one of several issues that caused Southerners to secede). However, the Southerners' use of slavery (which had been around for thousands of years in most cultures by that time) was also a privileged-based system, and was reluctantly sanctioned by the Federal government at the time of the founding in order to establish the Union. Over time, the Northerners came to despise the South's privileged system, and over time the Southerners came to despise the North's privileged system. The Civil War is an example of what a privilege-based society can lead to. It causes factions to form and contention to escalate, the limits of which are dependent upon the passions they extract from the breasts of men.

Considering what privileges mean and what they inevitably lead to, it can be seen that government officials do not have the authority to offer a privilege, or if they do, it would have to be a choice of last resort for the good of the entire community, and not just a faction within it. Nor do they have the authority to deny someone a right just because they don't like him or an activity he might choose to pursue. Therefore, the belief held by these officials that those fundamental rights not enumerated in the Bill of Rights reside in the government is not only false, but more importantly, dangerous to our liberties; for it stems from the supposition that government can arbitrarily grant or withdraw liberties, asserted as "privileges," as it sees fit. This is the basis of despotism and is the position of an enemy of a free State. The Constitution was created to prevent this eventuality, but when citizens do not understand the governmental system over which they preside, ambitious factions will strive to find ways to interpret and manipulate—i.e., usurp—law to their advantage or to their own sense of propriety (which occurred in democratic Athens, Greece). Animal rights and anti-gun special interests exemplify this and have deceitfully attempted to change the meaning of the Constitution and to undermine the integrity of the Founders in order to discredit our form of government, since it is meant to defend citizens from government.

Wildlife Harvest is a Right

The justification of wildlife harvest as a right is not necessary since it is a self-evident truth, for how could man have survived without it? The air is a natural resource, but no one attempts to limit the amount we breathe because the oxygen is replenished faster than we consume it. Natural resource harvest only requires that where the demand for a renewable resource, such as game animals, outpaces the replenishment of the supply, there must be limits on allowable take based on sound biological criteria in order to preserve the health of wildlife populations. No wildlife resource with healthy populations can be off limits to citizens since it belongs to no one until possession takes place.

However, now that we grow food in sufficient quantities, which reduces the need for subsistence hunting, there are those who want to eliminate harvest. This is short-sighted and ignorant. Should the time come when we may need to revert back to this way of life, whether temporarily (such as during a severe depression) or on a more permanent basis, because of some catastrophic pandemic (this occurred at the end of the Roman Empire, with large regions becoming completely depopulated), individuals would be utterly ignorant of how to acquire food and would eventually turn on one another and/or starve to death.

An important reason it is in society's best interest to support wildlife harvest for all citizens is that the conservation benefits it provides that cannot be realized in any other way.[56] Wildlife recreation is either consumptive—hunting and fishing—or nonconsumptive, such as birdwatching. An important distinction to make between them is that the taxes on hunting products, which are separate from permit fees, go toward wildlife conservation; whereas wildlife-watchers' activities contribute nothing toward this effort either through permits or taxes. This demonstrates that the users of wildlife are the true conservationists, and the wildlife watchers are, in economic terms, free-riders. Yet some factions of these free-riders attack the users as destroyers of our environment. Free-riders frequently complain the loudest and contribute the least.[57]

Another approach to limit citizens' rights to access of wildlife is derived from feudal Europe, where take and possession of wildlife were severely restricted for the lower class subjects, but were generously provided to the landed gentry by the king. In contemporary times, the need to meet property requirements in wildlife has been replaced with educational requirements. Scientists have far greater liberties when it comes to access and

---

56   As this relates to falconry, McDonald informs us that "the public display of falconry has proven to be a valuable tool in the prevention of the wanton destruction of raptor populations in countries of the New World."

57   In some cases, free-riders have a negative contribution. Consider what Cooper & Beauchesne (2007, p. 31) provide: "Peregrine Falcons are adaptable to urban environments and rarely experience enough disturbances from humans to cause breeding failure. However, there have been occasional nest losses associated with disturbance from construction (T. Maconachie, pers. comm. 2004), bridge maintenance, and **excessive visitation by bird watchers**." (Emphasis added)

use of wildlife than does the average citizen (of course, they would assert that their use of wildlife is for the good of society, as if working for society is the only good there is, and that individual use is for selfish ends. Does this ring of collectivism?). This is a form of privileged nobility this class enjoys at the expense of all others, not unlike the qualification statutes of England. This is unconstitutional and must be overcome. All should have equal access, regardless of class.

It is important that such truths be discovered and the light of day is allowed to disinfect our society of such poison. If we don't promote the use of wildlife and conservation based on enlightened self-interest reasoning, there won't be a sustainable force of public opinion to maintain it. When times get rough, subjective values will be the first to be sacrificed. Survival mode will kick in and priorities will change radically in order to meet contemporary exigencies. At which point conservation will fall in the scale of priorities, wildlife managers will lose their jobs, habitat will no longer be maintained, no new land will be acquired to expand habitat, endangered species funds will dry up, and citizens will then wonder why the environment is degrading because the span of time required for this to take place will prevent them from discerning cause and effect. They will simply lament on when times were better and wildlife populations were healthy.

> It is useful to give thought to why [wildlife] law was created and what problems it addresses. Why do we need wildlife law?…
>
> Historically, wildlife law has always had a multiplicity of objectives …: [conservation, preservation, and] recently, there has been a growing belief that species have an independent moral worth that we … have an obligation to recognize. (Goble & Freyfogle, 2002)

This last sentence is the source of contemporary animal rights beliefs, and while it can be agreed by most reasonable conservationists that wildlife species have significant value, this "moral worth" perspective must be kept within a very narrow compass, otherwise even dangerous bacteria and viruses will eventually be seen as having rights. Perhaps the termites eating my home, the aphids eating my garden vegetables, the feather lice found on my wild caught hawk should all have rights, making them off limits in my efforts to exterminate them from my property. The argument that the consciousness of sentient beings determines such limits does not confine the argument, as some might suppose. There are those in Switzerland who argue for the rights of plants, believing they have feelings too, which demonstrates that consciousness of individuals that compose a species is irrelevant to dogmatic environmentalist religious views. They will simply project any attribute onto the subject of their passions in order to deceitfully convince others that their cause is a worthy one.

> [Immanuel Kant] argued that the line between rational and nonrational beings was the crucial divide for ethics. Self-conscious, rational beings, he contended, possess the ability to form moral law and to act in conformance with the conception of such laws, (Goble & Freyfogle, 2002, p. 54).

Rights reflect a two-way street. By rationally respecting one another's interests, rights are created for mutually beneficial survival, which is a concept other species cannot grasp in relation to humans. Therefore, the right that other species possess is strictly the right to fight for their own survival. We cannot deny that instinct drives all species to fight to keep the fruits of their labor and to survive. Adaptation determines the winners from the losers. Whether we respect this instinct or not is not relevant to the present discussion. What is relevant is the part man plays in the survival or extinction of species. Rights of species, or individuals within the species, should not be the point of discussion since, if recognized, it may very well contribute to the eventual extinction of Homo sapiens because all species would be off limits to mankind. The focus should be on man's sense of responsibility in passing on to future generations a healthy and wealthy environment in which posterity may enjoy the fruits of this world. Our obligation is not to the various species, but rather to our own kind, to maintain the balance on this planet, i.e. enlightened self-interest, which means we must do our best to maintain healthy populations of all species that are not detrimental to man's survival, since it is through the interaction between species that a healthy environment is maintained. If this is not understood to be a truism, then if the animal rights argument were to eventually win the policy battle, the small number of sentimentalists who fought for the rights of animals will be the only ones left truly caring about wildlife. Their numbers will be insufficient to sustain a robust effort to support conservation efforts, and with no enemy to fight, their numbers will shrink. Since no one will be allowed to harvest wildlife, no one will be there to invest the capital into the all-important habitat, which is the primary requirement to preserve species. Keep in mind that the vast majority of extinctions—if not all of them— that can be attributed to man were due to the loss of habitat. The result will be a decline in the wealth of the environment, and mankind will be the poorer for it.

Kant further provides, "Our duties towards animals are merely indirect duties toward humanity.... If he is not to stifle his human feelings, he must practice kindness towards animals, for he who is cruel to animals becomes hard also in his dealing with men," (Lectures on Ethics, ca. 1775-1780). Of course, Kant did not mean that hunting, trapping, and fishing demonstrate cruelty to animals. He was speaking of inhumane treatment of animals, such as torture, an unhealthy living environment, malnutrition, etc. These demonstrate inhumane treatment and bring forth barbaric tendencies in men that can easily spill over into the human community. It is within this context that humane laws were enacted and it is within these boundaries that the application of these laws must remain. They cannot be expanded into the realm of animal rights since, as has previously been stated, the only rights we can recognize animals possess is their right to fight for their existence—the exact same right we possess in relation to them. We have no rights in their eyes and we would make fine Purina Human Chow if they had it their way. Our extinction would mean nothing to them. This is something that distinguishes us from them—we do recognize the loss of a species and feel the poorer for it.

In closing this chapter, it is instructive to mention the beginning of what appears to be a trend. Concerned citizens are disgusted with animal rights factions infringing upon their liberties, and are now demanding lawmakers enact legislation that protects their right to hunt. I am aware of six States that have decided to provide language in their constitutions to this end.

Minnesota's language is as follows: "Hunting and fishing and the taking of game and fish are a valued part of our heritage that shall be forever preserved to the people and shall be managed by law and regulation for the public good," (Minnesota Constitution, Article 13, section 12).

Additionally, in Virginia's Constitution, Article XI, **Conservation**, § 4, *Right of the people to hunt, fish, and harvest game*, it states, "The people have a right to hunt, fish, and harvest game, subject to such regulations and restrictions as the General Assembly may prescribe by general law."

Also, in the Montana Constitution, Article IX, **Environment and Natural Resources**, § 7, *Preservation of Harvest Heritage*, it states, "The opportunity to harvest wild fish and wild game animals is a heritage that shall forever be preserved to the individual citizens of the state and does not create a right to trespass on private property or diminution of other private rights."

In 2010, Arkansas, South Carolina, and Tennessee approved constitutional amendments in their November elections for protecting the right to hunt. As outdoorsmen become increasingly aware of the attacks against their rights, we can expect more States to follow suit.

It appears we are finally looking back to the founding principles for guidance in governing, to when there was far greater wisdom amongst representatives because of their studies of Natural Law political philosophy from the Enlightenment era. We can now see why many of the States originally provided language in their constitutions protecting the right to harvest wildlife. We simply need to adapt such language to contemporary circumstances so it is understood that management of harvest is essential to maintain the general welfare of the country, and that the opportunity to hunt is a right and not merely a privilege.

Immature red-tailed hawk.

Falconry Regulatory Regime

Kennedy's report (1987) on ownership and sale of domestic raptors provides a good account of the progress of falconry regulations.

Introduction: In the late 1960's and early 1970's regulation of raptors in North America underwent an intensive regulatory and legislative metamorphosis. In five short years, birds of prey, historically identified ... as vermin, became the most regulated wildlife on the continent. The flagship federal statutes were the Endangered Species Act of 1973 (ESA) and Migratory Bird Treaty Act Amendment of 1972 (MBTA). This legislation effectively prohibited the sale of all native raptors in the United States. Access to the birds was restricted to a few qualified individuals and institutions. For the most part, the individuals were falconers who legally possessed birds prior to the Acts....

Protection of Raptors Under Federal Law and Regulations: Legal recognition of falconry as a field sport occurred primarily during the 1960's and early 1970's.... Raptors themselves were unprotected by federal law until 1972. Persons who take ... raptorial birds may be affected by one or more of four federal laws: 1) The Migratory Bird Treaty Act, 2) The Endangered Species Act of 1973, 3) The Lacey Act, and 4) The Bald and Golden Eagle Protection Act. Of these laws, the two that most affect falconers and raptor propagators are the Migratory Bird Treaty Act and the Endangered Species Act.... The original Migratory Bird Act Convention signed by the United States and Great Britain (for Canada) in 1916 did not list raptors as a protected species.... By an exchange of notes in 1972, the 1936 Convention [*The MBTA was amended through this Convention in '36 when Mexico became a signatory to the Treaty*] was amended, adding the family Falconidae to the original list.... Falconry and raptor propagation [had been] regulated principally under the U.S. Code of Federal Regulations, Part 21, entitled "Migratory Bird Permits." The original falconry regulations under this section were designed by falconers and prohibited the sale of all birds of prey for falconry purposes. These regulations are listed in three sections: Section 21.29, Federal Falconry Standards; Section 21.28, Falconry Permits, and Section 21.30, Raptor Propagation Permits. The "Falconry Standards" section establishe[d] the minimum state standards for federally approved state falconry programs. The scheme was devised by falconers who participated in the development of the regulation.[58] It is based on a three-tiered system designed to protect the rarer, more fragile and more difficult species from inexperienced falconers. Based upon this system the regulation creates three classes of permits: "apprentice," "general," and "master" and provides criteria for the attainment of each. The "Raptor Propagation Permits" section was promulgated as a final rule in 1983 to allow the sale of captive-bred raptors among licensed falconers and raptor propagators. The "Federal Falconry Standards" section was amended at the same time to allow falconers to buy and sell raptors. When the original falconry regulations were promulgated in 1972, raptor propagation was a rare and uncertain science, and no provision for the sale of wild caught birds was needed since most falconers opposed it. By 1978, raptor propagation was common and reliable and the U.S. Fish

---

58   McDonald states, "This approach, adopted based on the fear of the loss of the right to practice falconry, should never have been the one proposed by American falconers. It was clearly contrary to the best interest of the art and of falconers. A few falconers at that time saw the danger and urged that all that should be required is a permit for take of raptors from the wild for use in falconry, unless endangered. They simply wanted falconry recognized as a legal way to hunt, just like hunting with guns, and that falconry be listed in the Federal regulations as a legal means."

and Wildlife Service sought to encourage propagation for its scientific value, for use as a management technique for wild populations, and for recreational use in falconry.

Now that we've reflected on the lay of the land, so to speak, let's consider how Federal wildlife managers treat falconers.

Falconry is the most highly regulated outdoor sport in the country, as Kennedy pointed out. Would-be falconers must find a sponsor who will oversee their training (if they don't find one, they cannot become a falconer, which is not legal since there is no general or public welfare issue at stake); they must take an extensive written test; meet shelter and equipment requirements and be inspected by an agency bureaucrat— who knows nothing of falconry or raptors—to ensure that the novice has met the requirements; go through a two year apprenticeship, with restrictions on which birds they are allowed to use; go through a five year "general" level classification before becoming a master falconer; contend with restrictions on the number of wild birds allowed to be possessed (regardless of the amount of accumulated years, which waterfowl hunters don't have to contend with), which is separate from what is allowed to be taken; accept the withdrawal of their Fourth Amendment right from unreasonable search and seizure – referred to as "inspections"; contend with certain raptors needing to be banded even though they are not threatened or endangered; submit a 3-186A form to wildlife managers for acquisition or transfer of any raptor; acquire a falconry license to possess and hunt with a raptor; acquire a hunting license to hunt with it; acquire a trapping license in most States to take a wild raptor; must not carry a firearm into the field with a raptor, which is a Second Amendment infringement; participate in no other activity with one's own bird than falconry; etc., and all of this for a private activity with private property, and with no impact on society. Compare this to what falconers have done for raptors and one must ask the question, what are falconers guilty of to deserve this kind of outrageous, Soviet-style treatment? Convicted felons have more rights than this. The possession of all other MBTA birds are not treated in this manner, so what provides FWS the authority to treat falconers in such a highly restrictive way? There is no justification for this either legally or biologically, and it is a clear violation of the Fifth Amendment takings protections:

The Fifth Amendment applies not only where the government has taken possession of private property, but also where regulation is so burdensome that it severely impacts a property owner's rights with regard to that property. As the U.S. Supreme Court recognized in 1922, "if regulation goes too far it will be recognized as a taking."[59] (Horn & Lampp, 2008)

FWS, in its 1988 Final Environmental Assessment in revising falconry and breeding regulations, stated in its abstract,

The Fish and Wildlife Service proposes to ... establish simpler, less restrictive regulations governing the use of most raptors. Both falconry and raptor propagation are small scale activities having little or no impact on raptor populations. Recent data indicate that most raptor populations have increased considerably from lows reached in the early 1970s [*the trend of which has continued up to the writing of this work*].... The degree of regulation imposed by the federal regulations governing falconry (1976) appears to be unnecessary for most species.

The 1988 revisions fell far short of the relaxation of Federal regulations that law and biology cried out for.

States have greater latitude in restrictive regulations—though they too have their limits—but the Feds have a very narrow compass in which they can operate if we are to embrace federalism principles.

Let's now consider the contributions made by falconers to raptor science and conservation to put things in perspective.

Falconers' Contributions to Man's Understanding of Raptors

Falconers were the primary promoters for the protection of raptors in the first half of the twentieth century, and they finally realized this objective in 1972, when they were able to recruit the birding community and together lobby Congress to include raptors in the MBTA. Some of the major contributions falconers have made since then include:

a) releasing peregrine falcons into the wild after discovering

---

59 *Pennsylvania Coal Co. v. Mahon*, 260 U.S. 393, 415 (1922)

how to breed them (discovered by Frank Beebe in 1967
– who was a falconer; who taught Dr. Heinz Meng – a
falconer; who instructed Dr. Tom Cade – a falconer, who
founded the Peregrine Fund which was made up of many
falconers) (personal communications with Beebe and
Meng, 2002)

b) commonplace breeding of many raptor species in
    captivity

c) major advances in raptor medicine by falconers who
    became veterinarians

d) those falconers who have become raptor biologists,
    have done, and continue to do, much of the important
    research on wild raptors, though certain lay-falconers
    have contributed more than many raptor biologists due
    to the scientific community's tendency to simply dissect
    rather than connect complex phenomena

e) educating the public about raptors and rehabilitating sick
    and injured raptors, thus furthering our understanding
    of raptor medicine and disseminating it amongst other
    falconers[60]

f) educating electric power companies of the hazards power
    lines pose to raptors and how to rectify this problem
    (This is probably the single highest contemporary source
    of raptor mortality attributable to man, and if a power
    company is responsible for the death of raptors, well, this
    is the cost of civilization. But if a falconer violates some
    irrelevant regulatory provision, the full force of the law
    must be leveled against him. Such hypocrisy demands our
    attention.)

g) improving the safety of airports by performing bird
    abatement services, which were initiated by Beebe.

The late Morley Nelson, who was a falconer, is quoted as having
said, "Falconry is responsible for all of this... all of my work with
Idaho Power to modify the poles [*to prevent electrocution of raptors*],
all of the Disney films we did [*to educate the public about raptors*],
the Snake River Birds of Prey Area [*which Nelson helped establish as*

---

60   McDonald informs us that "falconry played an important role in changing the public
attitude from the 1940's to the present. Falconers changed the raptor 'vermin' perception
into a valued ecological symbol. Falconers' presentations, magazine & newspaper articles,
and general public exposure via films, books, television, etc. made this outstanding
transformation a reality."

a raptor sanctuary], [*and*] the Peregrine Fund.... [N]early every major advancement in raptor research and conservation over the last 50 years can be traced directly to falconers and their love of the birds."

In short, without falconers, there would be little to no advances in raptor science and protection. Raptors would be an obscure and little-understood family of birds, and probably still labeled as vermin. Therefore, the promotion of falconry has a corollary effect of promoting the recruitment of professional and amateur raptor specialists, thereby benefiting society with our understanding of them. Any attempt to place obstacles in falconry's path is a disservice to raptors and to this branch of science.

The effort to reduce hunting age requirements by the various States in order to recruit dedicated outdoorsmen reflects the part falconry plays in this conservation cause. Falconry recruits highly dedicated conservationists who frequently remain committed to conservationism throughout their lives, so the promotion of falconry is in the interest of States' conservation efforts.

All fish and game departments have three primary duties: first, they are to manage our natural resources for present and future generations' access and use; second, they are to provide this access and use within the framework of sustainable use principles; and third, they are to promote conservationism—not protectionism— and recruit lay conservationists (who will then become the future supporters of fish and game departments) through managed access and use of our resources. The full support of falconry programs contributes to the fulfillment of these obligations to society.

The Reason for our Draconian Falconry Regulations

An examination of a research paper by a falconer, Ash (2005), is a good starting point to help explain why FWS, with their excessive falconry regulations, treats falconers worse than felons. Her paper analyzes falconry-related offenses and convictions "so that reality can be viewed objectively." She states:

> [Some] groups have put forth a ... theory that there is large scale corruption and conspiracy exporting wild taken raptors for massive profits abroad. It is frequently cited by officials that the falconry community must be kept in check and under tight controls else illegal trafficking in raptors threaten the wild populations of raptors.

There are an estimated 4,000 licensed falconers in the United States ... holding an estimated 5,000 birds.... Each year an estimated 1,000 birds are taken from the wild for use in falconry. This study is an analysis of the federal cases, citations, and violation investigations over a 64 month period.... [There appears to be only] 0.4% of the falconry population that was involved in any illegal activity in more than 5 years. The bulk of citations have no bird associated with them.

... It is very interesting to note that there are no violations in over five years pertaining to smuggling, soliciting, forgery, false records, conspiracies, export violations, or any CITES violations. Indeed there were no cases involving selling raptors, and no cases involving Europe, Asia, or the Middle East.

... [T]he proper conclusion is that the falconry community works hard to understand the letter, spirit, and interpretation of the law and there is minimal illegal activity, perhaps only well-intended individuals misinterpreting regulations, to catch.

There is a healthy captive breeding population providing falconers legally obtainable birds at affordable prices. Illegally acquired birds are not worth the risk due to the market pressures.

Operation Falcon

Ash's excellent research is a response to accusations leveled against falconers by the birding community throughout the 1970s and 1980s and by some gullible wildlife managers who fell for the birding community's deception, the effects of which we still live with to this day. The 1984 sting operation, Operation Falcon—the culmination of the deceit—is believed by many to have been a conspiracy between FWS's law enforcement division and the birding community to eradicate falconry at any cost. This failed because it was proven that no illicit international trade was taking place amongst U.S. citizens—a major embarrassment to FWS, who had spent many millions of dollars trying to prove there was. In the law enforcement community's mind, the falconry community was guilty and needed to be proven innocent before they would accept this as fact. This demonstrates how dangerous unchecked law enforcement personnel can be to citizens.

Over a period of years, the birding community had sent its representatives to State and Federal wildlife management meetings to spread rumors of extensive international illicit trade of raptors by falconers. Because of the birding community's deception, FWS implemented Operation Falcon, which was initiated to pursue and arrest the fictional smugglers. FWS's own expert raptor biologist, Jim Ruos, was not even informed of the operation when it was underway. If anyone would have been aware of illicit trade in raptors, he would have had insight given his association with the falconry community.[61]

FWS law enforcement division used the highly illegal tactic of entrapment (which is despised by jurists, who refer to such tactics as Outrageous Government Conduct). Their undercover agent baited otherwise innocent falconers to take raptors he offered them. For many falconers, he had to harass them on numerous occasions before they finally agreed to take a bird. Falconers who were given these birds were then arrested and, through plea-bargaining, FWS was able to obtain convictions of some falconers, which they surely would not have accomplished had they gone to trial. Many who fought and argued that it was entrapment won their cases. However, the cost to do battle with FWS was more than most could bear and many innocent people were harmed by illegal law enforcement tactics.

FWS frequently uses the scorch and burn approach, i.e., they continue the case until the citizen runs out of money (personal communication, Richard Epstein, 2007). Canada did not provide for plea-bargaining, and not one falconer was convicted there as a result of this operation because of the fact that there was no illicit international trade in North America, as the birding community and FWS had alleged.

It is unfortunate that no official has been called to answer before a court for the illegal conspiracy, for entrapment tactics, and for the irreparable harm done to the falconry community. Lives were destroyed and the falconry community was torn apart, the effects of which still linger to this day. The real crime was perpetrated by FWS Law Enforcement Division, and until they make amends with the falconry community by coming clean with the origin of their illegal behavior, a rift will remain and little collaborative work can be expected. It is a most unfortunate situation, but not surprising given the highly criminal behavior that had emanated from this

---

61   McKay, 1987.

Division in 1984. Let us hope that wiser individuals, who respect the rule of law, are now at the helm.[62]

Were falconers angels? Absolutely not! What sector of society can claim perfect observation of every rule that exists? As just observed, law enforcement is as guilty as any other sector of society. If deviations from the law by a few individuals were to determine the extent of our liberties, then all endeavors would be illegal. Falconers in the 1970s and early 1980s exchanged wild birds on a regular basis. Some exchanges may have been on the edge of regulatory provisions (it then becomes a question of whether such restrictions were legal), but we need to keep in mind that falconry had gone from absolute liberty in the 1960s, when raptors were considered vermin and wildlife managers would brag about how many they had shot, to absolute control in the 1970s, when our ownership of raptors was being denied by FWS because of the saintly pedestals raptors had been placed upon by environmental religious factions. Both were inappropriate perspectives for setting policies in twentieth century America, but because of social dynamics, they were dominant in their respective periods. Falconers were caught between these extreme forces and had to adapt to the cultural paradigm shift in a very short time span. It was an evolutionary process that took time to adjust to, whereas Operation Falcon was a violent convulsion that shook the very foundation of the falconry community and tore it into two opposing camps: those who were intimidated by FWS law enforcement and would do anything to keep them happy because they believed FWS had the power to eliminate falconry; and those who saw FWS as a rogue agency that needed disciplinary action and a great deal of authority pulled out from under their feet. This second group saw any attempt by FWS to eliminate or further restrict falconry as proof that this was an agency that had nothing but contempt for citizens rights and would therefore need to be removed from oversight of falconry altogether.

---

62   A thought to ponder: It took Western civilization a very long time to finally discover the dangers of an unrestrained military. We got a handle on this when we kept the military strictly under the control of the civil authority. For over a hundred years, American courts have been like a roller coaster when it comes to restraining not only the police, but also the "police powers." One can only hope we will look to the past for lessons to guide us in making decisions for the future. Too much power lodged in government, or any individual part thereof, is a very dangerous proposition. Power must be dispersed to be safe. This is why the Founders designed our system the way they did.

How Falconry Regulations Collide with the MBTA

It is necessary to consider the purpose of the MBTA and the authority the Service is vested with and how it affects falconry. As stated in the purpose of USC Title 16, Chapter 7, Protection of Migratory ... Birds, in Subchapter I, § 701, "The duties and powers of the Department of the Interior include the preservation, distribution, introduction, and restoration of game birds and other wild birds.... The object and purpose of this Act is to aid in the restoration of such [wild] birds in those parts of the United States **adapted thereto** [*this excludes hybrids and non-indigenous birds since they are not "adapted thereto"*] where the same have become scarce or extinct," which is an early form of endangered species act. The present purpose of the MBTA is to maintain healthy bird populations. Once birds have lawfully been taken from the wild, the Service's responsibilities diminish drastically. (Emphasis added.)

In Sections 703 and 704, respectively, the MBTA provides, "Unless permitted by regulations, the Act provides that it is unlawful to pursue, hunt, take,... possess, offer to or sell,... any migratory bird," and "[T]he Secretary of the Interior may adopt regulations determining the extent to which ... **taking** ... of any migratory bird,... will be allowed, having regard for ... distribution, abundance, [and] economic value," (emphasis added) but there is no mention of personal **use**, and as a strict liability statute, this is required. Let us consider what limits the Act provides for and what limits apply to the Act. It sets limitations on take, transportation, possession—only as it relates to illegal take, i.e., one cannot possess migratory birds that were illegally taken, which is more clearly stipulated in the ESA—and trade, but there is no provision for how lawfully-acquired migratory birds are to be used by permittees for private purposes. The Act manages social intercourse as it relates to commercial trade of migratory birds or their parts. Therefore, the personal use of legally acquired raptors, just like legally acquired waterfowl, is outside the scope of the MBTA's authority and intent. If it wasn't, it would be unconstitutional given the fact that government agencies are the servants of citizens, not their masters; the legislative, judicial and executive branches cannot change this. Citizens are not answerable to government and therefore do not require permission to pursue any endeavor that is not irresponsible—i.e., endeavors that do not conflict with the general welfare of society. As long as activities do not conflict with the general welfare, wildlife agencies must provide management mechanisms that offer citizens ample access to any resource they wish to pursue and use.

However, FWS interprets the MBTA, as it relates to falconry, as a statute that requires regulatory provisions that spell out what is allowable with raptors—not what is prohibited, as we see in waterfowl regulations. The same Act is interpreted and applied differently to these two endeavors. This is not only illegal because of its arbitrariness, but also illogical, since it would take volumes of texts to define what would be permissible if we took this regulatory approach to its logical conclusion. FWS asserts that if falconry regulations don't provide allowance for a falconer to charge money for public demonstrations with his raptor, for example, that such an activity would be illegal and would allow them to confiscate his raptor and revoke his permit. This is a taking; it is dictatorial and utterly unacceptable! No such provision applies to waterfowl. As a strict liability statute, FWS needs to cite the source of this omnipotent power. They assert it comes from the word *possess* in Section 703 of the Act, but as previously noted, the word is used to prevent an illegally taken bird from being possessed and to state that some harvest provision must be developed before a species is open for harvest. The word *possess* and the word *use* have very different meanings, and use is not provided for in the MBTA.

Next, it is necessary to take a closer look at where falconry regulations initially came from and what purpose they were meant to serve. The concept of Federal falconry regulations was initiated in the early 1970s by a faction of falconers who desired to control their sport. They found a receptive audience within FWS, though the States could just as easily have served this purpose; some States had formulated falconry regulations earlier than the 1970s. However, these individuals believed a Federal program would be more uniform and therefore easier to initiate and maintain; nevertheless, their perspective conflicted with States' rights.

Another reason this faction believed falconry needed to be strictly regulated was to provide, in their minds, a defense from the attacks of animal protectionist type organizations. Without regulations, it was believed that falconry might not survive the onslaught coming from the bird watching community (demonstrating that minority interests are not being adequately protected from powerful factions). Stan Marcus, who was a member of this faction and President of the North American Falconers' Association at the time, informed Murrin (personal communication) that he had asked the leaders of the Audubon Society, who had real problems with the art of falconry, what they wanted to see in falconry regulations. They told him what they desired, which he then incorporated in the falconers' proposed regulations in order to appease them.

This faction—some members of which were not falconers, but were actually from the birding community and might have been self-appointed plants or spies—asserted its own perspective on falconers rather than respecting the rights of others (this is also the faction that demanded the tundra peregrine should be prohibited from take even though the falconry community knew this subspecies was not in any trouble). The rules falconry has existed under do not represent the will of most falconers, nor do they protect their rights. These rules reflect the birding community's restrictions on an activity they despise and wish they could make illegal.

It is not suggested that we eliminate all regulations pertaining to falconry. Instead, we should establish management parameters at the State level—with minimal Federal involvement—that are sensible and achieve the desired goal of providing adequate protection to wild raptor populations without resorting to micromanagement tactics (waterfowl regulations are a good model as it relates to Federal involvement). Such tactics often do not discriminate between important and petty issues, which frequently causes resources to be expended in areas that do not warrant the time and expense, and potentially makes "criminals" out of falconers for issues that have little to no significance to society. This is not a matter to be taken lightly in a free society. At the same time, falconers do not desire the loss of their liberties in the name of conservation, when it has been adequately demonstrated they are not mutually exclusive. Managed properly, liberty complements conservation, as raptor propagation and organizations such as Ducks Unlimited thoroughly demonstrate, whereas prohibitive types of regulations arrest progress. Consider where the peregrine would be today if Frank Beebe had not been allowed to take them from the wild in the 1960s and discovered how to breed them in 1967.

The removal of Federal permitting in the 2008 revised falconry regulations was an important first step in the right direction.

Federal authority should be involved only to the extent that responsibility for the health of migratory bird populations is at issue, as the MBTA is intended for. Beyond this, States are better adapted to manage programs such as falconry, and States' rights principles demand such programs must be managed by the States. The Supreme Court expressed it perfectly when it stated, "[T]he theory and utility of our federalism is revealed [when] the States may perform their role as laboratories for experimentation to devise various solutions where the best solution is far from clear," (*United States v. Lopez*, 1995, at 15). States are more responsive to the needs of their residents, they can handle local issues with greater understanding and clarity, and they are better suited to handle issues that are not related to MBTA provisions.

The appropriate regulatory regime the falconry community should demand is for FWS to relinquish all authority over falconry, raptor education, raptor breeding, and abatement to the appropriate authority, which is the States. In *United States v. Enmons* (410 U. S. 411), the Court stated, "[U]nless Congress conveys its purpose clearly, it will not be deemed to have significantly changed the federal state balance." Congress did not convey the MBTA's purpose to extract all State authority over migratory birds so that FWS could assert the authority it claims over falconry. FWS should only have management authority over that which the MBTA provides for, which is *harvest numbers* and *commercialism* of indigenous, naturally occurring wild raptors (all other MBTA listed provisions fall under these two primary federal interests as subcategories)—both of which need to be regulated, but only to the degree regulation serves a true public—as opposed to factional—interest.

McDonald makes an important point regarding excessive regulation:

> The use of raptors domestically bred, does not fulfill the full requirements of the art of falconry, and much of the lore of this art has been allowed to "fade" as a result of regulation. It will, in my opinion, continue to regress as time goes by, until it will no longer be the art form we once knew and which history had passed down to America. To survive it must be free of regimentation, regulation and interference. Falconry is, in the final analysis, the art of individual dedicated artists, which over time finds its way into a "pool" we call the history of falconry. (2010)

Sharp-shinned hawk.

Non-Resident Take

Non-resident take is an important issue to many since various States have greater raptor numbers and types compared to other States. There are falconers in States that have highly desirable raptors and who have objected to opening their doors to non-residents, typically stating, without evidence, that their politics are unique and that things are more complicated in their State, or they simply don't want non-residents doing something wrong that might threaten the residents' falconry rights. If this last were to be an acceptable excuse, non-residents wouldn't be allowed in any State to pursue any activity whatsoever, since it might threaten the rights of residents. It becomes obvious that this is simply a red herring so that residents of those States with healthy numbers of highly desirable raptors may hoard their resources, placing themselves in the elite position of being a minority of people who possess these raptors.

Let's consider non-resident take from a legal perspective. The U.S. Constitution's Privileges and Immunities Clause, Article Four, § Two ("The citizens of each State shall be entitled to all privileges and immunities of citizens in the several States") provides a licensed falconer of one State the same rights and opportunities of resident falconers in their home States. Therefore, States are prohibited from denying non-residents the same opportunities they provide to residents, unless there is some compelling interest that may jeopardize residents' objective interests. But then the courts have stated that the least discriminatory methods must be employed.

One may ask why we would want non-resident take in those States whose doors have been closed. A person living in Illinois would travel to Iowa or South Dakota to hunt pheasants, since this is where the resource is located in sufficient numbers to make it worthwhile to pursue with a reasonable expectation of success. The same is true with any natural resource; for example, would one dig for diamonds in a Midwestern plain State? In addition, reciprocity issues are at stake. Passage peregrine falcon harvest is now a reality. If a State prohibits non-residents from trapping within its borders, its resident falconers will not be allowed take in other States where peregrines can be found. Also, we need to ask why we wouldn't offer non-residents access to raptors like we do other wildlife resources, such as pheasant. Are raptors more "special" than game birds? In addition, we must ask why raptor take by non-residents was ever made illegal. There was never any justification in it. It's not as if non-resident demand of raptors will compete with resident demand—the demand from both quarters combined simply has no affect on raptor populations.

Let's consider take from a harvest perspective. Harvest of wild raptors is very small, as the U.S. Fish & Wildlife Service's 2007 Final Environmental Assessment, Take of Raptors From the Wild Under the Falconry Regulations and the Raptor Propagation Regulations, reveals (see Table 1), which is due to the small size of our community, many falconers not acquiring a new bird every year, and the number of raptors purchased from domestic breeders being about the same as the number of wild taken birds. So there is no serious harvest pressure on wild populations, which informs us that there is no real need to closely regulate or monitor falconry or wild harvest. The falconry community should require FWS to reduce the regulatory burden upon falconers and to provide for wild-take that reflects biology rather than religion-based politics.

Table 1.

Reported Falconry Take of Wild Raptors in the U.S., 2003-2005.

Raptors Taken

Species	2003	2004	2005	Percent of 3-Year Total
Falconiformes:				
Golden Eagle	4	6	4	0.45
Cooper's Hawk	67	72	79	6.98
Northern Goshawk	52	46	60	5.06
Sharp-shinned Hawk	15	15	19	1.57
Harris's Hawk	50	32	44	4.04
Ferruginous Hawk	7	6	6	0.61
Red-shouldered Hawk	3	3	4	0.32
Broad-winged Hawk	0	0	1	0.03
Red-tailed Hawk	527	645	610	57.10
Short-tailed Hawk	1	0	0	0.03
Rough-legged Hawk	0	0	0	0.00
American Kestrel	100	101	143	11.02
Merlin	48	52	69	5.41
Peregrine Falcon	1	18	13	1.03
Gyrfalcon	8	19	7	1.09
Prairie Falcon	31	42	66	4.45
Strigiformes:				
Eastern Screech Owl	1	0	0	0.03
Western Screech Owl	0	3	0	0.10
Great Horned Owl	6	7	6	0.61
Snowy Owl	1	1	0	0.06
Totals	922	1068	1131	100

In addition, FWS's population estimates for the various raptors used in falconry demonstrate healthy populations that are unaffected by the low numbers taken by falconers (see Table 2).

Table 2.

Population Data for Modeled Species.
Population size estimates are modified from Rich *et al.* (2004).

Species	Canada-U.S. Population
Falconiformes:	
Cooper's Hawk	276,450
Northern Goshawk	120,050
Sharp-shinned Hawk	291,500
Harris's Hawk	19,500
Ferruginous Hawk	11,500
Red-shouldered Hawk	410,850
Red-tailed Hawk	979,000
American Kestrel	2,175,000
Merlin	325,000
Peregrine Falcon	10,000[3]
Gyrfalcon	27,500
Prairie Falcon	17,280
Strigiformes:	
Eastern Screech-Owl	369,600
Western Screech-Owl	270,100
Great Horned Owl	1,139,500
Snowy Owl	72,500

Proportion of Juveniles[1]	Number of Juveniles	Percent in U.S.[2]
0.50	138,225	60
0.30	36,015	25
0.50	145,750	35
0.25	4,875	100
0.30	3,450	80
0.30	123,255	95
0.30	293,700	50
0.60	1,305,000	45
0.60	195,000	15
0.30	3,000	25[4]
0.30	8,250	NA[5]
0.50	8,640	95
0.60	221,760	99
0.60	162,060	85
0.30	341,850	55
0.30	21,750	NA[4]

1 The percent juveniles were estimated from observed population structure in species-specific population models at equilibrium. See text and Figure 1.
2 Estimated from the applicable <u>Birds of North America</u> account.
3 Estimate for twelve western states in which take of nestling peregrine falcons is allowed, based on the results of population modeling.
4 Based on the entire North American population. The population numbers in the text and the allowed take used the numbers for the western U.S. population of *Falco peregrinus anatum*.
5 Not applicable. For this Arctic species the North American population value is appropriate.

Now, if we consider FWS's analysis of the harvest numbers raptors can conservatively sustain, it becomes quite obvious that actual harvest of raptors for falconry is so low as not to even be an issue of concern (see Table 3).

Table 3.

Harvest Data and Maximum Take of Species Taken for Falconry.

Species	Number of Juveniles	% in U.S.	Young Available for Harvest
Falconiformes:			
Cooper's Hawk	138,225	60	82,935
Northern Goshawk	36,015	25	9,004
Sharp-shinned Hawk	145,750	35	51,013
Harris's Hawk	4,875	100	4,875 0
Ferruginous Hawk	3,450	80	2,760
Red-shouldered Hawk	123,255	95	117,092
Red-tailed Hawk	293,700	50	146,850
American Kestrel	1,305,000	45	587,250
Merlin	195,000	15	29,250
Peregrine Falcon[1]	3,000	25[4]	3,000
Gyrfalcon	8,250	NA[5]	8,250
Prairie Falcon	8,640	95	8,208
Strigiformes:			
Eastern Screech-Owl	221,760	99	219,542
Western Screech-Owl	162,060	85	137,751
Great Horned Owl	341,850	55	188,018
Snowy Owl	21,750	NA[4]	21,750

Maximum Sustained Yield	Maximum % Take Level	Recommended Take Level	Average Taken (% of Allowed Take) 2003-2005
0.06	3	2,488	73 (2.93)
0.16	5	450	53 (11.78)
0.06	3	1,530	16 (1.05)
.41	5	243	42 (17.28)
0.01^2	1	27	6 (22.22)
0.01^2	1	1,170	3 (0.26)
0.09	4.5	6,608	594 (8.99)
0.03	1.5	5,872	115 (1.96)
0.01^2	1	292	56 (19.18)
0.16	5	150	11 (7.33)
0.01^2	1	82	13 (15.85)
0.06	3	246	46 (18.70)
0.01^2	1	2,195	0.33 (0.02)
0.01^2	1	1,377	1 (0.07)
0.01^2	1	1,880	6 (0.32)
0.01^2	1	217	1 (0.46)

1 Estimate for twelve western states in which take of nestling peregrine falcons is allowed, based on the results of population modeling. Take of wild peregrine falcons for falconry was only authorized in Alaska prior to 2004.
2 Insufficient survival data available, see text.

The FWS's 2006 Draft Environmental Assessment (DEA), in its analysis on the affects of harvest on raptors, provides, "[M]any raptor populations can sustain eyass or passage harvest rates of 10% to 20%, and sometimes higher."

In this DEA, the FWS points out that the take of nestling raptors by falconers provides "higher survival rates" for the remaining eyasses "than nestlings from un-harvested nests." The fact that falconers must leave at least one eyass in the nest demonstrates that nestling take will have no impact on raptor populations. In addition, the FWS points out, "[S]ome raptors taken from the wild by falconers are returned to the wild. Millsap and Mullenix reported that about 40% of falconer-harvested red-tailed hawks and American kestrels are intentionally or accidentally returned to the wild each year." Given the high juvenile mortality rate of raptors, one must conclude that falconers have a positive influence on survivability of raptors, especially if they keep them through the first year of the raptor's life.

All States should be open to all U.S. citizens for harvest of all raptor species that are not endangered. Those that are endangered should be made available to breeders so that they may build the breeding stock. There is no justification for non-resident prohibitions, and it is something all falconers should demand from their neighbors. Otherwise reprisals, such as prohibiting non-resident hunting and trapping for falconers from those offensive states, could be forthcoming.

Peales peregrine falcon.

The Poster Child of the
Endangered Species Act:
The Peregrine Falcon

I wish to consider the environmental forces that lead to the demise of the Eastern anatum peregrine falcon and the manner in which our country dealt with this situation. Though this may appear to deviate from the analysis of wildlife law, it is important to analyze factional forces and their influence on regulatory policy. Factional forces have come to dominate wildlife science and subsequent policy that are frequently based on deceit, which then influences the enactment of wildlife statutes and regulations. It is our opinion that these forces have, in many cases, done more harm than good because of the misleading propaganda that has emanated from certain quarters. It is most certainly a fact that these factions recognized a problem; however, their arguments and solutions deviated from sound civil principles and constitutional limitations—not to mention their manipulation of scientific information and the exploitation of it. Their intention, of course, has been to dominate the argument and control the applicable power for their own self-serving purposes rather than for the good of the country. The design of falconry regulations was directly influenced by this un-American and unhealthy situation.

Falconry regulations were formulated in large part because of the influence of the contemporaneous culture that surrounded the Endangered Species Act (ESA), which portions of the falconry community were deeply involved in. The ESA and falconry regulations were formulated at the same time, and there was a great deal of overlapping because of intense emotions in the culture of that period. Since the peregrine falcon was the primary symbol of both falconry and the ESA, falconry regulations were intertwined with the ESA regardless of what species of raptor falconers might have possessed. The draconian regulations falconers contend with, separate from any endangered species issues, mirror the intense regulatory nature of the ESA, but with no justification. There were simply those—inside and outside the falconry community—who put raptors on a pedestal and wanted to see them treated like royalty, whereas falconers, outside the elite clique, were to be treated like peasants.

It is important to reveal how a true public welfare interest can be manipulated by factions to extract rights and liberties, in the name of the welfare cause, in order to gain control of the political landscape and punish those who are not of the same political/ religious persuasion. The peregrine is not only the poster child of the ESA, it is also the poster child of abusive political manipulation. The hypothesis claimed by certain sectors of the scientific community, and the process in which the two North American subspecies of peregrines (the anatum and tundra peregrines[63]) were listed as endangered reveals ignorance in some individuals and manipulation by others to formulate policy that served those factional forces who had much to gain by the end result. Who these people were is not as important as the lack of defense our society has against such factional influence. Perhaps it would be more appropriate to say that we have the defense, but

---

63   "Recent genetic evidence suggests that Peale's Peregrine Falcon [sic] is genetically distinct from the other two subspecies, but that historically the Anatum and Tundrius subspecies could not be distinguished genetically. Further, current differences between these two subspecies are weak and likely due to the limited gene pool associated with the introductions and introgression from non-Anatum birds from the US. In terms of population genetic structuring, only two diagnosable genetic groups were identified in historical samples of Peregrine Falcons in Canada: *pealei*, and all other individuals.... Brown et al. (2007) state: 'Both mtDNA and microsatellite data show that *F. p. anatum* and *F. p. tundrius* were genetically indistinguishable historically and that contemporary samples are weakly, but significantly differentiated.' (p. ii) ... Microsatellite analyses suggest that the changes in genetic structure between Anatum and Tundrius are largely due to changes within Anatum alone ... and that this change is localized to northern Ontario and Québec, where reintroduced Anatum individuals, their descendents and possibly also birds from the US occur. The change in genetic structure of Anatum in this area is most likely due to the limited gene pool associated with the introductions and introgression from non-Anatum birds from the US (Brown et al., 2007). Breeding Peregrine Falcons of mixed subspecific pedigree, originating from the US, have been documented in both provinces," (Cooper & Beauchesne, p. 8, 2007).

our legislatures and courts frequently ignore the anti-factional principles underlying our system of government.

Peale's and Tundra Peregrines

To begin, let us consider two North American subspecies: the Peale's peregrine, which was never ESA listed, and the tundra peregrine, which was never threatened or endangered other than on paper.

Even though the Peale's peregrine never experienced a decline, because of the unjustified *similarity of appearance* provision in ESA regulations, it was protected along with the anatum. This is like saying, "Since Koreans and Japanese have a similar appearance, we should lump them together in any quota we may implement for immigration purposes." This would be unacceptable, and so it is with the *similarity of appearance* regarding wildlife. This was put in place for convenience of wildlife officials—or, perhaps, simply as another barrier to access of wild peregrines—and at the loss of rights by citizens.

Like many arctic birds, the tundra peregrine likely experienced cyclical variations in populations. While the cycle *appeared* to be at a low point for a few years, the tundra peregrine was lumped into the same declining category as the anatum and was therefore included in the endangered grouping.

Fyfe (Hickey, 1969, p. 105) states,

> Unfortunately, there are no long-term data available on the [tundra] peregrine in northern Canada which would indicate either an increase or decrease in the total population. Much of the area is yet to be visited by ornithologists, and most observations that have been recorded have been made during expeditions of but a few weeks duration.... [T]he peregrine is still a common breeding bird in the north.

This still holds true to this day. Cooper and Beauchesne (2007, p. 25) discuss surveys being conducted from 1970 to the present day in select areas throughout Canada and point out that most of Canada is not and never has been surveyed. They provide, "Many additional breeding pairs exist, especially Tundrius Peregrines Falcons [sic] that breed in a vast, relatively uninhabited Arctic landscape." They also provide on page twenty-five, "[T]here were no systematic surveys of Peregrine Falcons in North America before their decline." On page twenty-six, when discussing the present populations being robust, they mention, "Increased search effort may also contribute somewhat to the increasing population trends." This shows how little was known about the tundra peregrine prior to its listing and the lack of effort that was put forth by Canadian and U.S. governments to determine actual population numbers.

There was no long term data when the tundra peregrine was listed, yet some asserted there was a decline—a decline from what? Earlier expeditions in the century were cursory and sporadic, so no significant data could possibly have given a realistic picture of any trends. In the 1960s, scientists had no idea what they were observing. Were the tundra peregrine numbers "declining" to a normal level, or were they simply exhibiting normal population fluctuations? No one knew, yet they were listed as endangered! White (Hickey, 1969, p. 47 & 51) states,

> The density of peregrines along the Colville River, on the Arctic Slope, has not diminished since Cade's last survey in 1959; in fact, it may have increased [*in spite of the presence of DDT in the environment since the mid-40s and the cyclodienes since the mid-50s*].... The peregrines in Alaska do not appear to be decreasing. No evidence of decreasing population or reproductive capacity was noted there. The number of breeding adults seems to be maintaining itself at a constant level, and the population is considered numerically healthy. The migratory routes and wintering grounds of these peregrines are poorly known. Since the population apparently is not decreasing in Alaska ... accurate records should be made of population fluctuations.

Cade (Hickey, 1969, p. 505) provides,

> As has been abundantly pointed out by our Canadian colleagues and by White (Chapter 2), most of what has gone on in the Arctic in the way of research on falcons has involved quick surveys, very superficial in their treatment, of tens or hundreds of thousands of square miles of country in which we know there are a lot of peregrines; but we do not know precisely how many there are.... And we need, as

was mentioned by Aldrich, an intensive banding program … to determine more about what the wintering range of the population of peregrines is, because indeed this is still very poorly understood.… This kind of ecological research would be invaluable, I believe, in providing a background of information on the still relatively undisturbed and healthy populations of peregrine falcons.

White and Cade's summary of the tundra peregrine was made after DDT had been on the scene for around twenty years. If DDT was the cause of the demise of the Eastern anatum in the few short years after its introduction in the mid- to late '40s, then the tundra peregrine should have been affected by it *prior* to the 1960s. However, a temporary dip in count numbers occurred in the 1960s, which was used as an excuse to list this subspecies as endangered. The chronology doesn't add up, and it then becomes obvious that the listing of this subspecies was based on flawed reasoning or possibly to further an agenda.

Falconers have collected tundra peregrine migration data from 1939 to the present,[64] and while some of the observers' (McDonald, 1970, unpublished) counts indicate there was a slight decline in migration counts for a few years in the mid 1960s—which was due to the lack of personnel available to count peregrines during that period—their count numbers rebounded far too quickly for there to have been a serious decline in their population. At the same time, other counters' and banders' (Ruos, Rice, and Berry) data strongly suggest that there was little—if any—decline in the number of migrant peregrines during the mid 1960s. Rice and Berry's observations indicate that they captured three times more peregrines than were observed by the McDonald observers, which

---

64   Nye, A.G. Jr. (Nov. 18, 1969), *Assateague Island Peregrines*, private paper; Shor, W. (Feb. 11, 1969), *Peregrines Sighted in the Fall of 1968 Along the Atlantic Coast*, private paper; McDonald, B.B. (Feb. 1970), *Migration Population Study of The Tundra Falcon (Falco peregrines tundrius)* 1956-1969, private paper; *1967-69 Assateague Island, Maryland—Peregrine Observation Report*, J. L. Ruos, private report; *Assateague Island, Md.—Peregrines: Fall 1969*, J. N. Rice, II and R. B. Berry, presented at Cornell Univ. Conference Nov. 7-9, 1969, private report; Seeger et al., *Return of the Peregrine, 2003*. These data reveal cycles of tundra peregrine numbers. In addition, Cooper & Beauchesne (2007, p. iii) provide, "National surveys to examine population trends of breeding Peregrine Falcons have been conducted in Canada every five years between 1970 and 2005. The surveys show substantial increases in Anatum and Tundrius Peregrine numbers since 1970." Right around 1970 was allegedly the time when the tundra peregrine was on the decline—hence the reason for its listing. How could it have "recovered" from being endangered in a few short years?

was due to the lack of observers in the McDonald study during that period. Additionally, based on a consistent 1:5 ratio of birds-captured to birds-seen by Nye, Ruos, Rice, and Berry over a period spanning from 1939 to 1969, the number of peregrines that could have been counted were likely two to ten times greater than the McDonald observers recorded. It is highly probable that the years of the "decline" reported by some of the counters was simply due to either bad migration counting weather, bad counting locations, differing counting methods, or all three.

Weather patterns, pre-migration conditions, and methods of counting all affect the ability to observe migrating peregrines. When weather patterns and other conditions are ideal, peregrines tend to concentrate along established migration routes, known as leading-lines, where observers take their migration counts (White pointed out above that migration routes were poorly known). If weather conditions are not optimal for concentrating raptors along these leading-lines, raptors spread out over a broad migratory front, both inland and far out over water (some leading-lines are located along large bodies of water, such as Lake Michigan and the Atlantic Ocean, while others are located along mountainous ridges), where there are no observers to count them. These leading-lines are few in number and sporadic in their occurrence, therefore, they don't provide accurate information on populations. To complicate matters, the passage of very stormy weather associated with hurricanes and tropical storms sometimes grounds birds where they can be more easily seen and counted, and other times draws them out over the water beyond the counters' sight.

Seeger et al. (Cade & Burnham, 2003, pp. 220-21) mention the variation in factors relating to migratory bird counts affecting count numbers.

> It is apparent from our data that even in a completely recovered population, yearly counts on a highly standardized study such as ours can vary significantly. Contributing factors are local and continental weather patterns, and also the timing of events that prevent full conduct of the study…. Continental weather patterns play a major role in the overall number of Peregrines encountered at Padre [Island, Texas]…. These confounding factors further illustrate the value of our

long-term studies as such yearly aberrations are balanced and distributed over time and a more accurate index of populations emerges.

This summarizes the real picture, but this common sense explanation was not followed in the late 1960s and early '70s, when it was decided that the tundra peregrine was in "serious trouble."

Sulski, who has been studying peregrine migration for the last twenty-five years and has been conducting research on the same along Lake Michigan for the last eleven years, offers some interesting insight into the complexity of peregrine migration.

The following personal and literature documented observations on North American autumnal peregrine migration are offered in an attempt to answer the question of whether migrant peregrine count numbers are a reliable indicator of peregrine population numbers.

Peregrines begin their fall migration in early September and don't conclude their passage through the lower 48 U.S. states until late October or early November. For the most part, birds originating from higher latitude locations begin their migration at the early part of the season and reach their wintering grounds at lower latitude locations toward the end of the season. Like many raptor species, peregrines that originate at more southern breeding grounds tend to terminate their migration at more northerly wintering ground locations, and some lower 48 breeders remain in the U.S. throughout the winter. The literature has coined this phenomenon "leapfrog migration."

With a few exceptions, peregrines travel daily from the time they begin their migration to the time they reach their wintering grounds. Predicting a migrating peregrine's route at any particular point during passage is a complicated if not impossible matter because the path of migration is intricately tied to weather patterns and meteorological conditions that widely fluctuate often from hour to hour. Peregrines adjust to such changes and fluctuations in order to conserve energy during their migration. What complicates matters more is migrant peregrines gravitate toward coastal areas, and coastal weather conditions are often more complex than terrestrial conditions. Additionally, peregrines, unlike most raptors, are very comfortable migrating: 1) out over large bodies of water, including the Great Lakes, the Atlantic Ocean and the Gulf of Mexico; and 2) during heavy rain.

At the initiation of their migratory passage, peregrines in North America set their course according to the weather patterns at the time, especially the general wind direction and speed. If mid and low level winds are strong from the east, their course is more westerly. If the winds are strong from the west, their course is more easterly and often far out over the Atlantic Ocean. On clear days, an observer, at best, can sight flying peregrines at distances of no more than a few miles, less as a migrant's altitude increases.

While on passage, peregrines adjust their method of flight and their location in accordance with the set of meteorological conditions they encounter. Only a few of the many various sets of conditions are conducive to observing migrating peregrines. As a point of reference, the most ideal locations and conditions for observing migrating peregrines is along well defined, north-south oriented coastlines during moderate to strong winds (+15 mph) out of the southwest-west quadrant, accompanied by falling barometric pressure—pre-frontal conditions. Unfortunately, such conditions are uncommon and sometimes absent during some years. For the sake of brevity, rather than exploring in detail the many different sets and combinations of sets of conditions that affect where peregrines migrate and how such conditions affect peregrine accountability, the following are some examples of conditions that interfere with the ability to count migrating peregrines, and such poor conditions are much more common than ideal counting conditions:

- fog, haze or rain that obstructs the observer's visibility.

- no or low winds and no thermals, which tend to ground the birds.

- no or low winds and terrestrial convection thermals, which drive onshore breezes and cause birds to migrate inland.

- no or low winds and coastal thermals, which, depending on the temperature gradient magnitude and direction between land and water, cause birds to migrate inland or out over the water.

- winds parallel to the shoreline, which cause birds to drift inland and over the water across a wide front.

- strong onshore winds, which cause birds to drift inland.[65] (Sulski, unpublished, 2011)

Other scenarios that can explain variations in migrant tundra peregrine count numbers include temporary environmental conditions, such as bad weather in the breeding grounds that affect reproductive success, and low prey density during pre-migration, which affects the condition of migrants. Anctil et al. (2011) state, "Changes in climatic patterns may affect populations directly (e.g., influencing thermoregulation of individuals) or indirectly (e.g., influencing food availability)." The study area was around Hudson Bay. "Here, a long-term studied Peregrine Falcon population shows a highly variable annual productivity that seems to be correlated with the amount of summer precipitation." In the conclusion of this abstract, the authors provide,

These results indicate that both the direct and indirect effects of weather can strongly affect the condition of the young Peregrine Falcons. An understanding of how changes in weather, like an increase in precipitation, can affect animal populations is critical. These findings provide insight into the influence of changing weather pattern[s] on arctic-nesting Peregrine Falcons.

Ratcliffe (Cade et al., 1988, pp. 154-55) reinforces the observations that weather conditions have a profound effect on breeding success.

---

65   Further information can be found in Cooper and Beauchesne (2007, p. 17) who state "Factors influencing annual productivity include: (1) egg and chick mortality from cold, wet, and late spring weather (White and Cade 1971; Court et al. 1988b; Mearns and Newton 1988; Ratcliffe 1993; Bradley et al. 1997); (2) local yearly variation in prey abundance (Court et al. 1988b; Bradley and Oliphant 1991); (3) regional differences in overall prey availability (Ratcliffe 1993); (4) predation/disease: not quantified for any population but can be locally significant (Cade et al. 1989; Tordoff and Redig 1997)."

One feature has become clear during the last ten years. **Adverse spring weather can so appreciably reduce breeding performance as to resemble the earlier, pesticidally-induced depressions in output of young.** The last decade has been notable for cold, backward springs, sometimes also accompanied by unusually heavy rainfall.... [*And on page 150, he states,*] In 1981 an unusually cold and wet spring caused heavy mortality of chicks at hatching and during the early nestling stages. (Emphasis added.)

On the other hand, even during years of low productivity, if prey populations are low when peregrines are staging for migration and they leave their foraging grounds with insufficient fat reserves, more migrants will travel over land rather than out over water in order to forage en route, and migrant population counts can be higher than expected. Conversely, if prey abundance is high and weather is favorable, a greater proportion of migrants will be in good physical condition and can spend more time over water, out of sight from the counters.

Finally, methods of observation can also affect migrant count numbers. The McDonald paper, which indicates relatively low numbers of migrants in the mid 1960s, was based on the non-luring technique for counting peregrines. This method involved traveling in vehicles up and down various beaches along the Atlantic Coast, from the mouth of the Delaware Bay to the tip of Cape Hatteras to spot peregrines. However, there were those who practiced fixed-site counting from blinds, using luring techniques to capture and band peregrines, which gave different results.

In short, meteorological conditions dictate where peregrines migrate, and the number of migrant peregrines counted from year to year often has little if anything to do with the size of peregrine populations. That is why the scientific community relies on count data for little more than a crude qualitative measure of migration trends over extended periods of time. Even today, year to year fluctuations in peregrine count numbers for dozens of count sites across North America (see www.hawkcount.org) demonstrate that present robust and increasing populations of peregrines are not reflected very well in count numbers.

Other evidence used to claim a decline in tundra peregrine populations was gathered from a few isolated locations in the Arctic and subarctic. These pockets of habitat—i.e., stretches of rivers—that raptor biologists visited were like grains of sand on a very large beach, which any statistician would dismiss as insufficient information from which to draw any solid conclusion. We are informed (Cade, 1971) that the rivers observed were the Yukon River, the Colville River and its major tributaries, the upper Utukok, the Noatak River, and the Canning River. This is hardly representative of the entire arctic region where the tundra peregrine breeds, yet it was considered sufficient to influence its status as endangered.

Bromley (Cade, et al., 1988, p. 57) conducted an aerial survey of gyrfalcons in the central and eastern arctic regions of the Northwest Territories in Canada for four consecutive years—from 1982 to 1985. "During these surveys, observations of territorial and nesting Peregrine Falcons (F.p. tundrius) were routinely recorded." He concluded that "apparently numerically healthy populations exist in all surveyed areas and are reproducing at normal rates." It is highly improbable that the tundra peregrine could have "recovered" this quickly from the time of its "endangered" listing.

A final word on the subject of the tundra peregrine is provided by a deceased falconer. In a letter dated Jan. 14, 1970 by James Fritz (who was an attorney for U.S. Customs and a member of the Potomac Falconers Association), regarding the proposed protection of the tundra peregrine, he provided the following:

To: Members of the Potomac Falconers Association

Re: A NAFA [North American Falconers' Association] proposal concerning protection of the Tundra bird, and related proposals.

First, I write this letter as a party with an obvious interest in the outcome of this matter, not as a member of NAFA, which I am not.

Having heard and participated in frequent discussions with most or all of you on the subject in the past, I believe it is accurate to say that there is unanimous agreement that protection of the Tundra bird is unnecessary, or not capable of achieving its stated purpose, or both. It is equally true that, at present, we enjoy the right to trap the Tundra bird on an individual basis. It is our right to go and sit, or ride, for hours and days on some beach, squandering our time and resources where and how we please, within certain not overly oppressive limits.

The proposals referred to suggest that we forfeit that right, although there is some small chance that the right will be converted to a grudging and limited permission conferred on some of us by government from time to time, if we are successful in convincing certain strangers to us and to our sport that we are worthy.

Some of us believe that protection will come in any event and that we should go along with it, in the expectation that we can somehow convert a loss into a gain. Experience does not justify that expectation. When has surrender of a right to government benefited the individual whose rights were surrendered? When has cooperation with bigots, and I regard wild eyed conservationists and empire building enforcement officials and biologists as such, ever satiated or even alleviated their bigotry? Never. One's interests are not served by capitulation. One cannot retain a right by surrendering it. One cannot reasonably expect a privilege to be conferred where a right could not be secured. For these reasons I do not believe that it is to any of our interests that these proposals be approved by the NAFA membership.

But I also believe that something more than self interest is involved here. It is something so basic to us as individuals and as citizens that it is difficult for me to believe that it has been overlooked. It goes beyond our rights as citizens not to be deprived of a thing by government without just cause and it goes beyond our distaste for seeing a thing occur that will be injurious to us. I refer, of course, to the difference between right and wrong. If we agree that this protection is unnecessary we must also agree that it is wrong for someone with an unsubstantiated opposing viewpoint to inflict his belief on us. There is no room for equivocation here; the issue is plain. If we not only submit but participate in the achievement of something that is wrong, we, too, are wrong. We are ethically wrong. We have diminished ourselves as people. This, in persons with a general reputation for individuality and fair play, would be very unfortunate. I urge you not to allow sophistry, hope of advantage, fear or carelessness to bring you to that.

B. James Fritz[66]

Taylor (1822, p. xxviii) provides another perspective regarding

---

66   A copy of this letter was provided by Brian McDonald, who was a member of both associations and received a copy from Fritz in 1970.

the principles articulated by Fritz:

> The evils of [unconstitutional policies], may undoubtedly be graduated by compromises, like those of every other species of tyranny; but the folly of letting in some tyranny to avoid more, has in all ages been fatal to liberty. A succession of wedges, though apparently small, finally splits the strongest timber.

Anatum Peregrines

Next, let us consider the environmental forces that have caused the eastern population of the anatum peregrine subspecies to become extinct and how much of the evidence that was available was ignored. You may say, "I thought the peregrine was saved." "The American peregrine falcon was listed as endangered on June 2, 1970, under the precursor of the Endangered Species Act (35 FR 16047)."[67] However, the "American" peregrine is the anatum subspecies, and the eastern portion of the population (hereafter referred to as the Eastern anatum, which was so much larger than its western brethren[68] that it could be classified as distinct) became extinct, as a regional and unique group, sometime in the 1950s (McDonald, 2010), well before the anatum was listed as endangered. The western portion of the anatum population declined significantly because of natural environmental conditions. Nelson (Hickey, 1969, pp. 65-67) hypothesized that the lack of precipitation and rising average temperatures in the western portion of North America were the primary contributors to the decline of the Western anatum peregrine. He states, "There was practically no pesticide problem when the decline started." The precipitation problem, he informs us, began in the 1930s or earlier. Beebe's hypothesis of the need for higher humidity levels being critical to the survival of eyass peregrines (Beebe, 1960, p. 181) supports Nelson's hypothesis.

---

67 http://frwebgate.access.gpo.gov/cgi-bin/getdoc.cgi?dbname=2006_register&docid=fr13oc06-97

68   Beebe attributed the difference in size to its primary prey base, which was the passenger pigeon—a colonial breeding bird of the region. He hypothesized that the size of raptors is determined by the size of the primary prey base during the breeding season and the tiercel's (male falcon) ability to catch it in sufficient numbers and carry it back to the eyrie (a raptor's nest) efficiently. If tiercels are unable to do this, there can be no breeding success. The tiercel Eastern anatum was the perfect size to catch and carry passenger pigeons. The Western anatum did not have this evolutionary pressure for similar sized prey (Frank Beebe, Personal communication, 2005).

Heads of first year North American peregrines showing main subspecies characteristics.

Tundra: Small size, pale general tone, light crown, narrow black broken malar stripe.

Anatum: Medium size, contrastingly marked, dark crown, black malar stripe, rufous overwash.

Peales's: Large size, dark general tone, crown and malar stripe dark gray.

It is highly probable that the demise of the Eastern anatum population was due to egg-collectors (oologists), exterminators (such as game managers, pigeon racers, farmers, etc.), recreational activity after WWII on and at the eyrie sites (McDonald, 2010 speaks of repelling down cliff faces), loss of habitat (large scale deforestation of mature trees), and loss of a primary prey species (for the prey species hypothesis see Beebe below and in Hickey, 1969, pp. 399-402), all of which had catastrophic consequences for the Eastern anatum prior to any possible influence of DDT.

Falconers certainly had no influence on Eastern anatum populations (though some protectionists did try to include falconers in the blame), given the small number of falconers at the time and the number of peregrines taken, which McDonald informs us was no more than twenty to thirty eyasses per year in the late 1930s. And from 1939 onward, few if any eyasses were taken because of Bill Turner and Al Nye's discovery in 1938 of migrating tundra peregrines on Assateague Island.[69] McDonald (2010) states, "American falconry, had its active beginning in the 1930's. No discernable activity, for the most part, has been recorded prior to that period; therefore there was no impact on wild raptor populations." The population of falconers in the 30s was simply too small to have any effect. But egg-collecting was different, as a plethora of period literature informs us. Kiff and Zink provide:

> [W]idespread hobbyist egg collecting did not really take hold in North America until the 1860s.... The study of eggs ... was at its zenith on this continent from about 1885 through the 1920s ... and had completely faded from the American scene by 1970. Thus, the "oological chapter" of North American natural history lasted about a century.... Egg collecting was justified on both scientific and recreational grounds (Grinnell, 1906), and many of

---

69   Bill Turner's father, Landon, and a law enforcement officer, "Roddy" Gascoyne— unsure of the spelling—for USFWS, would fish at Fox Hill Levels on Assateague, and when the fishing for Red Drum was slow because of the outgoing tide, they would shoot sitting peregrines with a Hornet varmint .22 caliber rifle to pass the time, since this was socially justifiable given the belief that peregrines would take game birds. Landon Turner saved some of the dead peregrines and brought them home for his son to see since Bill was a falconer. It must have been heart-wrenching for Bill to see these dead peregrines, but it provided evidence that migrating tundra peregrines did rest on Assateague before moving on. These tundra peregrines then became the primary subspecies falconers would trap (McDonald, 2010).

the great lights of American ornithology ... collected bird eggs in their early years. (Kiff & Zink, 2005)

It appears that most outstanding naturalists got their start as young outdoorsmen of one sort or another. Raptor biology's best have similar backgrounds. Now that access to wildlife is regulated to extreme levels, it is highly doubtful we will see any extraordinary naturalists emerge in the future. The training ground has become so restrictive that it retards development rather than encourages it.

Hickey (1969) indicates egg-collecting was popular in earlier decades. A good example of this can be found in *The Oologist* (Sharp, 1919, pp. 39-43), in which the author of an article shares his story of anatum peregrine eggs being taken from a breeding pair almost every year from 1901 to 1913. Afterward they ceased to breed, though they were observed in the vicinity for some years after. It appears no pair replaced them, perhaps indicating the lack of a floating adult population in the region. The author also provides,

> Our race of ... Falco peregrine anatum seems to be pretty well distributed over North America. In most localities very rare; common nowhere. Perhaps we ... are as well favored with them as anywhere, yet even with such ardent collectors as Dixon and Carpenter on the job we have only found five pair nesting in a radius of twenty-five miles.

Also consider Reed (1904, pp. 11-12), who provides,

> At some time during youth, the desire to collect something is paramount; it has very frequently culminated in the indiscriminate collecting of birds' eggs, merely to gratify a passing whim or to see how large a number could be gotten together, without regard to classification. It is this in conjunction with the many natural enemies that birds have had to contend with, that has caused the great decrease in numbers of certain birds.

No mention of the primary cause of reduction in bird populations, which was habitat loss, as we have come to learn. Also interesting to note, market hunters aren't blamed in this case.

Rice (Hickey, 1969, p. 159), in referring to the Eastern anatum, provides, "In my opinion the egg collectors reduced by at least one-third a marginal population already restricted by its environment."

Berger et al. (Hickey, 1969, 170-71) point out that a major factor of the decline of the Eastern anatum

> was the prevalence for some 70 years of fanatic egg-collecting.... Frank Flick (1883) said of [a particular eyrie] 'I have known 30 persons to visit ... [the site] in one day looking for the hawk's eggs.'

Peterson (Cade, et al., 1988, pp. *iii-iv*) provides,

> The rarer the bird, the keener the collector was to acquire its eggs. The challenge was so great that some oologists specialized in Peregrine eggs. One collector in Philadelphia had a cabinet full of Peregrine eggs, drawer upon drawer representing years.... A Boston oologist was reputed to have 180 sets—more than 700 eggs! Sixty, 80, and 100 sets [*a set consists of a few to several eggs from a clutch that were taken from an eyrie at a given moment*] were frequent.... I was shown a cliff in California where a collector pitched his tent before the eggs were laid, so he would be there first. He told me that he had taken the eggs at the eyrie each year for 29 years.

Berry (Cade & Burnham, 2003, p. 53) referencing an ornithologist from the American Museum of Natural History of the 1930s, states, "Ernst Mayr ... felt there was little doubt that commercial egg-collecting was at the present time the worst enemy of our rare hawks," which at that time would have been primarily the Eastern anatum; however, McDonald mentions the goshawk would also have been considered a rare raptor of that period. Contemporaneous ornithologists did have a good feel for the egg-collecting activities, since collectors were both amateur and professional ornithologists, and both of these groups mingled and did indeed discuss such issues extensively as the oological literature shows.[70]

---

70   For example, "The history of ornithology in Alberta: An overview," In addition to amateur and professional collaboration, Semenchuk informs us "The popularity of the pastime was enormous. *The Oologist* had as many as 2500 subscribers," (Semenchuk, p. 12,

Bent (1938, p. *ix*)[71], in his highly respected bird books, acknowledges that a great deal of his information on eggs came from the "mass of records taken from the data in a large number of the best egg collections in the country."

Harvest of wildlife for the market took many forms, and egg-collecting was both an integral part and a problem that unregulated natural resource harvest created when human populations exceeded the carrying capacity of the land. A set of anatum peregrine eggs sold for eight dollars in 1922,[72] which was no small amount for the time (to put this into perspective, my immigrant grandfather was paid three dollars per week in the '20s and he had four children to provide for at this time in the city of Chicago). While this was too small a segment in the market hunting economy to be noticed, it probably contributed to the peregrine's inability to reproduce at sustainable numbers due to selective forces (any easily accessible eyrie would have been ravaged by collectors, so no breeding success could have occurred at such eyries). The only peregrines left in the east by the time falconry got a foothold in North America and biologists, such as Hickey, took note of raptors, were those eyries inaccessible to most people. With eyasses imprinting only on cliff sites in the 1930s, this would have been their preference when they would later seek a breeding site for themselves. The question begging an answer is: Were there enough cliff sites, enough breeding pairs,[73] and sufficient prey

---

1992).

71   See Bent's (1938) "Duck Hawk" chapter (pages 43-67) in particular, which provides a good deal of information on egg collectors taking anatum peregrine eggs.

72   "A competent collector with a fair scientific knowledge of birds and their habits, can always make a good average salary by collecting specimens of birds, their nests and eggs for public institutions, and for private collectors.... Such a collector ... can always thus finance an outing or a vacation trip into the far away wild places that he might not otherwise be able to visit," (The Donald R. Dickey Library of Vertebrate Zoology, 1922). This is when private citizens funded their own naturalist expeditions and truly dedicated individuals attempted to promote responsible use of these resources by others. When such activities were eventually restricted, government grants and jobs replaced these naturalist expeditions. One must ask, has the quality of scientific information improved since then? I am of the opinion that it has not. Instead of providing deeper insight into nature, much of the scientific community typically offers a wealth of data with little practical information from which society may benefit (this has been true at least since the writing of Lester Frank Ward's *Dynamic Sociology* (1883, pp. 24-25). This is due to the limits scientists place upon their community, i.e., artificial rules, where one scientific discipline is prohibited from reaching into another discipline. This inhibits the "connecting of dots." Private individuals are not bound by such artificial rules.

73   Hickey's research shows the count of active peregrine eyries in 1940 to be somewhere around 275 in the eastern U.S. and 126 in eastern Canada, with a 1.1 fledgling success

species in the 1940s to support a sustainable population, exclusive of DDT, and inclusive of other extermination forces such as loss of habitat, unsustainable egg-collecting, loss of the passenger pigeon as the primary food source during the breeding season, vermin status with the effort to exterminate, introduction of new diseases by invasive species from Europe, etc.?

Prior to the 1930s, there were tree-nesting peregrines in North America. Sielicki (2010) informs us that in Europe, this peregrine population was estimated at 4000 pairs. Over time, both populations were lost. In the U.S., the tree-nesting peregrines lost the necessary habitat since large, mature trees used by peregrines would have been harvested for timber or cleared for farming.

In addition to egg-collecting, there were widespread efforts to eradicate peregrines. In Europe, the effort to exterminate peregrines by pigeon racers could very well have eliminated the tree-nesting peregrine population. In the U.S., Berger et al. (Hickey, 1969, p. 171) point out, "[P]igeon fanciers are known to be archenemies of the peregrine." Hickey and Anderson (Hickey, 1969, p. 9) provide the following:

> There seems to be little doubt that, where it is found, the domestic pigeon is the favorite prey of the peregrine.... Its fondness for pigeons has placed the peregrine on the black lists of those keenly interested in racing pigeons as a sport.... The hatred of these people for the peregrine is at times fanatical, and their repeated destruction of peregrine nestings has been regarded as one of the chief factors in the reproductive failure of this species in Germany in the 1950's (Mebs, 1960).

Hickey further points to how large a population of pigeon fanciers there was and how they had bounties on peregrines. Beebe (1960), quoting Bannerman (1956), provides,

> It says much for the powers of recovery of the peregrine that it has successfully withstood the persecution meted

---

rate in two U.S. study areas—see page 189—with efforts to persecute the bird from many quarters. Whereas USFWS's 2007 *Draft Environmental Assessment & Management Plan: Take of Migrant Peregrine Falcons* ... shows eastern peregrines experiencing a 1.65 fledgling success rate—page 13, table 2—accompanied by Federal and State protections.

out to it in the years 1914-1918 and in 1939-1945 when a price was put upon its head owing to the menace it remained to pigeons carrying urgent messages of war.

In 1913, even scientists such as William Hornaday, Director of the New York Zoological Park, supported the destruction of peregrines, as well as other raptors, when he stated, "The goshawk is a bad one, and so is the peregrine falcon, or duck hawk. Both deserve death, but they are so rare that we need not take them into account," (Hornaday, 1913). Rare even in 1913! This example, and others, is evidence that the Eastern anatum was already in trouble. Of course, this is the year before the last passenger pigeon died in captivity, and as Beebe points out (see below), the loss of this pigeon would have, in all probability, been a major contributing factor in the Eastern anatum's decline.

Hickey's summary (1942, p. 202) supports Hornaday's claim that peregrines were rare. In addition, Davie (1898, p. 223) provides, "The Peregrine Falcon … is distributed throughout North America at large, but it can hardly be considered common anywhere.… The nests are placed in natural cavities in trees, and on the sides of rocky cliffs."

By the time tree nesting peregrines had become rare, ornithologists were just becoming aware of the peregrine as a bird worthy of study, and therefore assumed they nested almost exclusively on rocky cliffs. They were even given the inappropriate nickname of "rock peregrines" by some.

In addition to egg-collecting and extermination efforts, Beebe (Hickey, 1969, pp. 399-402) points to the dependence of nesting peregrines on colonial nesting prey species for their success. He refers to the northwest coast and the arctic regions, where dense colonies of birds thrive during the breeding season, and the breeding peregrine's dependence on such colonizing birds. He points to the loss of the colonial nesting passenger pigeon as a very important ingredient in the loss of the Eastern anatum. He makes the comparison to the northwest coast:

> Just how much, and how quickly large-scale human utilization of one of the important prey-species would reduce the peregrine population in [the northwest] would be difficult to say; but that it would have a profound effect, in time, is almost a certainty.

He further states,

> It may or may not be entirely coincidence that [the Eastern anatum] has virtually disappeared from that part of its former range that coincides, almost exactly, with the former range of the passenger pigeon, but the magnitude and rapidity of the environmental changes brought about by man in this region make it quite impossible to say just what combination of stresses have been really responsible.

Cooper and Beauchesne (2007, p. 32) support Beebe's hypothesis when they state,

> In Labrador, nesting Peregrine Falcons seem to be strongly associated with Black Guillemots [a colonial breeding bird], a potential prey source, (J. Brazil pers. comm. 2006) and are largely absent from otherwise suitable nesting areas when guillemots are absent.

Beebe does not attribute the demise of the Eastern anatum exclusively to the loss of the passenger pigeon, though he does assign great weight to the proposition. He offers the hypothesis that the loss of the passenger pigeon surely contributed to its decline because of the vast numbers of this bird and the love peregrines have for pigeons, as previously mentioned. This is certainly a logical supposition.

An important comparison to make between the passenger pigeon and the Eastern anatum is the timeline to extinction. There was a gradual decline in passenger pigeon numbers between approximately 1800 and 1870, which was due to the loss of habitat as forests were cleared, and which the pigeon was utterly dependent upon. Between 1870 and 1890 (westward expansion was at its height during this period) there was a catastrophic decline (this is, in all probability, the beginning of the decline of the Eastern anatum), which market hunters are blamed for. But in all likelihood, market hunters simply contributed to the trend.[74] Keep in mind that passenger pigeons were known to exist in the billions (Blumm & Ritchie, 2005, p. 118); market hunters

---

74   This was a period in which there were huge numbers of immigrants coming to the U.S., and habitat was being lost by westward expansion in many miles per year.

could not possibly have approached harvest numbers such as these, and the market simply could not have consumed such numbers. In addition, ask any pest exterminator how difficult it is to eradicate a species that has plenty of suitable food and habitat (think of European pigeons and starlings). Goble and Freyfogle (2002, p. 85) point out that market hunters had ceased harvesting pigeons when pigeon numbers were insufficient to support the economic cost of harvesting them. In other words, pigeons were so cheap that a large harvest was required to make the effort worthwhile. Yet pigeon numbers continued to decline afterward because, it can be presumed, of the loss of habitat and the loss of large colonies it needed in order to breed. This bird was simply incapable of adapting to a changing environment. Around 1900, the last wild pigeon was shot (this is the period when observers were stating peregrines were rare).[75]

DDT: A hazard or a scapegoat?

Let's consider the timing of DDT's entry on the American scene and the timeline of the Eastern anatum's demise.

- DDT had been determined to be effective as an insecticide by a Swiss chemist in 1939
- It was patented in the U.S. in 1943 (Bethell, 2005)
- It came into agricultural use in the U.S. after 1945 (EPA, July 1975)

However, Eastern anatum numbers had been in serious decline even before DDT was used in North America as previously noted. Global expansion of its use began in 1947 (Geisz, et al., 2008), just about the time when the Eastern anatum was, for all intents and purposes, gone. McDonald (2010) informs us that by 1950, there were virtually no peregrine eyries in the mid-Atlantic region. The timing of the entry of DDT on the agricultural scene paralleling the final days of the Eastern anatum gave the appearance there was a correlation. However, the alleged effect of DDT, i.e., egg-shell thinning, could not have caused such a crash in peregrine numbers in just a few short years.

Spencer (Hickey, 1969, p. 175) states, "A review of the literature on the peregrine in the eastern United States would seem to indicate that this group of birds may have ... [been] in

75   http://sciencenetlinks.com/media/filer/2011/12/06/passengerpigeon.pdf

trouble well before the middle of the 1940's.... The population appears to have been declining prior to the introduction of the chlorinated hydrocarbon insecticides. If this be true, only minor adverse effects would be needed to produce a steep mortality curve."

Rice (Hickey, 1969, p. 163) provides, "It is believed that insecticides may have caused the reproductive failure of the falcon, but this has not yet been proven." And to this day it has yet to be proven (Bethell, 2005, pp. 77-78).

A report by Porter and Wiemeyer (1969) suggests that DDT caused egg-shell thinning in sparrow hawks (kestrels). The kestrel was used because, among other factors, of its "close relation" to the peregrine falcon. What most have failed to notice is, if the kestrel's egg-shells were affected by DDT, why didn't the kestrel become endangered or at least threatened? It too would have eaten contaminated birds, rodents, and insects, yet its numbers have always been excellent. Also, why didn't merlins, sharp-shinned hawks, Cooper's hawks, and other bird-eating raptors become endangered across the continent? Though, after the introduction of the cyclodienes in the mid-1950s, Cooper's hawks did indeed decline in some regions dramatically. Many of these birds found in the lower forty-eight contiguous States and southern Canada would have been exposed to DDT-contaminated prey far more frequently and would have therefore built up much higher concentrations of DDT in their bodies than the tundra peregrine, which briefly passes through the lower forty-eight in a matter of days during spring and fall migrations to and from its breeding grounds in the arctic regions, where no DDT spraying occurred.

If one argues that the various peregrine prey species accumulate DDT in their bodies prior to migrating to the arctic, then not only should the prey species have experienced egg-shell thinning themselves—as Hickey referenced (Cade, et al., 1988, page 15), regarding experiments on mallards by Heath et al. (1969)—but all other raptors that bred in the arctic and subarctic that fed on the various contaminated prey should also have become at least threatened (the Peale's peregrine was also exposed to contaminated prey as Cade (1971, p. 53) points out), yet they didn't. Neither the arctic, subarctic, nor the various lower forty-eight raptor species that fed on birds became endangered because DDT may not affect raptor reproduction under natural conditions as it may under laboratory conditions. Therefore, we can assume that the

American kestrel.

peregrine was unaffected or minimally affected by DDT unless solid evidence is produced to the contrary. To my knowledge, no one has actually tested DDT on peregrines under controlled conditions to determine its effect on peregrine egg-shells or at what level the weakening of egg-shells may occur. Add to this the fact that DDT is still being used in Central and South America (Edwards), where tundra peregrines, North American passerines, and waterfowl reside during our winter months, and we can see that DDT is still in the food chain, yet peregrine numbers are well beyond any we have ever recorded.[76] Seegar *et al.* (Cade & Burnham, 2003, p. 220) state:

76   Cooper and Beauchesne (2007, p. 30) provide, "DDT/DDE was banned in Canada and the United States in the early 1970s and in Mexico in 2000 (G. Holroyd pers. comm. 2006), but is still used in other parts of the world including the winter range of some Anatum and Tundrius Peregrine Falcons (i.e., South and Central America; White et al. 2002). In addition, many prey species winter in the south where they may be exposed to and accumulate organochlorines, which may in turn be passed on to falcon predators on their breeding grounds.... The current impact of residual organochlorine pesticides in Canada on Peregrine Falcons is not well known. For instance, serum contaminant loads of some individual Tundrius Peregrine Falcons from Rankin Inlet, Nunavut exceed safe thresholds (e.g. 1.8-2.4 ppm in serum...)." But what is a "safe threshold," no one knows

During the course of our studies at Padre Island, we have taken blood samples from thousands of falcons which have been analyzed every six to 10 years.... We learned early on that Peregrines were becoming contaminated with organochlorine pesticides while wintering in Latin America (Henny et al. 1982). More recent blood analyses have shown that organochlorine concentrations in Peregrines captured at Padre are no longer the threat they were a decade ago. (Henny et al. 1988, 1996).

No longer a threat or never were a threat? Since no one has performed studies on peregrines under laboratory conditions, no one knows what the "threat" level is. This does not bode well for the DDT theory. Of course, all substances, including water, become harmful if not fatal at some point, so it is logical to assume that DDT would be harmful at some level, but no one knows what that level is because no studies on peregrines have been attempted. Bald eagles, ospreys, and pelicans may have been affected by DDT since they were typically exposed to much higher concentrations of the chemical because of the intense spraying of waterways, where these birds resided, in order to eradicate mosquitoes. Or if the waterways themselves were not sprayed, water runoff from surrounding fields may very well have carried the chemical in high concentrations into the waterways.

Addressing the final days of the Eastern anatum, Peterson (Cade et al, 1988, pp. *iii-iv*) states, "Shortly after 1950, my friend Richard Herbert, who had shown Joseph Hickey and me all the Hudson River eyries, noticed that although the birds laid eggs, the eggs failed to hatch." Peterson continues, "At eyrie after eyrie, the birds eventually disappeared.... By 1960 no one knew of a single active eyrie anywhere in the northeastern United States.... It was not clear what was wrong, and many explanations were bandied about."

With the introduction of DDT in the east in the mid- to late 40s and the absence of breeding pairs sometime in the 1950s, the DDT hypothesis doesn't hold water for the Eastern anatum. Based on Millsap and Allen's analysis (2007, pp. 29-32) of hypothetical scenarios that would lead to eventual extinction of various raptor

since no one has tested this on peregrines under laboratory conditions.

species, the likely scenario is that the population had been in very serious decline for decades before DDT's arrival. By sometime around 1950 or earlier, a sustainable breeding population was no longer viable (something that must be considered is the size of the gene pool at this point) and it was simply a matter of time before the last remaining pairs died.

It is important to point out that the decline of a species to a threatened level is typically over an extended period of time—not simply a handful of years, as has been suggested with the Eastern anatum if DDT were the culprit, since DDT was alleged to affect reproduction, not mortality.[77] In all likelihood, the last several years of decline was the result of the lack of a viable floating adult population. There were simply insufficient younger generations left to fill abandoned eyries, and it would have taken time for the breeding adults to no longer be viable breeders; hence their eventual infertility and perhaps weak egg-shells. What was probably being observed in the late '40s and early '50s was an infertile, aged last generation, not a population that was poisoned by DDT. The Eastern anatum's catastrophic decline occurred just when falconers and biologists were taking a genuine interest in them and were thus utterly ignorant of their population dynamics, habits, and habitat prior to this period. Hence the reason why so "many explanations were bandied about." The timing of DDT's arrival was convenient as a possible explanation, though off by a few years, and made for a good scapegoat when the rage amongst environmentalists was anti-capitalism, anti-chemical industry, and for all intents and purposes, anti-human.

Chemist and raptor biologist Lee Grater (personal conversation, 2011) states, "The introduction of the cyclodienes, which are strong and deadly neurotoxins, essentially obliterated the remaining individuals in the period of two to three years from 1955-58." It was the critical blow to the few remaining Eastern anatums, whose population was far too small to recover. Cooper's hawks were also decimated in certain regions by this neurotoxin, but there were sufficient numbers in the population at large to rebound once this toxin was removed from the environment.

---

77   Consider the tundra peregrine, which was alleged to have gone from a very healthy population, as reported by Cade, White and others (Hickey, 1969), to endangered within a few short years, back to normal levels within another few short years. Unless there was some very deadly toxic substance at fault, such as the cyclodienes as suggested by Grater, these exceptionally fast crashes of peregrine populations don't stand up to close scrutiny.

Findings in Britain Demonstrate the
Weakness of the DDT Theory

The following is a summary from *Peregrine Falcon Populations: Their Management and Recovery*, Cade et al., 1988, based on Ratcliffe's and Newton's findings in Britain.

In the chapter <u>The Peregrine Population of Great Britain and Ireland, 1965-1985</u>, on page 147, Ratcliffe points out that during the 1960s, "some parts of Scotland showed only partial decline [of peregrine populations], but only in the central Scottish Highlands had numbers remained around their normal level." Given that the Scottish Highlands are one of the most sparsely populated regions in Europe, perhaps the lack of human harassment (e.g., egg collecting and extermination efforts) might have been a primary factor in peregrine falcon population dynamics in Britain.

Also on page 147, Ratcliffe states, "The persistent organochlorine insecticides were **suspected** as the main cause of this unprecedented population collapse, **but largely on circumstantial evidence**." However, he points out that

> Restrictions on use of the most suspect chemicals (dieldrin, aldrin and heptachlor) as seed-dressings for spring-sown cereals in 1962 were followed by an arrest in the decline by 1964 and stabilization in 1965.... 1967 saw the first signs of a reverse trend.

However, was this due to the reduction in cyclodiene use, or public awareness and conservation efforts afforded the peregrine (which were parallel efforts), or both? Since they occurred simultaneously, it is hard to determine which one had a greater effect. Given that the Scottish Highland populations were relatively stable throughout the "crash" period, it would appear that human harassment may have played a very important role in the crash, unless the effects of insecticides are local, which would signify that the Highland population had less exposure to the insecticides from migratory prey and were therefore largely unaffected by them. Perhaps a comparison should be made between migratory prey species in the Scottish Highlands and the North American tundra, since both are so remote—especially as it relates to DDT. (Emphasis added)

The graph on page 148 of this chapter in *Peregrine Falcon Populations* shows the trend of peregrine populations in Britain from 1930 to 1985. From '30 to '39, populations were stable.

From '39 to the early '40s, there was a dip in numbers due to extermination efforts during the war, given the threat of peregrines killing carrier pigeons. From the early '40s to '55, there was an increase in numbers in spite of the introduction of DDT in 1947. In '55, the cyclodiene insecticides were introduced, and this was the point at which peregrine numbers began their crash. This lasted until '64, after restrictions had been implemented in '62. Further restrictions were put in place in '64, and again in '69. Then by 1976, their use had been reduced to an insignificant amount. Throughout this period, from '62 to '76, peregrine numbers were on a steady upward trend, and by '81, peregrine populations had recovered dramatically. This is strong evidence suggesting cyclodienes may have been the culprit in Britain, with DDT playing no part in the decline.

At the time of publication of *Peregrine Falcon Populations*, 1988, Ratcliffe stated:

> DDT is still quite widely used in Britain…. A point of interest is that population recovery has taken place against reduced but continuing contamination by organochlorine residues. The development of some degree of resistance to these substances is a theoretical possibility, but without supporting evidence. Within the varying spectrum of organochlorine compounds to which Peregrines have been exposed … we have always regarded the dieldrin group [cyclodienes] as the most significant in their population effects in Britain, because they greatly increase adult mortality. Peregrines had been exposed to DDT and gamma-BHC for at least eight years from 1947 onwards … but the population crash did not occur until dieldrin, aldrin and heptachlor were introduced into widespread agricultural use around 1956. Similarly, it was the restrictions on the use of these cyclodiene insecticides which so clearly appeared to halt the crash, and the further restrictions of 1964 and 1969 evidently fueled the recovery…. [T]he increase [of peregrine populations] to unprecedented levels in certain districts has taken place in the face of DDT/DDE contamination still high enough to produce detectable eggshell thinning and associated symptoms. (p. 153)

On page 155, Ratcliffe explains,

The increase of peregrines to unprecedented levels in certain regions requires explanation beyond the reduction of exposure to organochlorine pesticides. Other factors have allowed numbers to rise above the pre-war level. One obvious factor is that persecution is much reduced, compared with pre-1940 years, when egg robberies were heavy in many districts, and killing of breeding adults on grouse moors was rife.

The pressure of new [peregrines] seeking nesting places, and the relaxation of [human] hostility to Peregrines, could explain the many instances of first-time occupations of nesting places of marginal quality.... At least two instances of genuine ground nesting have occurred; a good many have occurred almost on the ground in "walk-in" sites, and one for two different years in a tree-nest.

This demonstrates the true breeding nature of peregrines when unmolested by humans, and, no doubt, the way it was in the U.S. before wildlife managers, game farm managers, and pigeon fanciers persecuted them, and before egg-collectors began wiping out their nests.

In the chapter <u>Changes in the Status of the Peregrine Falcon in Europe: An Overview</u>, Newton informs us, "Over much of Europe, DDT came into agricultural use in the late 1940s, and the more toxic cyclodiene compounds, including aldrin and dieldrin, were introduced in the late 1950s.... Their use continued unabated for several years [but] became progressively more restricted during the 20-year period between the early 1960s and early 1980s," (p. 227). He points out that annual quantities of organochlorine use have seldom been reported.

He continues on page 228, "The decline in Peregrine numbers became obvious mainly in the late 1950s, soon after the cyclodienes came into use. These highly toxic chemicals affected bird populations mainly by increasing mortality above the natural level. They were associated with many large-scale mortality incidents involving seed-eating birds and their predators."

On pages 229-30 he states,

Declines in resident populations were generally least pronounced in areas remote from farmland (e.g., the Scottish Highlands), where the falcons fed mainly on uncontaminated resident prey species [*perhaps cyclodienes kill prey species before they are able to migrate very far*], whereas extinctions occurred in the most arable areas, where pesticide use was greatest (e.g., southeast England and northwest France) [*and human populations and interference were greatest*].... Declines were acknowledged in other European countries, but without estimates of former numbers [*i.e., no previous knowledge to base trends or hypotheses on*], it was impossible to judge their extent.

A remaining uncertainty concerns the relative roles of DDT/DDE and the cyclodienes in the declines. The timing of the decline and the subsequent recovery, plus the known high toxicity of aldrin/dieldrin strongly suggest that cyclodienes were the primary cause of the population changes. The small number of Peregrines found dead and analyzed in recent decades included several with dieldrin residues (from aldrin and dieldrin) thought large enough to have killed them. This conclusion was based on analogy with various nonraptorial birds in captivity, where dieldrin emerged as 12-150 times more toxic than DDT, <u>depending on species</u> (Hudson et al. 1984). ... **[Peregrine] decline was not apparent until after cyclodienes came into use some 8-9 years after DDT....** (Emphasis added)

Even the most elementary population model confirms that decline in breeding numbers is more readily brought about by an increase in adult mortality than by a corresponding decline in breeding rate (Young 1969) [*associated with DDT*]. Where declines were monitored from annual counts, as in parts of Britain and Germany ..., the rates were too rapid to be attributed to poor breeding alone and must have entailed extra mortality (as high as 22% between 1961 and 1962 in northern England).

Little can be learned from the pattern of recovery, because in most countries, DDT and cyclodiene use were restricted at about the same time.... What is clear, however, is that recovery has taken place despite continued eggshell thinning and egg breakage, and despite a lower-than-"normal" reproductive rate. [*One must then ask if thin egg-shells and egg breakage are a normal occurrence with wild peregrines, with egg-shell thickness fluctuations being normal—as Beebe determined—which scientists have simply overlooked.*]

It is therefore plausible that, through their effects on mortality, the cyclodienes were the main cause of the Peregrine's decline....

The population declines were more closely linked with the use of cyclodienes (aldrin and dieldrin) than with DDT, and appear to have resulted mainly from increased adult mortality. (p. 233-344)

There are lessons to be learned from the listing of the peregrine and the enactment of the ESA. It becomes apparent that some scientists are honest and put forth hypotheses that appear to have merit based on contemporaneous information and events and that over time come to be accepted as the "truth," but eventually facts reveal a very different picture than what was first perceived.[78] However, there are those who use crises to further their own careers or causes (an individual who invested many years and dollars into an education that doesn't have high economic utility must ruthlessly compete for funding

---

78   Bielfeldt (2011) addresses this from a philosophical perspective: "Lessing's 'broad ugly ditch' concerns the ... *accidental truths of history to the necessary truths of reason....* Lessing's solution to the problem of the 'ugly broad ditch' is not to base deep truths ... on the contingent facts of history, but rather to reverse the situation and find in history an exemplification of the deepest truths.... These truths are ultimately grounded not in history but in *personal experience.* Lessing compares his solution to geometry: 'Is the situation such that "I should hold a geometrical theorem to be true not because it can be demonstrated, but because it can be found in Euclid?'

"A distinction used among twentieth-century philosophers gets at the issue about which Lessing is concerned. We must distinguish the *context of the origination* of a [commonly accepted] truth from its *context of justification.* Just because probability theory originated among men of rather unsavory reputation playing in the Italian casinos does not mean that probability theory is somehow incorrect. **Truth claims must be justified in the logical space of reason, not by an appeal to external historical circumstances. The context of origination (or discovery) of a truth simply is logically independent from the context of its justification.** To confuse the two is to commit the *genetic fallacy,* to claim that an argument is unsound [or sound] on the basis of the one giving it (and the purposes for which it is given), rather than on the basis of the evidence for the premises and the validity of the reasoning. (Emphasis added)

"... [T]ruth must stand on its own legs; it must not be dependent upon who said what when,"

wherever it can be found). The peregrine is a victim of both camps. There were those who believed DDT may have caused egg-shell thinning in wild peregrine eggs, but were open to alternative hypothesis, and there were those who blamed DDT regardless of the lack of evidence, since it served their agendas. Beebe demonstrated that the egg-shell thinning hypothesis was highly questionable because of the use of specimens from private and museum collections (which Hickey's hypothesis—see Cade et al., 1988, pp. 13-14—relied on to determine the average thickness of peregrine eggs) as a baseline. Specimens from such collections survived the "blowing" process of extracting the eggs' contents. Weak egg-shells—regardless of the thickness—do not survive this process, thereby skewing the baseline data. It can be imagined that wild peregrine egg-shells still break if the female ingests insufficient nutrients, such as calcium.

This raises an important question: Do we know if peregrine eggs broke in eyries prior to the introduction of DDT, and if so, what was the frequency? There is no data on this subject since no one was analyzing the thickness of peregrine eggs prior to DDT; so how can we say whether DDT caused eggs to break or some other factor caused it in wild populations—a factor that may be as old as the peregrine itself, such as availability of a proper diet.

Retired Army Major Bill Meeker, a breeder of falcons for over twenty-five years and President of American Falconry Conservancy, informs us that diet is extremely critical to healthy eggs in general (personal conversation, 2011). When asked if eggs break in domestic falcon breeding projects, he responded,

> Egg breaking is not a significant problem with raptor breeders feeding a high quality diet. The goal is to get strong viable eggs that will develop full term and hatch. A healthy egg can survive conditions that would otherwise kill many other eggs. It seems like common sense but the key to getting healthy eggs is nutrition. Some folks spend all their money on acquiring birds and placing them in fancy chambers with dual cameras, etc. Believe me, the birds aren't easily impressed. And if the breeder then stoops to feeding less than the best quality food in order to save money, it's one more variable to consider at the end of the season when he may end up with a basket full of infertile or dead eggs. The biggest birds, gyrs and

sakers, can do well with marginal food, some white meat, etc. Peregrines are smaller and require a higher quality food: dark meated quail, duck or pigeon which is great quality but requires careful inspection before feeding. Then Barbaries require even higher quality food and by the time you get to merlins and redheads there can be absolutely no compromise on food quality. What's interesting though is, **thinner shells are often more dense and consequently harder for full term embryos to break out of**. So a breeder really hopes to get a thicker but less dense shell that will allow the proper weight loss (around 15%) during incubation and remain soft enough for the eyass to break out. If a breeder is feeding the best food he can get, he will likely get high quality eggs with thick shells that are porous enough to allow for the embryos to develop properly and hatch healthy chicks.

Meeker concludes,

Something else I should say about thin, dense egg-shells is that when a person visits a peregrine eyrie and finds broken eggs, it doesn't mean they broke simply from being thin shelled. **Typically, the thick shelled ones break easier than the thin shelled eggs due to the thin shelled being denser.** Now, on occasion I've had females lay eggs that I had not inseminated. When I choose not to inseminate, I still let the females set until eventually the eggs split open due to decomposition. If someone measured the thickness of a shell chip in an eyrie and found it to be thin, and a portion of a broken egg exhibiting dark material suggesting it was fertile, he may deduce that the female broke it and killed the embryo. More than likely it simply died, spoiled, and then from inside decomposition, it broke. I suppose the thin shelled eggs on wild eyries could be REALLY thin shelled, but I'd have to see them broken BEFORE 32 days to buy that the female's weight did it, and that otherwise it was a healthy embryo. (Emphasis added)

None of this information was known when biologists were claiming that DDT was causing egg-shell thinning in wild peregrines. But we know it now, and this sheds new light on the subject and allows us to scrutinize earlier theories. Perhaps Beebe's hypothesis that the loss of the passenger pigeon was a significant factor in the demise of the Eastern anatum may also include the nutritional value that this pigeon provided, which peregrines were unable to acquire in sufficient quantities from other regional prey.

Related to peregrine egg-shell thickness: It is my understanding that the poultry industry would inform anyone who might inquire about the thickness of chickens' egg-shells—chickens that are of the same breed, provided the same food and water, same facilities, etc.—that they produce eggs with significant swings in shell thickness. Obviously, this must be true of all bird species. Meeker informs us that in some instances, chickens will lay eggs with extremely thin shells that crack very easily. This can happen with a bird that normally lays perfectly good eggs, or in some instances, particular chickens lay defective eggs on a regular basis.

The Eastern anatum was already near extinction prior to DDT's arrival onto the agricultural scene, and the Western anatum population experienced a decline prior to DDT's presence, with evidence pointing to climatic changes being the cause, as Nelson suggests. The Peale's peregrine never experienced any decline, and the tundra peregrine simply demonstrated cyclical variations in population counts, though not necessarily actual overall population numbers (perhaps they may have suffered in certain regions, such as where biologists were surveying them in the '60s). Therefore, we must look to other causes to discover the reason for the Eastern anatum's demise. It becomes apparent that the primary causes were: the loss of its primary prey base, the passenger pigeon, and the superior nutrition it offered; intense egg-collecting; efforts to exterminate peregrines by pigeon racers and wildlife managers, amongst others; the loss of nesting habitat due to the loss of old growth trees; with the final, fatal blow coming from cyclodienes, as suggested by Ratcliffe, Newton, and Grater.

Honest mistakes are to be expected; however, there are those who manipulate information to serve their own agenda and careers. Whether that agenda is focused on garnering monetary support for research or for erecting barriers in order to protect a faction's turf, a social evil is the result. Such evils cannot be allowed to enter the legislative process; if already present, they must be identified, and the deceit and ensuing laws and regulations must not be allowed to continue.

It is time to revisit Rachel Carson's hypothesis of the effect DDT allegedly had on the environment. There is sufficient evidence to put into question her conclusions and the subsequent influence these conclusions have had on environmental policies, wildlife statutes, and wildlife regulations.[79]

Falconry regulations have been dominated by peregrine ESA policy and politics, which were dramatically influenced by Carson's *Silent Spring*. It is time to reveal the flaws and demand that regulations be made sensible and grounded in unmolested science and based on sound constitutional principles. The ESA itself needs serious revision because of the abuse it has been subjected to by radical religious environmentalists as well as by ambitious and self-serving biologists.

The health of the environment and the rights of citizens go hand in hand—they cannot be separated. A toxic environment or an environment depleted of natural resources because of the actions of men exposes everyone, including the offenders, to a desperate and dangerous world. Therefore, the management of resources must balance the right of citizens to unmolested access and use of all resources (including peregrines) with sustainable use principles to ensure continued healthy wildlife populations for posterity to enjoy in whatever way fits their individual—as opposed to collective—preferences.

An interesting side note: When peregrines were bred to replace the extinct Eastern anatum through release projects, many of these peregrines were of different subspecies from different parts of the world. In most of the release projects, they were bred with little to no effort being made to ensure the purity of the subspecies. They were mixed randomly so that what is now promoted as the "recovered peregrine" in the urban areas of North America is actually a race of mongrel peregrines with no pedigree. There were many falconers who objected to this, but politics demanded that something be done quickly. Mongrel peregrines were less expensive than pure Western anatums (which

---

79   See: Edwards, J.G. (Fall, 2004). DDT: A case study in scientific fraud. *Journal of American Physicians and Surgeons*. Vol. 9, No. 3. pp. 83-88; also see Lieberman, A.; Kwon, S. (Sept., 2004). *Facts Versus Fears: A review of the Greatest Unfounded Health Scares of Recent Times*, American Council on Science and Health. pp. 8-12; also see Beebe, F.L. (1999). *The Hoax of the Century: The Endangered Falcon Scam*. Privately Published by Robert Herrick, Tulare, California. (available through http://www.anglebooks.com).

is the subspecies falconers preferred to see released, since it was the actual endangered race) and they were more readily available, so these dominated most, though not all, release projects.[80]

An interesting twist to this is related to the *similarity of appearance* provision used by FWS to prohibit access to an entire species when only one subspecies was endangered. The "similarly appearing" or "look-alike" rule prevented falconers from taking any peregrines, even of those subspecies that had robust populations, to ensure that no individual of the endangered subspecies would incidentally be taken. Yet at the same time, FWS was supporting the release of peregrines that were mongrels. On the one hand, they were attempting to protect an individual subspecies through excessive prohibitions; on the other, they were supporting the introduction of an entirely new class of peregrines—an exotic—that would compete with the purebred indigenous bird and could potentially eliminate it as a subspecies through the mixing of genes. This is how bureaucracies operate and is an example of why we must monitor and control them so as to prevent them from infringing on our interests and our rights.

After completing this chapter, a catastrophe occurred that reinforced the assertions made in this book regarding religious-based environmental policies influencing laws and regulations. In the spring of 2011, the Missouri River basin, with approximately ten million citizens within the river's reach, experienced a flood of epic proportions. Herring (2011)[81] informs us that this situation was completely avoidable, but because of the environmentalists' demands, a disaster of this sort was inevitable. Herring provides:

> Some sixty years ago, the U.S. Army Corps of Engineers …
> began the process of taming the Missouri by constructing
> a series of six dams. The idea was simple: massive dams

---

80   "Captive-bred Peregrine Falcons were reintroduced into Canada and the US, following the collapse of North American populations [of anatums] in the 1950's and '60's. In Canada, about 1,500 pure Anatum Peregrine Falcons were released during the reintroduction program (G. Holroyd pers. comm. 2006). In the US, 2500 Peregrine Falcons of seven subspecies, including *anatum, tundrius, pealei* and four exotics were released in 13 states including several (e.g. New York, North Dakota, Minnesota, Michigan, Wisconsin, Ohio) adjacent to Canada (Tordoff and Redig 2003). The introduction of subspecies from outside North America into the US raised concerns about the genetic integrity of Anatum Peregrine Falcons breeding in Canada," (Cooper & Beauchesne, p. 9, 2007).
81   http://www.americanthinker.com/2011/06/the_purposeful_flooding_of_americas_heartland.html

at the top moderating flow to the smaller dams below, generating electricity while providing desperately needed control of the river's devastating floods.

But after about thirty years of operation, as the environmentalist movement gained strength ... the Corps received a great deal of pressure to include some specific environmental concerns into their MWCM (Master Water Control Manual, the "bible" for the operation of the dam system). Preservation of habitat for at-risk bird and fish populations soon became a hot issue among the burgeoning environmental lobby. The pressure to satisfy the demands of these groups grew exponentially as politicians eagerly traded their common sense for "green" political support.

Things turned absurd from there. An idea to restore the nation's rivers to a natural (pre-dam) state swept through the environmental movement and their allies. Adherents enlisted the aid of the U.S. Fish and Wildlife Service (FWS), asking for an updated "Biological Opinion" ... that would make ecosystem restoration an "authorized purpose" of the dam system. The Clinton administration threw its support behind the change, officially shifting the priorities of the Missouri River dam system from flood control ... to habitat restoration, wetlands preservation, and culturally sensitive and sustainable biodiversity.

The Corps began to utilize the dam system to mimic the previous flow cycles of the original river, holding back large amounts of water upstream during the winter and early spring in order to release them rapidly as a "spring pulse."... [A] multi-year drought masked the full impact of the dangerous risks the corps was taking.

This year, despite more than double the usual amount of mountain and high plains snowpack (and the ever-present risk of strong spring storms), the true believers in the Corps have persisted in following the revised MWCM, recklessly endangering millions of residents downstream.

... [H]ad the Corps been true to its original mission of flood control, the dams would not have been full in preparation for a "spring pulse." The dams could further have easily handled the additional runoff without the need to inundate a sizeable chunk of nine states. The Corps admits in the MWCM that they deliberately embrace this risk each year in order to maximize their re-ordered priorities.

Perhaps the environmentalists of the Corps grew tired of waiting decades to realize their dream of a "restored Missouri River." Perhaps these elements heard the warnings and saw in them an opportunity to force an immediate re-naturalization of the river via epic flood. At present, that is impossible to know, but to needlessly imperil the property, businesses, and lives of millions of people constitutes criminal negligence....

In recent decades, many universities have steeped their Natural Sciences curriculum in the green tea of earth-activism, producing radically eco-centric graduates who naturally seek positions with the government agencies where they can best implement their theories. Today, many of these men and women have risen high in their fields, hiring fellow travelers to fill subordinate positions and creating a powerful echo chamber of radical environmentalist theory.

The ... Corps ... is a victim/tool of the above-described process [*and so is FWS*]....

There are many well-publicized examples of absurd [deference] to the demands of radical environmentalists resulting in great economic harm. The Great Missouri River Flood of 2011 is shaping up to be another—only this time, the price will likely be paid in lives lost as well as treasure. Ayn Rand said, "You can avoid reality, but you cannot avoid the consequences of avoiding reality."

... It seems that it is sanity, and not the river, that needs to be restored.

Herring's analysis of the situation is mirrored in many other agencies as well as many other circumstances. It is time to rein in the insanity that is rampant in our government agencies. If this means closing these agencies, laying off all who are within them, and then re-establishing agencies with reasonable people (but only if the agencies are ABSOLUTELY necessary) who are not of a radical eco-centric bent, then the sooner we get started, the better it will be for our country.

Conclusion

When citizens are educated in the sources of their freedoms, and familiar with attempts in history to limit these freedoms, they are better equipped to recognize new encroachments.
(Bechtle & Reitz, 2011)

Wildlife Law, Regulation, and Falconry provides insight into the manipulation of facts, policies, laws, and regulations as it relates to biology and wildlife management in the United States. Users of natural resources have had to endure the subversion of their rights by a government controlled by environmental religious factions (as well as by socialists, who would deny private property and private use of natural resources) known as protectionists; that is, people who are against any use of wildlife, with some even being against use of our natural resources in general. While conservationists are able to maintain a defensive position to a degree, they are losing the war as the protectionists incrementally extract rights that previously had been understood to be inalienable. The pendulum has swung from unmanaged harvest to draconian control. Aspects of the British system, in which the monarchy had both the proprietary and sovereign powers, have been adopted by some courts and wildlife management agencies because of the broad and sweeping powers it provides them. This becomes most evident as it relates to the assertion that States "own" wildlife and that access to wildlife is a "privilege," in the disparaging sense, which means they can assign or extract this privilege from citizens – as though they were subjects – at their pleasure.

The Public Trust Doctrine (trust) is being manipulated to add force to this position by placing wildlife under the umbrella of the trust so that eventually, wildlife harvest will be off limits to citizens since trust property cannot be alienated from the State (in Britain, prior to the Glorious Revolution, the king was the State, for all intents and purposes). The extraction of Fourth Amendment rights, whenever wildlife is at issue, further erodes the rights of wildlife users. Falconry regulations and the contemporaneous ESA, where these regulations are indirectly derived from, exemplify the tyranny that now dominates wildlife management—not because they provide protection to wildlife, but because of the manner in which they are used to attack citizens who deviate from the religious dogma that emanates from them. The prohibition of taking raptors in some States by non-residents is indicative of the tyranny just mentioned. No North American indigenous raptor used in falconry is threatened or endangered (the aplomado falcon and Harris' hawk are neither threatened nor endangered—they are simply rarer in the southern part of the U.S. because of this region being at the far northern edge of their range) and yet some States had, up until recently, prohibited take by non-residents.

The peregrine, the poster child of the ESA, provided the impetus to etch in stone, through the power of government, the religious dogmas of the protectionists. It allowed for them to use this Act to seize citizens' private property whenever an endangered species was found within the boundaries of their land, without compensation for the seizure – which is perfectly acceptable in their minds since no one should own property anyway. It offered them the ability to expand the ESA culture (i.e., severe protectionism) to all other wildlife management strategies (e.g., CITES and WBCA are interpreted by FWS with draconian limitations on citizens that are incompatible with citizens' rights). It also allowed protectionists to manipulate the judiciary, through activist judges who believe they should legislate from the bench,[82] to use the various wildlife acts in ways that proved useful to their agendas, regardless of citizens' rights. In addition, it allows wildlife biologists to use such acts to acquire funding for their pet projects. Therefore, it is in their best interest to pursue research

---

82   Or take the Justice Felix Frankfurter approach of "judicial restraint," which, in his mind, meant don't challenge legislatures' Acts when they attempt to socially engineer society.

on rare plants and animals and to support any effort to include them on the endangered species list; keeping them listed as long as they possibly can assures the stream of funding will continue flowing throughout their careers.

The use of the peregrine is a perfect example of Quigley's (1961) explanation of *institutions*. Citizens who were concerned about wildlife started off with good intentions and formed a loose coalition of nature lovers. They established a form of social organization, which Quigley defines as an *instrument*, and pursued the means to protect wildlife from over-harvest. However, in time, those good intentions evolved into the pursuit of power and career opportunities for those who became part of the institution. This leads to the erection of barriers that serve the institution at the expense of society.

An additional perspective is instructive, as it relates to institutions and over regulation. Herrnstein and Murray (1994, pp. 541-42) inform us that a cognitive elite has been growing in power and influence since the middle of the twentieth century, and in the name of doing good, they've complicated our society to the point where it is very difficult to navigate through our culture without the assistance of expensive specialists who are part of the cognitive elite. They provide:

> As of the end of the twentieth century, the United States is run by rules that are congenial to people with high IQs and that make life more difficult for everyone else. This is true in the areas of criminal justice, marriage and divorce, welfare and tax policy, and business law, among others. It is true of rules that have been intended to help ordinary people—rules that govern schooling, medical practice, the labeling of goods, to pick some examples. It has happened not because the cognitive elite consciously usurped the writing of the rules but because of the cognitive stratification…. The trend has affected not just those at the low end of the cognitive distribution but just about everybody who is not part of the cognitive and economic elites.
>
> The systems have been created, bit by bit, over decades, by people who think that complicated, sophisticated operationalizations of fairness, justice, and right and wrong are ethically superior to simple, black-and-white

versions. The cognitive elite may not be satisfied with these systems as they stand at any given point, but however they may reform them, the systems are sure to become more complex. Additionally, complex systems are precisely the ones that give the cognitive elite the greatest competitive advantage. Deciphering complexity is one of the things that cognitive ability is most directly good for.

We have in mind two ways in which the rules generated by the cognitive elite are making life more difficult for everyone else. Each requires somewhat more detailed explanation....

First come all the rules that make life more difficult for people who are trying to navigate everyday life. In looking for examples, the 1040 income tax form is such an easy target that it need only be mentioned to make the point. But the same complications and confusions apply to a single woman with children seeking government assistance or a person who is trying to open a dry-cleaning shop. As the cognitive elite busily goes about making the world a better place, it is not so important to them that they are complicating ordinary lives. It's not so complicated to *them.*

The same burden of complications that are only a nuisance to people who are smart are much more of a barrier to people who are not. In many cases, such barriers effectively block off avenues for people who are not cognitively equipped to struggle through the bureaucracy. In other cases, they reduce the margin of success so much that they make the difference between success and failure. "Sweat equity," though the phrase itself has been recently coined, is as distinctively an American concept as "equality before the law" and "liberty." You could get ahead by plain hard work. No one would stand in your way. Today that is no longer true. American society has erected barriers to individual sweat equity, by saying, in effect, "Only people who are good at navigating complex rules need apply." Anyone who has tried to open or run a small business in recent years can supply evidence of how formidable those barriers have become. [*Acquiring a falconry permit is a formidable barrier that requires navigation, and once acquired, potentially requires legal counsel – should FWS need "reprobates" to cite to justify FWS's existence – for permit infractions unrelated to wildlife issues.*]

Credentialism is a closely related problem. It goes all the way up the cognitive range—the Ph.D. is often referred to as "the union card" by graduate students who want to become college professors—but it is especially irksome and obstructive for occupations further down the ladder. Increasingly, occupations must be licensed, whether the service involves barbering or taking care of neighborhood children. The theory is persuasive—do you want someone taking care of your child who is not qualified?—but the practice typically means jumping through bureaucratic hoops that have little to do with one's ability to do the job. The rise of licensing is both a symptom and a cause of diminishing personal ties, along with the mutual trust that goes with those ties. The licensing may have some small capacity to filter out the least competent, but the benefits are often outweighed by the costs of the increased bureaucratization.

It can be seen that wildlife law has certainly been affected by the influence of the cognitive elite. To what extent, I'll leave for another to analyze at another time. For now, suffice it to say that wildlife laws and regulations have become excessively complicated, which creates legal landmines across the landscape that citizens must navigate through. Those less cognitively endowed are at the greatest risk of stepping on a mine.

It can be surmised that the environmental protectionists have taken full advantage of the changes the cognitive elite made to our structure of government to twist our system to serve protectionist ends. It has allowed them to erect barriers of every imaginable sort that confound common sense and reason, which then makes it very easy to interpret laws and write regulations in whatever way the bureaucracy, made up of protectionists, desires. If a user attempts to apply regulations based on the plain language of an Act and this doesn't fit into the bureaucratic protectionists' scheme, they will simply say your interpretation is wrong, and since all things in life are "relative" in the minds of statists, he who has the power controls the interpretation, regardless of the intent of Congress, the rule of law, or the Constitution.[83]

In their concluding chapter, Herrnstein and Murray (1994, p. 546) suggest a return to a simplification of policies, laws, and regulations.

> As matters stand, the legal edifice has become a labyrinth that only the rich and the smart can navigate.... The time has come to make simplification a top priority in reforming policy—not for a handful of regulations but across the board.

Falconry, as well as all other outdoor sports, has been under attack for many decades. These attacks are warrantless and demonstrate the fragile balance that liberty is exposed to. That common and ancient enemy of all republics, factions, has not been restrained as of yet, and until mankind identifies factional influence in the political realm as a social evil of the highest order, there can be no peace, harmony, safety, or security in our country. One might ask, "Isn't any political interest by its very nature factional?" The answer is an unequivocal no! We need to look to Bracton's definitions of law to grasp this. There is *natural law*, which is applicable to the entire Earth and encompasses objective law; *human law*, which is applicable to all humans and encompasses objective law; and *civil law*, which is applicable to cultural regions, encompassing both objective and subjective law (see notes on page 39). This gives us a better understanding of that which is objective versus subjective moral projections asserted by factions, which give the appearance of being law because of government's collaboration (however, certain subjective law, such as which side of the road one drives on, is neutral and has neither a negative nor positive effect, but picking a side is objective in its benefit to all). Objective law benefits the entire society, providing peace, harmony, safety, and security to all, which are the ends that laws and regulations are meant to accomplish. Factional subjective law (which is a form of corruption) benefits only those with a particular moral perspective unique to the faction's adherents (think of the feudal lords of England, who prohibited non-Normans from hunting

---

[83]   This is reminiscent of the old Roman maxim, "Whatever pleases the prince has the force of law." Whereas today it needs to be adapted to "Whatever pleases those in power has the force of law."

and possessing weapons in order to protect game for their own use and to ensure there could be no effective rebellion). It provides little to no benefit to society, only peace of mind to those who assert the unique factional subjective morality. Criticisms against those who violate subjective dogmas are acceptable, so long as the dogmas are not allowed to enter the realm of law and governance. In other words, they are free to speak publicly of their disdain for particular endeavors and perspectives, but they are not free to use government to restrain individuals, groups, or sectors from pursuing activities that do not infringe upon others (if their ethics and arguments are convincing, let other citizens adopt them because of the merits of their argument rather than by force). As soon as a subjective moral perspective is allowed to cross this line, it becomes an illegal, factional force that must be resisted with great prejudice so that all other citizens may see that such behavior is utterly intolerable in a free society. Those who attempt to assert their factional, subjective will upon others through law must be ostracized in a very forceful manner so that everyone will understand the offensiveness of such behavior. It is better to suffer minor transgressions where potential harm may be more localized[84] than to suffer the broad destruction that subjective morality causes when backed by the power of the State.

It is our hope that what has been provided in this work will prove useful to those who need to defend themselves from both legal and political factional attacks; however, a strictly defensive position is not a winning position. More importantly, it is hoped that what has been provided here may offer the means to go on the offensive, to enact laws and set policy that will be friendly to individual liberty and utterly destructive to factional forces that attempt to manipulate the public forum. This is the next great step forward that mankind must make if civility is to rule our existence and liberty is to succeed. Until this takes place, political, economic, or military contention will dominate the human landscape, with great suffering being the consequence. And as always, the weak will suffer the most.

Adams (1776) summarized the purpose of government when he provided,

---

84   Where local communities can address local problems through local laws. Municipalities have far greater discretion in making laws than do State or Federal governments where constitutions restrain their powers.

[T]he divine science of politicks is the science of social happiness, and the blessings of society depend entirely on the constitutions of government.... [T]he happiness of society is the end of government ... [and] that the happiness of the individual is the end of man.

Adams concludes, "[S]ome forms of government are better fitted for being well administered than others." The present work in the hands of the reader is meant to help us see this fact and to work toward recovering our constitutional free government from the hands of factions presently dominated by statists.

A final thought regarding America's destiny

We must consider the fate of America, given our deviation from first principles. There is evidence that the United States is following in the footsteps of the decline of Rome. It is imperative that we consider what some of these causes were if we hope to prevent a similar fate. Edward Gibbon, in his 1776 classic, *The History of the Decline and Fall of the Roman Empire*, provides an explanation of Rome's demise. He cites uncontrolled immigration, where the northern peoples brought their uncivil manners with them; the transformation into an ignorant population incapable of performing the jobs necessary to operate communities (immigrants and slaves took care of the manufactures, food production, and services for them); a purely abstract educational system; excessive taxation to the point where the peninsula was dramatically depopulated; and an effeminate populace incapable of defending itself, which allowed the northern hordes to invade the peninsula with no resistance. These were the primary causes of the fall of Rome. America gives the appearance of heading down this same path. History is bound to repeat itself if not rightly understood.

Power (2000, pp. 15-16) provides us with some thoughtful insights:

The fact is that the Romans were blinded to what was happening to them by the very perfection of the material culture which they had created. All around them was solidity and comfort, a material existence which was the very antithesis of barbarism.... How could they imagine that anything so solid might conceivably disappear? Their roads grew better as their statesmanship grew worse and central heating triumphed as civilization fell.

But still more responsible for their unawareness was the educational system in which they were reared.... The education ... consisted in the study of grammar and rhetoric, which was necessary alike for the civil service and for polite society; and it would be difficult to imagine an education more entirely out of touch with contemporary life, or less suited to inculcate the qualities which might have enabled men to deal with it. The fatal study of rhetoric, its links with reality long since severed, concentrated the whole attention of men of intellect on form rather than on matter. The things they learned in their schools had no relation to the things that were going on in the world outside and bred in them the fatal illusion that tomorrow would be as yesterday, that everything was the same, whereas everything was different.

A safe and secure society, such as the Roman Empire or the United States, provides the environment in which relativism can flourish, and experiments in law and social engineering can take place. This is not at all an unnatural course for such a society to follow, since it is believed, perhaps fatally, as Rome demonstrates, that everything will work out in the end, so there is nothing to worry about even if relativism and collectivism are fatally flawed. The fall of various civilzations over the millenia informs us this way of thinking is the beginning of the end for them (see Quigley, 1961).

Opulence tends to extinguish the love for liberty, as we've observed in Rome and are presently observing in our own country. The unwillingness to defend liberty within our polity will be our undoing, as it was Rome's. It is not too late to turn around and resurrect our founding principles; but make no mistake, the point of no return is fast approaching. Either the love for liberty is revived in the hearts of Americans, or the heart of America will cease to beat. Something to ponder: What will happen to the West if the fall comes? Are we doomed to relive the Dark Ages? If so, how long would it last? And will it spread to all regions of the world, not unlike the Great Depression of the 1930s, but far worse? This is a very serious issue that must not be dismissed. The Romans dismissed the signs and paid dearly for their arrogance.

The question we must now consider is, are we going to make corrections for our suicidal course, or will we follow Rome and collectively walk right over a cliff? This would certainly fulfill contemporary collectivists' wishes that we either get there together or not at all.

References

Adams, J. (April 1776). Thoughts on Government, Applicable to the Present State of the American Colonies. In G. e. Wood, *John Adams: Revolutionary Writings 1775-1783* (pp. 49-56). 2011: The Library of America.

Agency, U. E. (July 1975). *DDT Regulatory History: A Brief Survey - to 1975.*

Anctil, A., Franke, A., Alogut, P., & and Bety, J. (2011). Effects of meteorological conditions on the growth and survival of young Peregrine Falcons. *Gyrfalcons and Ptarmigan In a Changing World* (p. 88). Boise State University.

Arendt, H. (1948/1976). *The Origins of Totalitarianism.* New York: Harcourt, Inc.

Arnn, L. (2010, December 28). Retrieved from imprimis@ hillsdaleconnect.org.

Ash, L. (2005). Longitudinal analysis of cases, violations, and citations involving the MBTA regulations from Jan. 1, 2000 through Apr. 20, 2005. In *The Modern Apprentice.*

Bechtle, J., & Reitz, M. (2011). *To Protect and Maintain Individual Rights.* www.amppubgroup.com: AmP Publishers Group.

Beebe, F. (1960, May-June Vol. 62, No. 3). The Marine Peregrines of the Northwest Pacific Coast. *The Condor,* p. 181.

Bent, A. (1938/1961). *Life Histories of North American Birds of Prey, Vol. 2.* New York: Dover Publications.

Berry, R. B. (2003). History and Extinction of the Appalachian Peregrine. In T. J. Cade, & W. Burnham, *Return of the Peregrine* (pp. 35-55). Boise: The Peregrine Fund.

Bethell, T. (2005). *The Politically Incorrect Guide to Science.* Washington D.C.: Tegnery Publishing.

Bielfeldt, D. (2011). *The Ugly Broad Ditch.* Brookings, SD: Institute of Lutheran Theology.

Blackstone, W. (1979, first published 1766). *Commentaries on the Laws of England, Vol II.* University of Chicago Press.

Blumm, M., & Ritchie, L. (2005). The pioneer spirit and the public trust: The American rule of capture and State ownership of wildlife. *Rule of Capture Symposium.* Lewis & Clark Law School.

Bracton, H. (1256). *On the Laws & Customs of England.*

Cade, T. J. (1971, December). A Case of Myth-Representation. *Hawk Chalk,* pp. 47-57.

Cade, T., & Burnham, W. (2003). *Return of the Peregrine.* Boise: The Peregrine Fund.

Cade, T., Enderson, J., Thelander, C., & White, C. (1988). *Peregrine Falcon Populations: Their Management and Recovery.* Boise: The Peregrine Fund.

Carson, C. (1988). *Basic Economics, 2nd Ed.* Phenix City, AL: American Textbook Committee.

Carson, C. (1983). *The Colonial Experience: 1607-1774.* Wadley, AL: American Textbook Committee.

Carson, C. (1985). *The Growth of America: 1878-1928.* Phenix City, AL: American Textbook Committee.

Conway, W. (1994). *The Adventures of Daniel Boone's Kid Brother - Squire.* New Albany, IN: FBH Publishers.

Cooper, J., & Beauchesne, S. (February 2007). *Update: Committee on the Status of Endangered Wildlife in Canada on Peregrine Falcon.* British Columbia: Environment Canada.

Davie, O. (1898). *Nests and Eggs of North American Birds: Ornithological and Oological Collecting.* The Landon Press, 5th ed.

Dickson, B. &. (2005, Nov.-Dec.). Who calls the shots: The courts continue their struggle to find the right mix of state and federal authority that best serves the public's interest in wildlife. *Montana Outdoors.*

Dorsey, K. (1998). *The Dawn of Conservation Diplomacy: U.S.-Canadian Wildlife Protection Treaties in the Progressive Era.* University of Washington Press.

Edwards, C. (n.d.). *http://www.pollutionissues.com/Co-Ea/DDT-Dichlorodiphenyl-Trichloroethane.html.*

Epstein, R. A. (2006). *How Progressives Rewrote the Constitution.* Washington D.C.: Cato Institute.

Epstein, R. (1997). Babbitt v. Sweet Home Chapters of Oregon: The law and economics of habitat preservation. In *Supreme Court Economic Review.* The University of Chicago Press.

Frank, J. (1930/2009). *Law & The Modern Mind.* New Brunswick, NJ: Transaction Publishers.

Frederick II, & edited by Wood, C. A. (circa 1250/1943). *The Art of Falconry.* Stanford University Press.

Gabriel, R. (1956, 2nd ed.). *The Course of American Democratic Thought.* New York: The Ronald Press.

Geisz, H., Dickhut, R., Cochran, M., Fraser, W., & Ducklow, H. (2008). Melting glaciers: A probable source of DDT to the Antarctic marine ecosystem. *Environ. Sci. Technol.,* 3958-62.

Goble, D., & Freyfogle, E. (2002). *Wildlife Law: Cases and Materials.* New York: Foundation Press.

Guelzo, A. C. (2003). The History of the United States. *The Great Courses.* The Teaching Company Lectures.

Haakonssen, K. (1996). *Natural Law and Moral Philosophy: From Grotius to the Scottish Enlightenment.* Cambridge: Cambridge University Press.

Hale, M. (1713/1971). *The History of the Common Law of England.* The University of Chicago Press.

Hall, W., Albion, R., & Albion, J. (1946). *The History of England and the British Empire.* Boston: Ginn & Co.

Hardin. (1968, Dec. 13). The Tragedy of the Commons. *Science,* p. 1243.

Herring, J. (2011, June 22). The Purposeful Flooding of America's Heartland. *American Thinker.*

Herrnstein, R., & Murray, C. (1994). *The Bell Curve: Intelligence and Class Structure in American Life.* New York: Simon & Schuster.

Hickey, J. J. (1942, April). Eastern Population of the Duck Hawk. *Auk,* pp. 176-204.

Hickey, J. (1969). *Peregrine Falcon Populations: Their Biology and Decline.* Madison: The University of Wisconsin Press.

Horn, W., & Lampp, D. (2008). *Ownership of Raptors: What Does it Mean to Falconers?* American Falconry Conservancy.

Huffman, J. (2007). *Speaking of inconvenient truths - A history of the public trust doctrine.* Lewis & Clark Law School.

Hume, D. (1778/1983). *The History of England.* Indianapolis: Liberty Fund.

Kant, I. (ca. 1775-1780). *Lectures on Ethics.* Louis Infield Trans. 1930.

Kennedy, R. F. (1987, Spring). Falconry: Legal ownership and sale of captive-bred raptors. *Pace Environmental Law Review.*

Kiff, L., & Zink, R. (2005, July). History, present status and future prospects of avian eggshell collections in North America. *The Auk, Vol. 122, Issue 3*, pp. 994-99.

Kliebard, H. M. (1999). *Schooled to Work: Vocationalism and the American Curriculum.* New York: Teachers College Press.

Kozxinski, A. (2000). Administrative Search. *Macmillan Reference USA.*

Locke, J. (1690/2000). *Two Treatises On Government.* Birmingham, AL: Palladium Press.

Maitland, F. (1950 ed.). *The Constitutional History of England.* New York: Cambridge Univ. Press.

Maranto, R., Redding, R., & Hess, F. (2009). *The Politically Correct University: Problems, Scope, and Reforms.* Washington D.C.: The AEI Press.

McKay, P. (1987, Oct. 31). Operation falcon: A special report. *The Whig-Standard Magazine: Criminal Justice.*

Millsap, B., & Allen, G. (2007). *2007 Final Environmental Assessment: Take of Raptors From the Wild Under the Falconry Regulations.* U.S. Fish & Wildlife Service.

Monroe, J. (1867/1987). *The People, The Sovereigns.* Cumberland, VA: James River Press.

Nagle, J. (2005). *The Spiritual Values of Wilderness.* University of Notre Dame Law School.

Novak, W. J. (1996). *The People's Welfare: Law & Regulation in Nineteenth Century America.* Chapel Hill: University of North Carolina Press.

Nygren, A. (1949). *Commentary on Romans.* Philadelphia: Muhlenberg Press.

Palmer, D. (2010). *Looking At Philosophy.* New York: McGraw Hill.

Parsons, W. (1948). *The First Freedom.* New York: Declan X. McMullen.

Payne, K. (n.d.). Falconers Hope to Stay in the Hunt. *kpayne@ dailypress.com.*

Perspectives, M. F. (2011). *Moving People to Work: Leveraging Talent Mobility to Address the Talent Mismatch in the Human Age.* ManpowerGroup.

Porter, R., & Wiemeyer, S. (1969, July 11). Dieldrin and DDT: Effects on sparrow hawk eggshells and reproduction. *Science, Vol. 165*, pp. 199-200.

Power, E. (2000). *Medieval People.* Mineola, NY: Dover Publications.

Quigley, C. (1961/1979). *The Evolution of Civilization.* Indianapolis: Liberty Fund.

Reed, C. (1904). *North American Birds Eggs.* Doubleday, Page & Co.

Rogge, Ben; Coase, Ronald; Hartwell, Max. (2000). The Industrial Revolution. *Film III: A Magnificent Century.* U.S.: Liberty Fund and Wadlow Grosvenor Productions.

Sax, J. (Jan. 1970). The public trust doctrine in natural resource law: Effective judicial intervention. *Michigan Law Review*, 471-566.

Sayre, F. (1933). Public welfare offenses. *Colum. L. Rev. 55*, 67.

Semenchuk, e. (1992). *The Atlas of Breeding Birds of Alberta.*

Sharp, C. (1919, March 1). Duck Hawk Notes. *The Oologist, Vol. 36, No. 3.*

Sielicki, J. (2010). Tree nesting peregrines. *The International Journal of Falconry*, 20-23.

Skousen, W. C. (1962). *The Naked Communist.* Salt Lake City: The Ensign Publishing Co.

Smith, A. (1776/1981). *An Inquiry Into the Nature and Causes of the Wealth of Nations.* Indianapolis: Liberty Fund.

Story, J. (1840/2001). *A Familiar Exposition of the Constitution of the United States.* Birmingham: Palladium Press.

Strayer, J., & Gatzke, H. (1979). *The Main Stream of Civilization: 1350 to 1815.* Harcourt Brace Jovanovich.

Sumner, W. (1883). *What the Social Classes Owe to Each Other.* Harper & Brothers.

Taylor, B. (2011, Summer). Gaian Earth Religion and the Modern God of Nature. *Phi Kappa Phi Forum*, pp. 12-15.

Taylor, J. (1822/1992). *Tyranny Unmasked.* Indianapolis: Liberty Fund.

Tober, J. (1981). *Who Owns the Wildlife.* Westport, CT: Greenwood Press.

Tucker, S. G. (1803/1999). *View of the Constitution of the United States.* Indianapolis: Liberty Fund.

Ward, L. F. (1883). *Dynamic Sociology.* NY: Appleton & Co.

Zoology, T. D. (1922). *The American Oologists' Exchange Price List of North American Birds' Eggs 1922.* Lacon, IL: R. Magoon Barnes Publishing.

$29.95

ISBN 978-1-888357-26-4

52995>